A History of
GREAT YARMOUTH

Aerial view, showing the Marina, the Jetty and Wellington Pier.

A History of
GREAT YARMOUTH

Frank Meeres

Phillimore

2007

Published by
PHILLIMORE & CO. LTD
Madam Green Farm, Chichester, West Sussex, England, PO22 2DD
www.phillimore.co.uk

© Frank Meeres, 2007
ISBN 978-1-86077-457-7

Printed and bound in Great Britain

Contents

Acknowledgements

M ost of the photographs in this book are from the archives held at the Norfolk Record Office. I am grateful for the permission of the Record Office to reproduce them here. They are listed below with their NRO reference numbers.

The stunning photograph 145 was taken by Mike Page. Photograph 3 comes from the *Eastern Daily Press* Library. Images 6, 23, 57, 68, 98 are from a collection owned by Mrs Linda Steward. Photograph 144 was taken by David Symonds and given to me by Stephen Earl, who is in the boat, having sailed her from Orford.

Thank you all for permission to publish these striking images:
4. Y/C 36/1; 5. MC 1050; 7. Y/BE 5/13; 8. Y/BE 5/11/1; 9. Y/BE 5/11/2; 10. Y/BE 5/12; 13. Y/BE 5/28; 14. MC 578/12; 16. Y/BE 5/21; 18-21. Y/TC 86/12; 25. MC 530; 28. Y/D 71; 29. Y/TC 86/12/65; 30. MC 530; 31. ACC 2003/213; 32. Y/D 71; 36. Y/D94/39; 38. Y/TC 87/65; 39. MS 453. 41. MC 2033/11/14; 42. Y/D 71/7; 43-4. MC 575/1; 45. MC 2098/1; 47. NWT uncat; 48-9. Y/TC 86/12; 50. MC 2033/11/9; 51. Y/TC 86/12; 53. DCN 59/44/14; 54. Y/TC 86/12/64; 55. Y/TC 79/24; 56; S0 141/1; 58. MC 2033/3/11/1; 59. MC 2033/11/9; 60. Y/BE 5/13; 60a. MC 578/13; 61-2. BR 191/2; 63. MC 530; 64. Y/D 77/19; 65. MS 4206; 66. BR 272/135; 67. BR 272/136; 69. Y/D99. 70. ACC 2006/145; 71. BR 272/128; 72. MC 578/9; 73. Y/D 36/13/3. 74. Y/TC 69/6/5; 75-6. BR 272/127; 77. MC 530; 78. BR 272/141; 82. Y/ED 643; 85-6, Y/ED 854. 92. Y/BE 5/14; 93-4. Y/TC 69/23; 96. BR 272/135; 102. Y/BE 5/21; 103. Y/ED 8/7; 105. Y/BE 5/1; 108. NWT uncat; 109. BR 272/135; 110. BR 272/138; 111. MC 1987/2; 113. Y/TC 86/12/79; 115. ANW 23/23/1; 117. NWT uncat; 118. MC 90/1; 119. BR 272/121; 124. MC 528/14; 128-30. MC 340/9; 131. MC 340/8

The following photographs are from a collection of uncatalogued photographs by the Yarmouth Planning Department now at the Norfolk Record Office, overall reference ACC 2004/307: *frontispiece*; 2, 24, 26, 27, 35, 79-81, 83, 84, 87-91, 97, 100, 104, 107, 112, 114, 120-3, 126, 132, 134, 136-9, 141-3. Other images are taken by or in the possession of the author.

Chapter One

The Environmental History of Greater Yarmouth

Any book describing the history of any part of Britain inevitably concentrates on the last 2,000 years when man has made his impact. However, standing on the coast of Greater Yarmouth watching the waves on the seashore, it is easy to see that this is just a part of a very much longer story. The landscape is never still, sea levels rise and fall, climatic conditions change. The very boundary between sea and land has always been in flux – and is changing today more rapidly than ever before.

It is the North Sea that has determined the shape of Greater Yarmouth and the people who have lived there. That great observer Charles Dickens saw how close was the connection between land and sea, writing in *David Copperfield* of David's first sight of the town:

> I was quite tired, and very glad, when we saw Yarmouth. It looks rather spongy and soppy, I thought, as I carried my eye over the great dull waste that lay across the river, and I could not help wondering, if the world were really as round as my geography book said, how any part of it came to be so flat … I hinted to Peggotty [David's old nurse] that a mound or so might have improved it; and also that if the land had been a little more separated from the sea, and the town and the tide had not been quite so mixed up, like toast and water, it would have been nicer. But Peggotty said, with greater emphasis than usual, that we must take things as we found them, and that for her part, she was proud to call herself a Yarmouth bloater.

Henry James also saw its power, commenting that 'the North Sea moves for ever, like a ruminating beast, an insatiable, indefatigable lip'. In friendly moods, the sea is a highway, carrying goods around the coast of Britain and over to Europe, only just over 100 miles away. It has also been as productive as any farmland, and the wealth of Yarmouth was largely built upon its catch, the 'little darlings' – the herring. In less friendly moods, storms in the North Sea have cost the lives of many sailors and fishermen, and on many occasions the sea has engulfed the lands beside it.

The Geology

The earth itself, although it seems solid to us, is an active entity. The continents are on the move as the 15 tectonic plates on which they rest slide over a layer of soft mantle. The stresses that result show up in the form of dramatic events such as earthquakes and volcanoes. These are most common along the edges of plates, but nowhere is immune. The power within the earth has occasionally manifested itself in the form

1 *Nodules of flint in a round church tower, typical of East Anglia. This is Bradwell church.*

of an earth tremor even in Greater Yarmouth. On 23 May 1865, the shock of an earthquake was felt from Scratby to Lowestoft, while on 7 June 1931 an earth tremor was felt in Yarmouth and Lowestoft at 1.30 in the morning: chimney stacks were brought down.[1]

Over millions of years, rocks form and disappear. About 270 million years ago, a down-warping of the earth's crust formed a basin, so laying the physical foundations of the present North Sea and the lands surrounding it. Within these rocks are petroleum and natural gas. These are *fossil fuels*, formed from living things. Decaying plants and animals sunk to the sea floor, and over millions of years were transformed by the heat and pressure of new layers of sediment forming above them. These resources are finite in quantity: once used, they cannot be replaced.

Norfolk is built upon a layer of *chalk*, tilting towards the east: at the west of the county it is at the surface, but at Yarmouth is 150 metres (500 feet) below ground. Chalk is a sedimentary rock: it was laid down about 200 million years ago in great prehistoric seas, which covered the whole or greater part of East Anglia. Within the chalk are *flints*, which make up the only building stone to be found in East Norfolk. Flints are hard, and liable to give off razor-sharp splinters if split, but each flint originally formed around the remains of a sea creature, a sponge formerly floating above the bed of the sea. Every time you look at a flint building, whether the Yarmouth Town Walls or any of the many flint churches of Greater Yarmouth, the stones themselves are a reminder that this land was under the sea for many millions of years.

In the last 200 million years, the chalk has been covered by sands, clays and gravels, also formed under water, either beneath the sea or at the bottom of freshwater estuaries. In more recent times – over the last 1.5 million years – the surface of the land has been shaped by ice: the Ice Ages. The climate of the area has alternated between cold and milder weather, and in the cold times enormous sheets of ice have spread down from the north, scraping off the surface, and, as they melt, having long-term effects on the drainage patterns of the area around the North Sea.

Rock movements and temperature changes have resulted in continual changes in the pattern of land and sea. When many millions of tons of water are 'locked up' in the form of ice sheets, the levels of water in the oceans are much lower, so that more land is exposed. Ice has advanced onto Norfolk on three occasions in the last 500,000 years

2 *A more sophisticated use of flint – knapped and squared, that is, cut into small squares. This is the* Duke's Head *on Hall Quay.*

– the Anglian, Wolstonian and Devensian Ice Ages. In the last of these, the ice-sheet only reached the coastal fringe of north Norfolk, but the rest of East Anglia naturally experienced an extremely severe climate.

By approximately 10,000 years ago, the ice sheets over much of Britain had melted for the last time (so far at least: it is too soon to know if the Ice Ages have ended for ever, or if we are in an inter-glacial period, and the ice will eventually once again advance southwards). As the ice melted, it left behind large deposits of sands and gravels which now cover the bed of the North Sea and the surface of most of Norfolk and Northern Europe. The southern part of the sea was left as exposed marshland, and the major east-west flowing rivers of East Anglia were tributaries of the Rhine. Men and animals were able to wander across from the Continent, reindeer and mammoths at first, and later, as the weather got warmer, wild boar and cattle.

Gradually, as the ice melted, the basin began to fill until about 9,000 years ago Britain became an island: it was then that the coast of Norfolk began to take its present shape. The process is still continuing, aided by the fact that the whole island is tilting. The landmass of Britain was pushed down by the weight of ice upon it, and, as the north-west of Scotland was the most heavily weighed down, *isostatic rebound* is now causing that area to lift: while the north and west edge of Britain is rising, the east side of the country is sinking at a rate of two millimetres every year. In addition the sea level is rising as the icecaps continue to melt. This rise has not been constant: as we shall see, even in historic times there have been periods when sea levels have fallen. Today, around the shores of East Anglia the rise in sea level is about four millimetres a year. Putting the two together, the sea is in effect rising at a rate of six millimetres a year. This does not sound very much, but over a century it works out at sixty centimetres, or about two feet. This makes an enormous difference to a landscape much of which is only a very little above sea level – and, as we shall see, the rise is increasing dramatically in present times.

The sea itself is on the move, with currents and tides affecting its contact with the land. The main currents in the North Sea run anti-clockwise, that is southwards along the east Norfolk coast. Left to itself, the sea will erode the cliffs at Weybourne, Cromer and Sheringham, and the material of which they are made will fall into the water. Some of this material goes out to sea to form banks in the North Sea; some of it is carried further down the coast. As Happisbugh cliffs erode, the eroded material is washed south by the current, to settle further along the coast – and to form a barrier there to the attacks of the waves.

As well as these long-term effects, there is also the issue of flooding. The sea is of course tidal, and tides are caused by the gravitation of the moon and, to a lesser extent, the sun. The highest tides are experienced when both bodies are pulling together: spring tides, which occur once every month, not just in the spring. Very often, these tides come and go without causing flooding, but if there happens to be a combination of low pressure and winds from the northwest along with the high tides, the result can be disastrous, as in 1287 or 1953.

Early Man

If we take a sufficiently long-term view, everybody in Britain is descended from immigrants, indeed from Africans as the human race first developed there, spreading out across the world. The first human beings to reach Britain – and Norfolk – came about 700,000 years ago, arriving from the south and taking advantage of a warmer period between two Ice Ages. These are the people of the *Old Stone Age* – small family groups, probably nomadic, hunting small animals, trapping larger ones, and gathering edible plants. Evidence for these people has recently been found just outside the area of Greater Yarmouth, at Pakefield to the south and Happisburgh to the north. It is worth pausing to reflect that the Old Stone Age lasted forty times longer than the rest of human history, from about 700,000 years ago to about 10,000 years ago. If the chapters in this book were in 'real time', all the activities of man described in the next seven chapters would have to be squeezed onto the last page!

By the latter date, the ice was melting for the last time, as we have seen. The region was slowly colonised by plants once more, first grasses and ferns with isolated trees, and then forests of birch and pine, followed by lime, elm and oak. People moved northwards into these forests and learned to develop tools from flint – the *New Stone Age*. Gradually they began to make small clearings in the forest: man was for the first time beginning to affect his environment. As plant-life died, it fell into boggy water and partly decomposed to form *peat*, to be of great economic importance in the area in the Middle Ages, and to lead to one of its most dramatic landscape features, the lakes known as the Broads. The formation of peat may thus itself have been partially triggered by human activity – deliberate woodland clearance.

3 *Nature's power: lightning over Yarmouth Harbour in 1994. Gorleston lighthouse is in the centre of the photograph.*

About five thousand years ago, new peoples arrived from Europe bringing with them farming skills. They developed more specialised tools, and began to mine the flint they needed to make them: you can still these mines in Norfolk at Grimes Graves near Thetford. By about 2,500 B.C., people learned to use soft metals to make tools – the *Bronze Age*. Bronze-Age sword fragments have been found in a hoard at Gorleston. Bronze is an alloy of copper and tin. These metals are not found anywhere in East Anglia, so that they must have been imported, but once objects made of these metals were here, they were re-forged when necessary: Bronze-Age man has lessons for our own time on the importance of recycling! These people also made round barrows in which to bury their dead, and in the Greater Yarmouth area these were built on the relatively high ground south of the Waveney and north of the Bure. Some of these barrows can still be seen around Belton Heath and Burgh Castle: Mill Hill bowl barrow is the earliest in date of the 13 scheduled ancient monuments within Greater Yarmouth.

Gold was also imported and used for luxury items such as bracelets and cloak fasteners. The gold came along recognised trade routes from Germany or even Ireland: the small horde of gold items dating from the seventh century B.C. found at Caister was Irish in origin.

In about 500 B.C., farmers from Holland and Belgium arrived in the area, bringing with them the use of iron. This enabled them to produce much more sophisticated tools. It was these *Iron-Age* people who were living in the area when the Romans arrived, and when we move from what is traditionally called 'pre-history' into historical times. The Romans found a landscape very different to that of today. Between their settlements at Caister and Burgh Castle there was no land at all, only the entrance to a vast estuary stretching over what are now flat lands toward the relatively high ground – sometimes rather grandly called a cliff – running between Acle and Reedham. The

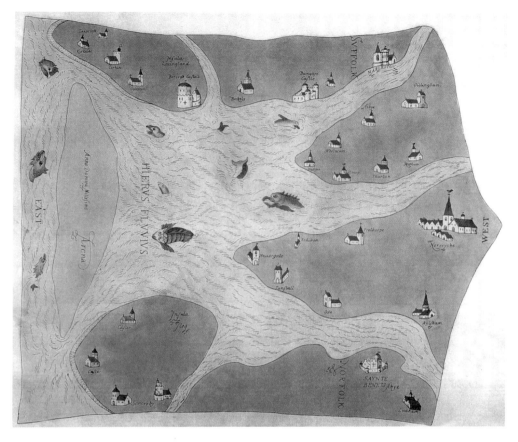

4 *The Hutch Map, drawn up by Thomas Damet before 1600 and intended to show Greater Yarmouth at the time of the first millennium, A.D. 1000. It shows the site of Yarmouth as a sandbank at the mouth of a great river estuary.*

Romans exploited the situation:'Water was by far the cheapest form of transportation, and most of the goods moved around Norfolk would have gone on shallow wooden river boats which sailed from the coastal ports up rivers like the Bure, Yare, Wensum.... In return, goods from manufacturing centres like Brampton were shipped down river to be loaded on to seagoing vessels and distributed to other parts of the province, or overseas.'[2]

The Middle Ages

About A.D. 400, there was a return to colder conditions. A rise in sea level led to the depopulation of Flanders and Netherlands due to flooding. Anglo-Saxon migrants across the North Sea were helped by high waters making estuaries and inlets from Flanders to Jutland more navigable. Some 50,000 to 100,000 Angles and Saxons came to Britain in the fifth and sixth centuries: by the eighth century they controlled the whole of England, having pushed their predecessors to the periphery. They were followed in the ninth and tenth centuries by immigrants from Scandinavia, whose impact on the area of Greater Yarmouth is obvious today in the place names, as we shall see. The latter probably brought with them two ideas that have shaped the economy of the area ever since: the dependence on a fish diet and the digging out of peat to use as fuel.

The eighth and tenth centuries saw phases of continental climate, with drier and warmer summers and colder winters. That of the tenth century marked the beginning of a long warm period lasting to the end of the 14th century. It was at this time that the sandbank on which Yarmouth now stands emerged from the sea. It was, of course, an island: there was an outlet from Breydon Water at Grubb's Haven, between Yarmouth and Caister, and the southern outlet of the Yare was at the other end of the sandbank four miles south of the present harbour mouth, near the village of Corton.

Man first made a major impact on the landscape of Greater Yarmouth in the early Middle Ages as a result of digging out peat. Patrick Armstrong sets the scene:

> The gigantic scale of production can be judged from the fact that account rolls reveal that for a time in the fourteenth century 200,000 turves per year were sold from South Walsham. At about the same time diggings belonging to St Benet's priory, Holme, produced 260,000 in one year. Norwich Cathedral priory was meanwhile consuming some 400,000 turves per year. Norfolk had a relatively dense population in the Middle Ages and on the coast there was a thriving salt industry where turf was used for the evaporation of sea water. The combined demand from the domestic, monastic and industrial users in the area would have been quite sufficient to account for the excavation of the broads in about three centuries.[3]

In the tenth century the sea level was more than 1.5 metres lower than it is today. A rapid re-submergence in the late 13th and 14th centuries led to the embanking of rivers and the cutting of drainage ditches to prevent the flooding of the adjacent marshes. This rise in water level also led to the abandonment of the deep peat cuttings, which filled with water to form lakes. The man-made origins of the Broads were forgotten, and they were assumed to be natural features of the landscape. It was not until the 1950s that research by Joyce Lambert and her colleagues proved that they were indeed artificial in origin.

There were several severe floods in the Middle Ages, but they are poorly recorded. In 1287, there was a surge of the North Sea much greater than that of February 1953, described later: the church at Yarmouth was flooded to a depth of four feet. Just outside our area, at Hickling, 108 people were drowned and the floodwaters reached a level one foot higher than the altar in the church at Hickling Priory. Oliver Rackham suggests that this may have been a key moment in the area's history: flooding caused by the surge could have been the immediate cause of the abandonment of the peat workings.[4]

There was a definite decline in weather conditions in the late Middle Ages, with many severe storms – there were at least four sea floods on the Dutch and German coasts of the North Sea in the 13th century, causing 100,000 deaths, and further tragic floods over the next two centuries. The effects on Britain were equally dramatic, but apparently without the great loss of life. The ports of Ravenspur and Dunwich were permanently lost to the sea. The colder weather led to the failure of vineyards and, more seriously, to the abandonment of settlements. The amount of rain led to successive years of very poor harvests, leading to appalling famines peaking in 1315-17. There was a further famine almost as bad in 1437-9.[5]

5   *Ormesby Broad, a landscape created by man. The artificial nature of the lakes of East Anglia was forgotten until the 1950s.*

The changing weather conditions may also have been the ultimate origin of the Black Death, which had such a devastating effect on Yarmouth, as described in Chapter Two. Severe flooding in central Asia in 1332 is thought to have destroyed human settlements and those of wildlife including rats over a wide region, forcing the latter to seek new habitats and thus leading to the spread of the disease across Europe. Once established, the plague returned on many occasions. Other diseases, including varieties of influenza, also swept through the medieval population, helped by unsanitary conditions and by poor nutrition.

The close relationship with the North Sea was exploited in several ways by the people of medieval Greater Yarmouth. One was the extraction of salt, an essential part of the medieval economy as in the days before refrigeration it was the only way to preserve meat or fish. Many saltpans are recorded in the area in Domesday Book of 1086. Another was to make use of the wind blowing across the North Sea: Greater Yarmouth was one of the areas of Britain leading the way when technology began to harness wind power for the first time in Europe. There were windmills in Flegg by about 1200, owned by Hickling Priory and used for grinding corn to make bread: saltpans and windmills are described in more detail in Chapter Six.

At this time, man was starting to impose himself upon nature in order to maintain a harbour at Yarmouth. By the time of the Black Death, the southern entrance of the Yare had silted up and an artificial entrance was made near Hopton. This was the first of many attempts to create a harbour. The 'fight with the tides, sand and silt', as A.W. Ecclestone describes it, was lost six times over the next two hundred years until the present line of the harbour was established in 1567. This has given the town the shape it has had for almost 500 years, with over two miles of quay between Haven Bridge and the abrupt east turn to the sea. The long piers jutting out to sea to protect

6 *The harbour mouth in stormy weather.*

the harbour entrance have blocked the drift of sand southward with two effects: the sand has built up north of the harbour entrance to form Yarmouth beach, but the long narrow spit south of the entrance has been eroded and pushed to the south, helping form Lowestoft Ness. So man has made a massive impact on the landscape of Greater Yarmouth from at least the Middle Ages, interfering with natural processes to his own perceived advantage.[6]

The Little Ice Age 1500-1700

Dr H.H. Lamb, researcher into the history of weather at the University of East Anglia, has called the 16th and 17th centuries 'The Little Ice Age', a period of many storms including those of 1588 and 1634, which led to permanent losses of land on continental coasts around the North Sea, and the great storm across all of Britain in December 1703. The conditions caused the terrible harvests of the 1550s, the malnutrition that resulted helping the spread of the influenza epidemic of 1557-8.

In January 1607, a great flood, now thought to have been a tsunami, hit the Severn Estuary drowning over 2,000 people. Its after-effects reached Norfolk: the sea broke in between Yarmouth and Happisburgh, devastating the farmland behind. The historian Francis Blomefield records that:

> At this time there were such violent inundations occasioned by the high winds that incredible damage both to houses, men and beasts, was done in many parts of England, and in several places to this county … . A part of the sea shore lying between the towns of Great Yarmouth and Happisburgh lying low, and being sand only, was lately broken down and washed away by the violence of the tides, so that the sea broke in every tide, and with every sea-wind came up the Norwich river into

the very body and heart of the county of Norfolk, drowning much hard grounds and many thousand acres of marsh, upon which the great part of the wealth of the county depends…. By means of the salt water the fisheries between Yarmouth and Norwich, as well in rivers as in broads, were much damaged, so that the great plenty which used to maintain many poor men was gone.

Two thousand helpers were mustered to repair the breaches in the banks. The disaster led to the establishment in 1609 of Sea Breach Commissioners, given the task of trying to maintain the sea defences.[7]

On 8 February 1683, a storm severely damaged Yarmouth parish church: 'the Pinnacle of the Steeple at the Great Church was broken down, the steeple rent by the violence of the Thunder, and afterwards fired by the Lightning which burnt down the Cross and continued to burn for four hours; so much of the Steeple is fallen down that it's feared the sailors, who are abroad, when they return upon that coast, will be much incommoded for want of their ancient Sea-mark.'[8]

November 1703 saw the greatest storm ever known on the east coast. According to A.W. Ecclestone, more than 400 ships were caught in Yarmouth Roads: some drifted north after their masts were lost but most were destroyed. The ships included three men-of-war, one of which, the *Reserve*, was escorting a number of Russian ships.[9]

However, the Little Ice Age also brought great benefits to Greater Yarmouth. The storm of 1588 broke up the invading Spanish Armada, against which Yarmouth, like other coastal towns, had been forced to take defensive preparations. More fundamentally, there was an increase in prosperity caused by the colder weather. The great shoals of herrings undoubtedly moved out of the Baltic and into the North Sea at about this time, although the cause is disputed: Lamb suggests that the reason was the change in climatic conditions. The sudden disappearance of the plague after 1666 in Yarmouth (and in Britain as a whole) could also be connected with the colder winters: the cooler weather conditions between March and June each year may have made it harder for the plague to re-establish itself in the following summer.[10]

1700-1950

The weather conditions improved over the following two centuries. The warmth of the 1730s helped agricultural improvements in Norfolk, with an increased diversification of crops, especially the introduction of roots such as turnips.

By the 18th century, wind power was being harnessed for a new purpose, draining the marshlands. All the windmills whose towers can be seen along the Broadland rivers today are 18th-century or later in origin. They have scoop wheels to take excess water up from ditches into the rivers, which flow at a higher level than the surrounding land. In the 1930s they were replaced by electric pumps (a few had been replaced by steam powered engines in the 19th century). Drainage enabled marshland to be used to grow crops or pasture animals, and of course the decline in marshland habitat was accompanied by a decrease in the plants and animals that flourish in that environment. Although the process has been going on for many centuries, the more sophisticated technology of the later nineteenth and twentieth centuries massively increased the rate of change.

There was a severe flood in 1791, resulting from a storm that tore nine breaches in the banks between Horsey and Waxham. One wherryman recalled that he could not sail on the 'North River' (the Bure), because the banks were invisible, 'tops of the reeds being his only guide'. As a result, the defences were repaired under the direction of William Smith, later famous as a geologist. He was an early advocate of the use of natural methods and materials:

> After considering a variety of plans which had been proposed for stopping the breaches by timber! By stone! By clay banks! etc, he examined the operations of the tides and storms on the coast, compared the levels of the high and low parts and finally proposed to make all the new artificial embankments as like as possible to the natural embankments thrown up by the sea (and wind) on the same coast, to make them of the same materials, and to give them such directions as might best shelter the new work by the old … By watching the aggregation of sand and pebbles on the shore, he found that, at particular seasons and by unusual storms, the bed of the sea was disturbed, and the sand became covered by pebbles or shingle scattered with much uniformity. These shingle beds were effective in binding down the sand which would otherwise have drifted with the wind, and he resolved in this respect to imitate his great teacher – Nature. Accordingly carts in great numbers were employed in removing sand and making great mounds across the gaps, and then, especially when the tides threw up shingle, the sandy bank was sealed down with a bed of pebbles. On these unresisting slopes the mightiest storms of the German Ocean now break harmless, and a very slight annual charge is sufficient to maintain the form and substance of the work.[11]

The shingle-covered bank created as a result can still be seen along the coast today.

Because of better recording due to sources such as local newspapers, many details are known of storms in the nineteenth century, and their tragic consequences. Many of the tales stress the helplessness of man before the forces of nature, with deaths occurring within sight of witnesses powerless to intervene. Two Gorleston tragedies are typical. On 4 January 1854, in a severe snowstorm and great gale, 50 vessels were driven ashore including the *Abraham*, which foundered only a short distance from Gorleston Pier. The crew hung onto the rigging for three hours but no boat was available to go to their rescue and eventually they succumbed. On 18 January 1881, a snowstorm and gale led to another disaster. Thousands of people watched as lifeboat crew tried to rescue seven people from the *Battle of Corunna*, including a woman, until: 'With aching hearts they had to leave the dreadful scene. As the chill afternoon light failed, all efforts had to be abandoned and the hands on this coal vessel died in a frozen state.'[12]

In contrast, many memories of Yarmouth holidays in the early 20th century recall days of glorious weather. There may well be a factual basis to this: 'It was during the second and third decades of the new century that the climatic warming became noticeable to everybody'. However, extremes of weather continued to occur. Floods in 1922, caused by a combination of a spring tide and north-west gales, led to flooding on the North Drive, in Blackfriars Road, and in Gorleston. The sea caused severe erosion at Caister, with a quantity of land in front of the Manor House disappearing. In January 1928, a flood ravaged the east coast and 14 people in London were drowned: the tragedy led to the Thames flood prevention scheme, which was not, however, finally completed until 1977.[13]

7   *Repairing the defensive wall around Breydon Water, 1930.*

The worst flood in this period occurred in 1938. On 12 February, the high tide tore a 473-metre (517-yard) gap in the sea defences at Horsey, flooding 7,500 acres of farmland: 'The immediate cause of the disaster was obviously the inability of the bank across the Hundred Stream, weakened by wind-drift of its sand and by wave erosion, to withstand the attack of the storm-driven breakers at a period of exceptional high tides.' Much of the area flooded was north of the Hundred Stream, and therefore not in the area discussed in this book, but there was flooding south of the Stream too, especially in Winterton and Somerton, where only the slightly higher ground known as the Holmes remained above the water.

The catastrophic effect of salt water on animal and plant life was recorded in detail, perhaps for the first time:

On the night of the flood, which was bright moonlight, the first thing noticed was a mass of dead worms being washed off the land. This complete destruction of earthworms is likely to be one of the most serious results of the flooding, not only to the many creatures which feed on them but to the soil itself, for they are of great value in keeping the land aerated and drained.

Hares and rabbits, utterly bewildered, were swimming or galloping (where they could find ground on which to gallop) in the hope of reaching a bank or an island. Very few survived and even those that reached a temporary place of safety, such as a bank just clear of water, gradually starved or died from lack of fresh water. Nearly all rats, mice and moles were destroyed, but a few water rats which probably entered the year after the flood found a living on the young reed when there was no other green thing to eat. A few stoats escaped and there was no lack of corpses or of

8   *The floods of 1953: High Mill Road, Southtown.*

weakened survivors to provide them with a meal. Insects and other tiny creatures also suffered badly.

The sea water had a disastrous effect on many plants as well. It lay on fields for up to three months, and meant that it was several years before arable crops or even grass could be grown as normal.[14]

The winter of 1947 was an extremely severe one: a stretch of ice 700 yards long formed in the River Yare at Reedham, cutting the route between Yarmouth and Norwich. Ice skaters travelled along the Waveney between Beccles and Oulton. Ice floes were seen off the Norfolk coast. On 1 March 1949, strong winds caused a storm surge, which battered at the defences on the east coast, cracking some of the sea walls.

The struggle to keep out the sea involved an enormous cost in time and money. In 1949, the *Yarmouth Mercury* boasted of the scale of the work being undertaken:

> The sea wall which is now being built at Caister to protect from any further erosion by the sea, which has steadily eaten its way over a hundred yards inland since 1941, is one of the most massive civil engineering works to have been built in this part of Norfolk, and indeed, as to mass, it is comparable with the pyramids of ancient Egypt.[15]

1950 Onwards

Weather conditions have become increasingly more extreme in the second half of the 20th century, and scientists now accept that this is the effect of *global warming* caused by the activities of the human race. The amount of greenhouse gases in the atmosphere is increasing due to carbon dioxide emitted from planes and cars, and from factories.

This holds the heat, making the earth hotter, and leading to changing patterns of rainfall and rising sea levels as the ice melts in the Arctic and Antarctic. As a result, the sea level is no longer rising 60 centimetres a century but by at least 1 to 1.5 metres: some think that the rise could be as much as five metres by the end of the century! It is predicted that by 2080, temperatures in south-east Britain could be between two and five degrees centigrade higher than they are now, with an increase of rainfall in winter by up to 35 per cent, but with only half the rainfall in the summer months that the area currently receives. Some of the potential effects of this on Greater Yarmouth are obvious, others have not yet been fully considered.

The worst floods on the East Coast for many centuries occurred on 31 January 1953. Dorothy Summers brilliantly describes the drama of the moment, not just the sight but also the smells and the sounds:

> The river started to overflow about 8 pm, and people stood awestruck watching a tremendous wave like the bow-wave of a fast ship curving away on either side of the granite supports of haven bridge. A raging flood of water tore towards Southtown and Cobholm. In Ferry Lane bordering the Yare people made futile attempts to erect barricades to protect their homes; the water smashed through, electricity failed, and the streets were plunged into darkness, masking a scene of hideous confusion. A surging mass of evil-smelling floodwater swept along the streets and through houses. Hen coops and rabbit hutches, the animals inside them trapped and drowning, flew past at a tremendous rate, along with boilers, full and empty fish barrels, and debris of every description. Above the din of the roaring water enormous baulks of timber from woodyards bordering the river could be heard crashing against doors and walls.[16]

Further experiences of the 1953 floods are given in Chapter Four. The new defences at Caister stood the test: '[they] deserve a special mention, if only because they stood out in startling contrast to the dismal conditions in evidence elsewhere. The village was protected by a well-nigh impregnable sea-wall, and was safe against all but the most outrageous attack. The wall had a strong foundation, a sloping revetment and a curved wave-return section at the top.'[17]

Extremes of weather conditions continued. The winter of 1962-3 was the coldest since 1740, while the summer of 1976 was the second hottest then recorded, only exceeded by that of 1826. Rainfall in the previous year had been about half the average, resulting in the Great Drought of 1976. The Drought Act came into force in August allowing water companies to restrict the use of water and a special minister was appointed, who exhorted people to save water by sharing a bath with a friend. In fact, the salvation was a natural one: the autumn of 1976 turned out to be one of the wettest on record.

The exploitation of the North Sea fossil fuels mentioned earlier began in the 1970s, but the transport of crude oil is a risky business. The fragile relationship between man and nature in Greater Yarmouth was illustrated in May 1978, when a major oil spill threatened shellfish on the coast – and also severely to interrupt that year's tourist trade. On 6 May, the oil tanker *Eleni V* collided with a French bulk carrier in thick fog ten kilometres off the Norfolk coast. She was carrying 12,000 tonnes of heavy fuel, 5,000 tonnes of which spilled into the sea. Eleven vessels were sent to attempt to

9   *The floods of 1953: the swimming pool on Yarmouth sea front filled with sand carried in by flood water.*

disperse the oil but this proved ineffective as the fuel was so viscose that it would not break up: on the night of 7 May the oil reached the shore. It had to be physically scraped off the beaches. Where possible, special vehicles were used for this, but where access was difficult or the coast was rocky the oil had to be scraped or shovelled by hand into plastic bags for disposal. The total cost of the clean-up operation was £2 million.

A combination of high tides with strong winds is always liable to lead to floods. January 1976 saw a surge similar to that of 1953, although the tide was not quite so high. The sea wall at Caister suffered severe damage: the works may have been on the same scale as the Pyramids but they did not last quite as long!

On Thursday 15 October 1987, the weather forecast in the *Eastern Daily Press* predicted 'winds moderate to fresh', but in the early hours of Friday 16 October, a hurricane struck Britain: 13 people died. Yarmouth avoided the very worst of the weather but the night was dramatic enough. At Bradwell, one toddler was buried in rubble and slates after the chimney in his grandparents' home in Beccles Road collapsed, bringing down part of the roof. The storm blew out large parts of the wall and roof of the Butterfly Centre on Yarmouth seafront, causing between £4,000 and £5,000 worth of damage and closing the Centre for the rest of the season. Over 200 butterflies and 30 birds escaped: about 30 of the butterflies were found alive on various parts of the Sea Front over the weekend but the rest were lost.[18]

There was more flooding in Yarmouth on 21 February 1993. Sirens – which many people thought old-fashioned when they were installed in 1986 – sounded in

10 *Hopton Beach on 9 May 1978, after the* Eleni V *oil spillage: the groyne is preventing the oil drifting north.*

Yarmouth. They did their job: as Yarmouth councillor Michael Castle said, 'very few people in Yarmouth slept through those sirens. The effect they had was a very big plus'. Water came over the sea wall, and Riverside was closed. The jetty car park and promenade were under water. Evacuation centres were set up at local schools. About 400 people in Gorleston were taken to local schools, although some refused to leave their home to the annoyance of the emergency services. The floods accelerated coastal erosion: five bungalows were lost at Hemsby. They caused damage to flood defences in East Anglia estimated at £1.2 million, and raised the long-established question of the wisdom of erecting a flood barrier or tidal barrage across the Yare. In 1977, a barrier had been recommended some 300 metres upstream of the Haven Bridge, but a 1983 report had favoured siting it much nearer the mouth of the river, to save on the cost of upgrading and raising the level of the quays on both sides of the river within the town.[19]

In August and September 2006, three exceptional storms led to a series of flash floods in the town. The local water authority pointed out that such a storm normally happened only once every hundred years, not three times in a month! They commented: 'We strongly believe that that the extremes of weather we are currently experiencing, both drought and flood, are evidence of a changing climate.' In the worst storm, on Monday 24 September, up to two inches of rain fell in six hours. There was nowhere for the water to go: one local spokesman said that it was 'like trying to get a bucket of water into a teacup'. Many people blamed the increase in the built-up area. Tony Overill of Caister parish council said: 'There is nowhere for surface water to go with the extra housing developments …. If you get rid of natural drainage and put concrete around, the area will flood.'[20]

Conservation

For many centuries, the wealth of Yarmouth depended upon fish. Conservation issues have been a concern for centuries. As early as 1488/9, an Act of Parliament had tried to prevent people using 'unreasonable nets and ingines' to catch huge quantities of very small fish in havens and creeks 'to the great hurt of all our liege people within this realm, and especially to the inhabitants of Norfolk and Suffolk'. The mid-19th century saw a massive increase in trawl fishing off Yarmouth, and this worried some fishermen. According to Nall, the number of boats involved doubled between 1853 and 1865: 'No mode of fishing has given rise to more angry controversy, from the alleged wholesale destruction of spawn, and young fish it is charged with occasioning.' Trawl fishing affected especially fish that live near the bottom of the sea, such as haddock and sole.

By the beginning of the 20th century, concerns were starting to be raised that over-fishing the North Sea might have dire long-term effects on the herring itself. Arthur Patterson was probably the first to raise the issue. He noted the increasing catches of herring and concluded: 'I am confident things are being generally overdone and I feel convinced that disaster will sooner or later overtake the herring fishery. Will not the increased ingathering glut the markets, or, what is more probable, will it not sooner or later break up the herring shoals or drive them further afield.'[21]

It was not just the herring that was a vulnerable species: mankind itself could fall prey to diseases that might kill millions. Bubonic plague disappeared from the country in the seventeenth century. The most-feared diseases of the 19th century, cholera and typhus, were conquered by the massive Victorian efforts to supply clean water and the removal of sewage. Other diseases could not be combated by cleanliness. The great influenza pandemic of 1918-19 killed more people than died in the First World War: its effects on Yarmouth are described in Chapter Four.

Meanwhile, the Broads and rivers were going through more environmental changes in the 20th century than in the previous 600 years. These were caused by man. Before 1900, the Broads had clear water, but, as increasing amounts of nitrates from farm fertilisers and phosphates from sewage found their way into the system, the situation altered: water weeds grew and the broads began to look cloudy due to the presence of *algae*, microscopic plants thriving in the 'enriched' waters. Marshy areas around the broads were no longer harvested for their produce – reed and sedge for thatching and marsh hay for cattle. This neglect led to invasion by sallow and alder shrubs, whose shade killed the natural plants of fenland. In the rivers, increased motor boat traffic led to erosion of the river banks. This was made worse by the disappearance of reeds and sedges that had grown along the banks in previous centuries and acted as a protective barrier. Sheep and other animals that had grazed on this now grazed the banks themselves, yet another destructive factor. Oliver Rackham wrote:

> The Broads are no longer the Paradise of my childhood: plants such as water-soldier are nearly extinct, and even frogbit and hornwort are rarities. Fish, insects and birds have similarly declined. The disappearances are attributed to pollution by the sewage of upstream towns and of boats, and by fertilisers washed out of agricultural land, which not only destroy the plants but indirectly affect the animals and increase the silting. Motor-boats make matters worse by stirring up the mud and by eroding river-banks, which adds to the silting. Many Broads have no motor-boats or no sewage, but significantly the only one still in reasonable health is Upton Broad,

which is both private and isolated from field-drains. Part of the sewage pollution has now been remedied, but this by itself is not enough: such vested interests are concerned that there is little immediate hope of reversing the causes of decline of the Broads, still less of undoing the decline itself.[22]

The unique nature of Breydon Water as a home of an amazing variety of birds was well-known in Victorian times – sadly, many a 'naturalist' was only too keen to add a rare bird to his collection by shooting it and having it stuffed. Birds such as bitterns and avocets were even sold as game birds on Yarmouth Market. Towards the end of the 19th century, some local people were beginning to think more about conservation as we understand it today: the Breydon Wild Bird Protection Society, was founded, appointing its first 'watcher', or warden, in 1888. This was the first bird protection society in Britain. Almost a century later, in 1978, the Broads Authority was set up, with powers to protect the area and its wildlife. It is a joint committee that includes Norfolk and Suffolk County Councils and six district councils including Great Yarmouth. It was reconstituted with greater powers in 1989: at last the Broads had been given a status similar to those of the National Parks first founded in the 1940s.

Ormesby, Rollesby and Filby Broads make up a closed system, known as the Trinity Broads: there is no access by motor boat from the main river system. Because of this, their water quality is less damaged than elsewhere on the Broads, and they are still home to a rich array of rare aquatic plants, swamp communities and breeding and wintering birds. Such a closed environment is especially vulnerable to pollution and needs to be very carefully protected. In September 2006, a local duck farmer was fined over £9,000 for allowing effluent to overflow into a drain leading straight into Ormesby Broad, with potentially catastrophic results.[23]

In the 1990s people began once more to harness the power of the wind, with wind farms at Scroby and West Somerton: the purpose this time was the production of electricity. There were objections on grounds of ugliness, and also of noise, and the proponents of wind farms defended themselves vigorously, predicting – correctly – that the farms would actually be tourist attractions. In regard to noise, the promoters of Somerton were precise: 'the level of noise at any residence will be less than 45 decibels, the same level of noise as in a public library', while those of Scroby were more poetic: there would be no mechanical noise, only aerodynamic noise 'similar to the noise of wind in the trees.'[24]

Far left: **11** *Resident of sandy heaths: the natterjack toad.*

Left: **12** *Resident of Broadland: the swallow-tail butterfly.*

Conclusion

Today, several parts of Greater Yarmouth are designated as areas to be preserved for future generations. Some are Sites of Special Scientific Interest (SSSI) – Breydon Water and Great Yarmouth North Beach. Others are National Nature Reserves (NNR) managed primarily for the purpose of nature conservation – Winterton Dunes, Martham Broad. Many small areas are designated County Wildlife Sites, privately owned but with their status taken into consideration in planning applications.

These areas are still a paradise for nature lovers. At Breydon Water, where salt water meets fresh water, there are vast mudflats made of mud and silt carried downstream by the rivers that meet here. Birds to be seen include great crested grebe, heron, widgeon, oystercatcher, golden plover, with many geese and swans in winter. The rivers, lakes and ditches of Broadland offer reedbeds, dragonflies and damselflies and butterflies.

The coast, 22 kilometres (14 miles) long, is mainly sand, with sand-dunes, cliffs or man-made defences behind. Marram grass has often been planted deliberately to stabilise the dunes. There are some pebbly beaches as at Yarmouth North Beach, where rare species include a breeding colony of little terns, one of the rarest seabirds, and the woolly hawkweed: the only other site where this plant is found in Britain is at Canterbury in Kent. There are also areas of lowland heath, especially at Belton Common, with smaller areas at Fleggburgh Common and at Winterton. Bracken, gorse, ling (heather) are found here, with many species of butterfly and also adders and grass snakes (the latter near to marshes).[25]

Most people in Greater Yarmouth will have thrilled at the sight of a heron in flight, or the shining reds and blues of dragonflies and damselflies near a patch of water. Two species already very uncommon outside our area are the natterjack toad, to be found in the sand dunes at Winterton, and the swallowtail butterfly, to be seen in the Broads. These species have as much right to live here as does man, and man has a duty to protect the environments in which flourish the *food webs* of which they are part. The natterjack needs unpolluted pools on sandy heaths, the caterpillar of the swallowtail feeds on milk parsley, which grows among reeds at the edge of rivers and lakes. If these environments are cleared away, then the wildlife associated with them will disappear for ever.

Mankind's own vulnerability as a species remains. If there is anything certain in life, it is that one day there will be another influenza pandemic. It remains to be seen if man's response in Yarmouth will be any more effective than it was in 1918 – or than it was against the waves of plague in the medieval town.

So the land continues to sink and the sea to rise, the latter almost certainly accelerated by global warming. What should we do about it? One answer is what is called *natural process*, that is simply to do nothing, and let 'nature' take its course. This solution is naturally not well-received by those with property near the edge of a cliff. Whatever solution is proposed must take the whole of the coastal region into account, or it is worse than useless. Natural process has been interrupted by the piers protecting Yarmouth Harbour, and more recently by defence works at Sheringham, Cromer and Bacton, and also by the scheme at Sea Palling, where reefs were constructed in 1995 to prevent flooding and help the beach maintain sand deposits. The consequences of these interruptions to the flow of sediment further down the coast of Greater Yarmouth and beyond are yet to be properly assessed.

13 *Proposed tidal barrier to control flooding, 1983: the cost of the barrier would have been £12 million, with a further £7 million to raise and renew river banks and walls.*

A related issue, also controversial, is the practice of offshore coastal dredging: millions of tons of seabed material are being removed from South Cross Sands, which is only seven kilometres from the Yarmouth shoreline. It is argued that this is removing the first line of defence against coastal erosion, as these offshore sand banks reduce the impact forces that the waves have when they reach the shore. Despite these fears, and in spite of protests by Yarmouth Borough Council, the Government has granted permission for dredging work to continue until 2011.

It is against the backdrop of these long-term issues that the story told in the rest of this book needs to be placed.

Life Stories

ARTHUR HENRY PATTERSON

Patterson was born in 1857 in Row 36: his father William was a shoemaker, originally from Norwich. His mother died when Patterson was three years old, and although he had at least seven brothers and sisters none reached the age of 21. After his mother's death, the family moved to Charlotte Street. Patterson went to a Primitive Methodist day school, and first took an interest in nature when in the churchyard he came across a sparrow that had been caught in a brick trap some boy had built: to the annoyance of another boy who was with him, Patterson let the sparrow go. He saved up two pence to buy his first nature book, *Gleanings From Natural History*. He recalled that 'the contents of the book ate into me like a fever and gave me a passion for nature'.

Patterson worked as a School Attendance Officer for 32 years, retiring in 1926. He wrote an enormous number of books, newspaper articles and drawings and cartoons on natural history subjects, much of which was published under the pseudonym of 'John Knowlittle'. Patterson's love of the natural world shines through all his work. He wrote in his diary in 1889:

> Just been with my three eldest children for a saunter as far as the Bure Walls – as much for a sight of a bunch of common reeds growing in a ditch by the Gasworks. If there be anything in the vegetable kingdom that bewitches me it is the reed, when quietly reflecting itself in the unruffled pool or swaying and sighing before the blast

of the roughening wind. If I ever get a fit of the 'blues' I always when convenient at any time of the day go and sit down by these reeds and regain my equilibrium.[26]

Patterson married Alice Paston, the daughter of a sawyer and Methodist lay preacher, in 1881: the couple had seven children including a son, Gerald, who was killed in France in 1916. He died in October 1935, and is buried with his wife in Gorleston Cemetery, in a plot then in view of Breydon Water. He is commemorated with a plaque at Patterson Close.

ANDREW LEES

Lees was born in Yarmouth in 1949: his father was a borough councillor and ran a hotel. Lees went to university in Cardiff, and then worked as a field scientist in Wales for the Nature Conservancy Council, returning to Norfolk in 1981.

Lees played a key role in preserving the landscape of the Norfolk Broads, at that time threatened by schemes to drain the area and turn it into a huge cereal-growing prairie. He set up Broadlands Friends of the Earth and

14 *Arthur Patterson rowing on Breydon Water in 1922. The picture was taken by fellow-passenger Judith Ferrier. Breydon Railway Bridge can be seen behind Patterson.*

became its first chairman. He succeeded in having large stretch of marshland declared an environmentally sensitive area in 1985: for the first time in England, farmers were rewarded for following traditional forms of land-use and management. The Broads were safe for future generations thanks to the work of Lees and his friends.

Lees then extended his concern to national environmental issues, taking particular interest in water pollution and in the destructive effects of the use of toxic chemicals. His interests spread into international matters as well. He exposed the illegal dumping of toxic waste in Nigeria, and became national campaigns director for Friends of the Earth in 1990.

In 1994, he went to Madagascar, where a mining company was planning to destroy a huge area of forest and sand dunes. On New Year's Eve 1994/5, he was alone in Periky Forest on the island, taking pictures. His body was found later and brought back home to Norfolk for burial: an autopsy revealed that he had died of heat exhaustion.

There is a memorial to Lees at the place where he began his environmental work, at Pant-y-sais fen. It bears words that Lees himself spoke: 'At some point I had to stand up and be counted. Who speaks for the butterflies?' He is remembered in Madagascar too. His friend Jonathan Kaplan wrote: 'I returned to the island to make a documentary about Lees and his work. Retracing the journeys he had made, I met villagers he'd spoken to, and recorded the beauty of the mangroves and lagoons threatened by the dredgers. The place where we'd found him had become a shrine. A tall rock stood there, and a post on which a zebu skull was impaled – sacrificed to Lees' spirit, which was considered a resident in the forest for eternity.'[27]

Chapter Two

'Silver darlings' – Yarmouth before 1759

B y about A.D. 900, the sandbank on which Yarmouth is built had begun to emerge from the sea. At first there were just five houses or huts on the beach 'for the reception of fishermen' during the season. Such temporary 'lodges' for seasonal fishing were not uncommon: they occur in Devon and Kent, for example, and give Winterton its name, as we shall see. A small chapel was put up for the use of this fisherman: the first register of Norwich Cathedral Priory specifically says that it was only used during the time of the herring season. It was on the shore beside the first harbour, Grubb's Haven. This was well to the north of the present church, near the racecourse. Its site is marked by Midsands Cross, almost certainly originally erected as a marker to guide boats into the Haven. The church was dedicated to St Benet, which is an abbreviated form of Benedict.[1]

Domesday Book records that by 1086 Yarmouth was a small but flourishing settlement, with a church, 70 burgesses – and 24 fishermen belonging to the neighbouring manor of Gorleston: a total population of perhaps 400 people.

From these small beginnings, Yarmouth emerges once more in recorded history just over a century later, by which time the settlement was of sufficient importance to receive a royal charter from King John, granting it the status of a borough. It was in the year 1208 that the town received this first grant of local self-government. Paul Rutledge assesses its significance:

> This meant, in effect, that, subject to good behaviour, to the prompt payment of an annual *fee-farm*, or fixed rent, into the Exchequer, subject to the overriding authority of the local justices, and subject also to the special jurisdiction of the barons of the Cinque Ports, the Yarmouth burgesses were free to manage their own affairs. They were free of attendance at shire and hundred courts, they were enabled to hold a *hustings*, or civil court, once in the week, to try the pleas of the crown among themselves, to choose their own reeves, and (by implication) to appoint their own coroners. They also received important economic privileges, among them the right to have a merchant gild … . The office of reeve was soon submerged in that of the four bailiffs who had probably originated as subordinate officials.[2]

The charter included right of toll (that is, of holding a market), and promised that Yarmouth 'shall be a free borough forever'. The fee farm to be paid to the king was £55 a year.

Before the reform of Municipal Corporations in 1835, a person (invariably male) had to be a freeman to take part in the government of the town. Freemen also enjoyed a privileged position within the community. They were exempt from customs dues levied by the town, only they could act as traders or craftsmen in the town, and only they could vote in Parliamentary elections. Admissions of freemen or free burgesses of the Borough of Great Yarmouth have probably been made ever since the town received its first charter in 1208. The first freeman whose name is known from the records is John Fraunceys of Caister, admitted in 1312. From 1429 onwards, the names of new freemen are regularly recorded in the Chamberlains' Accounts and Assembly records. From 1706 until the present day the names of freemen are recorded on separate parchment rolls.

The Cinque Ports authorities claimed to have jurisdiction over Yarmouth and sent officials to Yarmouth during the herring-fishing season. Relations with the Cinque Ports were always difficult, and led to violent conflict on several occasions. In just four years during the reign of Edward I, 380 men from Yarmouth were killed by men from the Cinque Ports, along with 280 Suffolk and 387 Norfolk men: the Ports lost 306 of their own men in the same period. The most serious single outbreak of violence was in 1297, while ships from both areas were serving together as part of the English national fleet. The Cinque Port ships attacked those from Yarmouth: between 17 and 37 ships were lost. The links were finally broken in 1662 when the Cinque Ports stopped sending representatives to the town.

The town has been known as 'Great Yarmouth' for over 700 years: the first known reference is in a document of the time of King Edward I, that is, between 1272 and 1307. Today, the designation is used to distinguish the town from Yarmouth in the Isle of Wight, but that was not its original meaning.

15 *The borough seal, showing on one side Saint Nicholas, the patron saint of the church, attired as a bishop, and on the other a single-masted warship. Note the three herrings in the sea beneath the ship. This seal was used for borough documents from the late 13th century until 1852.*

It was called 'Great' to distinguish it from the settlement known as 'Little Yarmouth', on the west bank of the river Yare. This is the area now called Southtown, described in Chapter Five.

The first reigning monarch to visit Yarmouth was Richard II, who came to the town in 1382. This was at a time of national crisis, in which Yarmouth played its part. In the 1380s the country was in very great danger of invasion from France: the danger was as real as that of the Spanish Armada, Napoleon or Hitler in future centuries. Yarmouth naturally played a key role, with an English admiral based in the town to defend the country. In 1385, everyone in the town was ordered to contribute to repairs to its defence. In 1389, with the threat at its height, the authorities in Yarmouth were ordered to operate a scorched earth policy if the French landed: ships belonging to

16 *The Hutch, a medieval chest given to the town in 1601, in which the borough records were kept for many hundreds of years. It is now in the Town Hall.*

Gorleston and Southtown were to retreat behind a chain stretched across the river, and everything outside the town walls was to be burned to the ground to prevent its use by the invading army. Fortunately the danger passed and there was no invasion.[3]

Under the royal charter of 1494, the borough obtained for the first time a separate commission of the peace. Thereafter, major criminal cases could be tried by the town's own justices in their sessions.[4]

In the 1530s and 1540s, the town's income was about £110 a year. This came from 'the profits of justice, customs and harbour dues, rents and the market, assembly fines and fines for the admission of freemen'. The money was spent on 'the fee farm and other fixed dues, wages and fees, charges incurred in the administration of justice, and repairs to common property including the Tolhouse, counting-house, crane, market-house, pillory, and public quays beside the bridge.' Two other sources of income for the town were *heyning money* and the *half-dole*. Heyning is the same word as heightening and refers to the difference between the wholesale price of herrings coming into the harbour and the market price: this profit was shared between the town and the individual broker, and the town received about £30 a year from this source. The practice came to an end in 1709. The half-dole, which brought the town an average of £19 a year, also came from the herring industry. The profit of each herring catch was divided into *doles*, which were shared between owner and crew. One dole was set aside as a tax. Half of it went to the parish church, the other half to the town.[5]

Yarmouth played an important role during another event of national importance, Kett's Rebellion of 1549. Rebels from Beccles and Bungay marched to Yarmouth and briefly held the town bailiffs captive, but were soon forced to withdraw to their main camp at Mousehold Heath. Kett sent a commission of one hundred men to Yarmouth demanding support and supplies but the town would not admit them, instead sending to London for armed men to assist the defence of the town. Other letters from Kett, including one demanding a last of beer 'to maintain your poor neighbours', were also ignored and Kett decided to take the town by force. On 17 August a large body of rebels arrived on the Southtown Road with cannon they had captured at Lowestoft. F. W. Russell takes up the story. The rebels stopped at the north end of Gorleston:

> Intending to batter the town from thence; which being perceived, a party of townsmen were privately detached to set fire to a large stack of hay on the west side of the haven, which being duly executed, raised a prodigious smoke, and the wind being northerly, drove the said smoke directly upon the face of the enemy, which so blinded them, that they did not perceive the Yarmouth men coming upon them; whereby many of the rebels being unprepared, were slain, and thirty taken prisoners, who, with the six pieces of ordnance, were immediately brought to Yarmouth, and confined in close hold.
>
> The rest, being exceedingly irritated by the above disaster, dared to approach the very walls of the town, and to destroy as much as possible all the materials for the new haven, then in making across the Denes near the south gate, to which they did irreparable damage; but being driven thence by the ordnance from the walls and mounts, they fled and never appeared about the town afterwards.

Yarmouth was in the headlines again just four years later, this time for its involvement in a succession crisis. Edward VI died on 6 July 1553. He wanted Lady Jane Grey, a Protestant, to be his heir and had issued letters patent to that effect: however, the Third Succession Act of 1544 laid down that his sister Mary was to succeed him. As Mary was a Roman Catholic, this situation split the country. Yarmouth was no exception. We can see this even today by studying the borough archives. On 11 July, the clerk wrote: 'It is agreed at this present assembly by the common assent of the assembled house that tomorrow at 8 of the clock before noon all the whole house shall meet together here in the common hall and then and there to take order for the proclamation.' However, the last six words have been struck through and replaced with the words 'to make a plan and definite agreement whether the Lady Mary her grace shall be proclaimed Queen of England'. We can see the indecision of the town authorities. They ordered that the town wall be strengthened and the watch increased, and sent men to Norwich to see what attitude was being adopted there. The borough eventually decided to declare for Mary. Meanwhile the Duke of Northumberland had sent a fleet of six ships with a thousand men-at-arms on board to try to capture Mary, who was at Framlingham in Suffolk. The fleet was driven into Yarmouth harbour by the weather, and there the entire force – officers, sailors and troops – declared for Queen Mary.[6]

In the Civil War, Yarmouth supported Parliament against King Charles I. John Carter, a Yarmouth bailiff, was living in the house on the Quay now the Elizabethan House Museum. He persuaded Yarmouth Corporation to melt down its civic plate to raise money for the Parliamentarian forces. In 1648 the Parliamentary leaders – including Oliver Cromwell – are supposed to have met at Carter's house and decided that the king must be tried and executed. One authority is a letter that Hewling

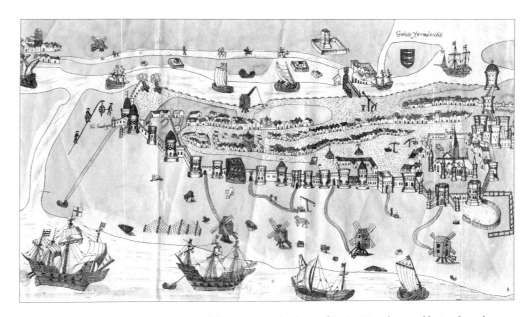

17 *Yarmouth in about 1588, showing defences against the threat of Spain. Note the guns blazing from the South Mount – and the number of windmills on the Denes.*

Lawson wrote to Dr Brooke in 1773: 'I remember when I was boy they used to show a large chamber in the house of Mr Carter, which had also been the house of his father, in which, as the tradition went, the infamous murder of Charles I on the scaffold was finally determined. A meeting of the principal officers in the army was held in this chamber. They chose to be above stairs, for the privacy of their conference, they strictly commanded no person should come near the room, except a man appointed to attend; their dinner, which was ordered at four o'clock, was put off from time to time till past eleven at night; they then came down, took a very short repast, and immediately all set off post, many for London, and some for the quarters of the army.'[7]

Cathedrals were abolished under the Commonwealth and the Yarmouth authorities tried to take advantage of the new situation. In 1650, the Corporation petitioned Parliament asking: 'You will be pleased to grant to us such a part of the lead and other useful materials of that vast and altogether useless Cathedral in Norwich, towards the building of a workhouse to employ our almost starved poor, and repairing our piers.' In 1651, £500-worth of damage was done to the Haven in a storm, and a further appeal was made to Cromwell for money in 1656. Help was not forthcoming so the Corporation decided to sell the town's gunpowder, for which they received £100: the money was spent on essential repairs.

On the death of Oliver Cromwell in 1658, the Corporation wrote to his son Richard recognising him as the new Lord Protector and describing Oliver as 'your most renowned father, the prince and leader of his people'. Not unnaturally, it changed its tune when Charles II was restored to the throne. A letter was sent to him welcoming 'with unspeakable joy' his restoration 'so long trampled upon by a treasonable usurpation'. Charles II clearly harboured no grudge against the town: he visited Yarmouth in

September 1671, the first royal visit for three hundred years. (A planned visit by Queen Elizabeth in 1578 had been postponed because of an outbreak of plague.) The Corporation hired the house of James Johnson to house him and his party: ironically Johnson was a ringleader of the Parliamentarian party and had opposed the King's visit. The King fed heartily on 'sea-made' herrings, probably meaning herrings cured on ship rather than on land. Ornaments in the shape of gold herrings added splendour to the scene: the entertainments cost the town £1,000. The town did not have to wait so long for its next visit from a reigning monarch: King William III landed in Yarmouth on 18 October 1692 when returning from a campaign in Flanders.[8]

In 1684, Yarmouth's first mayor was appointed under a charter issued by Charles II: he was George Ward. The town bought a mace for him to carry, and also a sword with figures of justice and law upon its pommel, to be carried before him: these are among the town's treasures on display in the Town Hall. In 1688, King James II annulled Yarmouth's right to have a mayor, and the town was once more governed by two bailiffs, but Queen Anne's charter of 1703 restored to the town the right to have a mayor, and actually named the first one: Benjamin Eagle.

Fishing

Yarmouth's wealth was based on the herring fishery, the mainstay of Yarmouth from its beginnings until well into the 20th century. The herring is a *pelagic* fish, that is, it lives in the upper layers of the sea. It swims in huge shoals, feeding off plankton. It spawns in shallow seas: each herring can lay 10,000 eggs or more. The herring is mature at three or four years of age and can live for ten or eleven years. There are various ways of preserving the fish. *White herring* are cured – the fish are gutted and salted and packed into barrels. *Red herring* are made by salting and smoking whole herring above wood fires in specially-built smoke houses, with a distinctive chimney shape: Time and Tide Museum is in one of these buildings. The fish are smoked using oak shavings, which gives them a distinctive flavour: the process takes at least ten days. Ash was sometimes used instead of oak for the home market.

The herring moved around Britain during the year, and the fishermen moved with them. In early summer, they were off the west coast of Scotland, and by mid-summer they were off the Shetlands and the north coast, moving round to the coast off Yorkshire. By September or October the fish were off Yarmouth and Lowestoft. Thus the Yarmouth fishing season began in September: it ended when the fish moved off in November or December: by Christmas, the herring season was over for another year.

So many herrings were caught each year that they could not be counted individually. Instead they were reckoned up in *lasts*, and more recently in *crans*. A last was defined under the Statute of Herrings of 1357 as consisting of 10,000 fish. In more recent times it is usually taken as 13,200 fish, or 12 barrels each of 1,100 fish. A cran is a measure based on a basket that could contain as many as 1,200 to 1,500 herrings.

In the Middle Ages, there were many days in the year when it was not permitted to eat meat, including the whole 40 days of Lent. Fasts also included Advent (the 30 days before Christmas), Fridays, and sometimes Wednesdays: according to Colin Spence, there were 215 fast days in the year. Fish was the obvious alternative to meat (the poor would not be greatly affected as they could afford to eat very little meat in any case). As

Spence says: 'The arrival of the Vikings, who lived largely from a fish diet, on the east coast of England further developed the fishing industry, including the smoking, salting and drying of fish. By 1066 herrings had become an important part of the economy and Yarmouth became the centre of the trade.'[9]

Herrings were also an important staple food because they were one of the few items in the medieval diet that could be kept for a long while without going off. The army fed on them: in 1429 Sir John Fastolf was attacked by the French when he was taking supplies to the English Army, and the battle has become known to history as 'The Battle of the Herrings'.

Medieval household accounts frequently refer to herrings as part of the diet of the house. The nuns of Carrow Priory, just outside Norwich, bought theirs in Yarmouth and paid a few extra pence to have them brought to the priory, no doubt by boat. Members of the household of the Earl of Northumberland including the children's nurse had a dish of sprats or three white herring for breakfast every day during the non-meat periods of the year. Long-term lay residents at Thetford Cluniac priory in 1315 were entitled to have six herrings on each fish day, the same as the prior and twice as much as each monk.

The importance of the fishing industry in Yarmouth is shown in the frequent use of three terms for specialised buildings in medieval documents:

> *Fishusa*: (fish-house, where the herring are cured by smoking).
> *Salthusa*: (salt-house, for the storing of salt).
> *Berghusa*: (barfe house, a shed open at the side where herring are salted on the floor and washed in vats).[10]

On 4 July 1204, King John issued his Assize of Customs imposing a duty of one-fifteenth on exports and imports in all ports (not on coastal trade). The tax was dropped after a few years, but does give a good idea of the profits being made by ports along the east and south coasts, especially those dealing in fish. Yarmouth paid a tax of £54 15s. 6d., so its total income must have been just under £822. This valuation placed Yarmouth twelfth in the list of eastern and southern ports, a long way behind East of England rivals Lynn and Boston. We know that the herring was already the basis of the wealth of the town: 'In John's time it became more frequent to accept renders in kind rather than in money in whole or part payment of debts … Yarmouth paid in herrings.'[11]

The Dutch were also exploiting the herring, and links between the two areas were strong. In 1568, Queen Elizabeth issued a licence to named Dutchmen, in danger of religious persecution in their own country, to settle in Yarmouth and to fish and prepare herrings according to their own customs: 30 master fishermen were allowed to settle, with their families, to be replaced by others if they died or left the town. The Dutch were allowed their own chapel in which to worship. In 1574 rather less welcoming orders were issued: the Dutch fishermen had to pledge that neither they nor their families would become chargeable to the town, and that, if they left, they would take their whole family with them. They were allowed to operate only ten *pinks*, and each one had to have at least three Englishmen among the crew.

The Dutch brought new technological developments with them – the drift net, the 'buss' (a form of vessel adapted for deep-sea fishing, about 70 feet long, with high freeboard and ample decks), and improved techniques for the preservation of fish. The Dutch developed the buss in the 15th century: the first Norfolk busses were built in response in the early 17th century.[12]

Herrings were so much a part of medieval life that they featured in several proverbs. The still common use of the phrase 'red herring' to denote a false trail derives from the practice of using the fish to divert dogs following a scent. Other sayings included 'Packed as close as herrings in a barrel' and 'As straight as a herring's backbone'. The fish was thought to be good for the health, leading to the Dutch proverbs 'Herrings in the land, the doctor at a stand', and 'Fresh herrings banish illness as the sun dispels the mist'. One 17th-century Dutch doctor wrote that a good fresh herring 'supports digestion, removes phlegm and excites appetite'.

18   *Blackfriars' Tower: the path through the tower was made in 1807.*

Although by far the most important, herring were not the only fish caught by Yarmouth men. The longest fishing voyages undertaken were in pursuit of the whale. Yarmouth ships took part in fishing for whales off the coast of Greenland from the 17th century. The earliest voyage was in 1626 and the trips were undertaken in defiance of the Muscovy Company who claimed to have a monopoly in the trade. This led to bloodshed in 1634. Two Yarmouth ships were installed at Horn Sound in Spitzbergen when a Muscovy Company ship arrived. The Muscovy men overturned the coppers in which the Yarmouth men were boiling the whale flesh to make blubber. A fight ensued in which several of the Yarmouth men were killed, including Richard Colledge: nine years later Colledge's brother was still seeking compensation for the murder, telling Parliament that his 'blood still cries for vengeance'. Whaling declined in the later 17th century but the 18th century saw a revival in the trade.[13]

Trade

The second leg upon which Yarmouth's prosperity rested was as a centre of trade. It served as the entrepot not only for the countryside around, but also for Norwich, 20 miles up the river Yare. The two key places that reflect this history are the Harbour and the Market Place.

Much of the limestone used to build the Cathedral and Castle in Norwich came from Caen in Normandy. It was brought in ships to Yarmouth, off-loaded there into boats and carried up the river to Norwich. The importance of water transport to the economy of both towns is well illustrated by what happened in 1607 when the river Yare was frozen over for 40 days: it cost 24 shillings to send a cargo to Norwich by road, ten times the sum that it would have cost to take it up the river.[14]

People from all over Europe were to be found in medieval Yarmouth. Two sanctuary cases at Yarmouth Blackfriars indicate the cosmopolitan flavour of the town. John the Scot hid there after breaking out of Yarmouth gaol, having stolen £30-worth of goods from merchants from Winchelsea and Flanders. Godfrey Gom also escaped from gaol to the Blackfriars: he had murdered a man from Gascony in the town. As was customary, both men were given 15 days to leave the country. Medieval mercy was strictly limited, however: if they did not leave, or if they returned to England, they would be summarily hanged.

The first known wine merchant in Yarmouth was William Oxney, bailiff of the borough in 1350. In 1339 he paid 27s. 6d. for the freight of one tun (cask) of wine from Bordeaux. Although Yarmouth was not a major wine importer, wine was brought in for local consumption. In 1576, for example, customs accounts show that 17.5 tuns (4,410 gallons!) of wine were landed from the *Robert of Lynn*, for George Smyth and Drew Drewery of Norwich. In 1665, French, sweet and Rhine wines and sack were being imported, paying customs at ten pence a tun.

Like every town, Yarmouth has had its cycles of wealth and poverty. One of its peaks was in the early 14th century. In 1332, the subsidy paid to the Crown by the town was £102, the fourth highest rated provincial town in England, and well above the £84 at which Norwich was assessed. The prosperity came to a sudden end in 1349: the cause was the Black Death, described later. In the 1520s, Yarmouth was ranked twentieth among the provincial towns of England. This was the low point in the town's fortunes, however. In 1545, the Duke of Norfolk described Yarmouth as 'the prosperest towne, the best builded with moste substancyall howses, that I Know so near the sea in all your Majestie's realme'. By 1662, the town's ranking had risen to seventh amongst provincial towns.[15]

As we saw in Chapter One, the entrance to the river Yare has frequently silted up, with disastrous consequences to the town. There have been no fewer than seven different entrances, or havens, at different dates. The sixth silted up in the mid-16th century, causing the waters of the Yare to flood through the town. Drastic solutions were needed. A channel was dug through the sand on the site of the fifth haven in the 1560s. Henry Manship, a historian of the time, says that more than a thousand Yarmouth people, including women and children, voluntarily gave their labour, proof of the sense of community within the town. In 1567, the town consulted the Vice Admiral of England, Sir William Wodehouse, for his opinion on how this new haven could be made permanent. He decided that foreign expertise was needed, advising the town 'to send over sea for a cunning workman well known to be very skilful in such waterworks, as in Sealand and Holland'. They sent for Joas Johnson of Middleburgh. He devised 'the great stoppe', whereby the south-flowing waters of the Yare are forced to make a sharp left turn at Gorleston and disgorge into the sea between two piers that prevent the sand from blowing south and blocking the entrance. By his advice 'there began to be wrought with great timber, brushwood, iron, planks and stone to drive it into one certain course, and the current that was forced to run into the sea between the two great main piers': the quay at Gorleston is still called Brush Quay today.

Johnson was paid four shillings a day to supervise the work, four times as much as the carpenters and sawyers working on the project: labourers received eight pence a day. The work was not completely paid for until 1613, but Johnson's vision has created a masterpiece of industrial engineering, which has endured for half a millennium, and he has probably had more effect on the landscape of Greater Yarmouth than any other individual. Johnson's southern pier, which had become known as 'the Old Dutch Pier', was finally replaced in 1962 by the

19 *Blackfriars' Tower and the south wall of the town.*

present concrete structure, which does not allow water to pass through it. Since then, many argue, Gorleston beach has been rapidly eroded: possibly the old Dutchman was wiser than the 20th-century engineer![16]

To raise money for the new harbour, in 1567 the Yarmouth bailiffs decided to gamble on the first lottery to be held in England. One of the bailiffs, Ralph Woodhouse, bought 15 shares with ratepayers' money. Another bailiff, Thomas Betts, bought a further 47 tickets. The draw was held outside St Paul's Cathedral in London on 11 June 1569: no prizes were won by the Yarmouth ticket holders. The financial aspects were finally put in order in 1670, when the First Haven Act set up *Port and Haven Commissioners*, who could impose dues on all cargoes except fish and use the money to maintain the harbour.

The sheer number of ships in the harbour stunned visitors. Defoe commented: 'The ships ride here so close and as it were keeping up one another, with their head-fasts on shore, that for half a mile together they go cross the stream with their bowsprits over the land, their bows, or heads, touching the very wharf, so that one may walk from ship to ship as on a floating bridge, all along by the shore side, the quay reaching from the drawbridge almost to the South-gate is so spacious and wide that in some places it is near one hundred yards from the houses to the wharf.' Doctor Alexander Carlyle, a visitor from Inverness, wrote in 1745: 'the Quay, which is on the west side of the town and lies parallel to the beach, is the most remarkable thing about the town. Here the largest colliers can deliver their coal, and the street behind it has some of the handsomest houses in the town.'[17]

Naturally, the great bulk of Yarmouth's trade was with the Low Countries and Scandinavia. Apart from herring, by far the greatest export was cloth. Some ships did venture further, going down the English Channel and to the Mediterranean. We have a record of one further-flung voyage in 1700: the town sent a ship to Jamaica containing bricks, pitch, beer, cheese, iron goods and leather, presumably for the owners of sugar plantations there. The venture does not seem ever to have been repeated.[18]

The importance of Yarmouth as a port can be seen in the archives of Felbrigg Hall. In 1612, two large tombstones were brought to Felbrigg church from London: they came by sea to Yarmouth, and then up the river Bure to Coltishall. When William Windham, the owner of Felbrigg Hall, died in 1689, his widow Katherine paid Grinling Gibbons £50 for a monument to be erected to him in Felbrigg church, with a further £1 19s. to 'bring it home': it came via Yarmouth. In 1752, Ashe Windham decided totally to renovate Felbrigg Hall. He asked his agent Robert Frary to charter a ship from Wells or Yarmouth to bring up the new features from London – a chimney piece, two carved tables, the ironwork for the new staircase and his paintings. However, one painting was not to be included: 'my great Van de Velde I cannot trust to the seas so that alone shall go by land'.[19]

Yarmouth was a crossroads, a place of embarkation for travellers to and from the continent, and a stopping place for shipping between London and Scotland. Many an adventure started or ended in the town. Julines Herring in 1637 was just one of many reformed clergymen forced to travel to Rotterdam from the port. William Greenhill came the other way in the same year, bringing with him several barrels full of 'seditious' books. In July 1648, Sir John Boys sailed with Prince Charles to Yarmouth to attempt to rouse support in Norfolk for the king and raise the siege of Colchester: the scheme came to nothing. There were rumours in Yarmouth that Charles I's wife, Henrietta Maria, would land with foreign troops in support of her husband, but this never happened. In 1665, a plan of the admiral Owen Cox to sail for the Mediterranean came to an abrupt halt when his ship the *Nathan* foundered off Yarmouth with the loss of all hands.

In 1681, Prince James (later King James II) was travelling from London to Edinburgh on the *Gloucester* when the ship struck a sandbank off Yarmouth. There was only one lifeboat: John Churchill, later Duke of Marlborough, held the sailors back at sword point as James made sure that a large tin trunk containing his memoirs was loaded into it, followed by the most important passengers. The men were left to fend for themselves: over 200 drowned. Later rumour accused James of taking his favourite dog Mumper on board the lifeboat but this was not true: Mumper was seen by eyewitnesses floundering in the water alongside the drowning sailors.[20]

Communications slowly improved over the centuries. Transport was mainly by water, for people as well as goods: a daily service by river between Yarmouth and Norwich was available in 1668, costing sixpence a head. In 1417, the first bridge was built over the river Yare, replacing a ferry. A drawbridge was erected in 1553, but had to be replaced in 1570 after it had been carried away in a high tide. By the 17th century, coaches to London were running from the *Duke's Head* inn on the Quay.

20 *The Market Place in winter: the market has been held on the same site for at least 800 years.*

These journeys were long and dangerous. In 1689, for example, at 4 a.m. on 1 July Dr Davies left London for Yarmouth. The coach stopped at Bishop's Stortford for lunch and at Bury St Edmunds for the night, arriving at Yarmouth at 7 p.m. the following evening. The return journey took him even longer. He left the *Duke's Head* at 5 a.m. on 21 October, had lunch at Harleston (which, he noted in his diary, cost one shilling!), and stopped for the night at Botesdale. On the second day he had lunch at Newmarket and reached Bishop's Stortford at 8 p.m., spending the night there. The coach set off for London at 8 a.m., but got stuck in the mud going through Epping Forest. The passengers had to walk into Epping itself, where they had lunch. They finally reached London at 7 p.m., on the third day of the journey.[21]

More localised trade was carried out at the Market Place, still on the same site today as it has been for eight hundred years. A market is presumed to have existed at Great Yarmouth before the granting of King John's charter. Henry Manship, writing in 1609, says, 'Yarmouth hath, time out of mind, enjoyed by prescription a very fair market'. The market's origin, then, is *prescriptive*, that is, arising from or recognised by long-standing custom or usage. The Market Place is the largest open-air market in England. In 1385, the area was paved and a Market Cross built to provide shelter from the rain, and also as a centre for punishing petty criminals by means of a cage, a pillory and stocks. The Cross was replaced in 1509 and again in 1604: this version is shown on Butcher's painting of the Market Place.

The running of the market was regulated by the Borough court and its records show what it was like. In 1281, John, a servant, complained to the court that while he was walking through the fish stalls in the market a man named Nicholas assaulted him with a stick. In the same year, Felicia Nigrum was in the market carrying a jug of water when Walter de Clippesby took the jug and broke it over her head. In the following year William Sterre was attacked by John de Portsmue, who stabbed him between the shoulder blades with his dagger. Other crimes were economic rather than physical. In 1391 Alice Goodgroom was 'a great forestaller of butter, cheese and eggs wherefore there is a great dearth in the Market', while John Lokard was hoarding oats. Both of these people were attempting to create an artificial shortage of goods, so that they could push up the prices they charged the hungry consumer.

In 1546, the Town constructed a large building for the use of country butchers. In 1551, the Butchery proving a success, slaughter-houses were built on the east side of the Market Place, and it was ordered that meat could only be sold in this area of the market, under penalty of a fine of 20 shillings. Carlyle commented: 'The market people are clean beyond example; and the butchers themselves dress with great neatness. In short there is nothing to offend the eye or any of the senses in Yarmouth market. Very genteel looking women were providing for their families.'[22]

21 *The Tolhouse, the oldest civic building in Britain.*

The Built Environment

The only building in Yarmouth roughly contemporary with the 1208 charter is the Tolhouse, the oldest civic building in Britain. It was built as a private house and its external stairway to the main entrance can still be seen, but was in public use by the early 13th century. The borough court was held here, and the basement was the town gaol. In 1552, it was ordered that the building be repaired 'as fast as may be'. It was also used for the Admiralty Court, which was established under Queen Elizabeth's charter of 1559 to handle maritime cases: this court was abolished in 1835.

The Guildhall was built between the church and the Market Place: this is where the Borough Assembly met. It was re-roofed in the 16th century, using the roof from a dissolved college for priests at Mettingham. The old roof was itself re-used within Yarmouth: the roof truss on the outside wall behind the *Duke's Head* is a relic of it. The Town Hall was begun in 1715, and included an Assembly Room 61 feet long. The architect was John Price.

22   *The South Gate. The contraption on the tower is a semaphore system linking Yarmouth with London.*

King Henry III granted the town leave to build a town wall and ditch in 1261. Large portions of the wall survive, and are well worth a visit: the wall and towers along Blackfriars Road are one of the most impressive sections of medieval town wall in Britain. The wall, with its 16 towers and ten gates, was not completed until 1391. It was paid for by the levying of a special rate, but many Yarmouth citizens chose to leave money for it in their wills. The most important of the gates were the North Gate, the only means of vehicular access to the town before the bridge was built, and the South Gate, providing access to the South Denes.

The section of town wall around the churchyard is in fact the wall of the priory precinct. It is in a different style from the rest of the town wall with square turrets. King Henry's Tower within the churchyard was used as an ossuary chapel – when new burials were made in the churchyard any bones found would be placed here. Eventually they would be burnt, a medieval practice that has given us the word 'bon[e]fire'.

The Assembly Minutes show that the town was spending money in the 1540s on strengthening its defences. Two of the town guns were sent for repair and gunpowder was bought and distributed to the three bulwarks. Ships were commandeered to block the mouth of the harbour. Parts of the town wall were *rampired*, or strengthened with earth banks as a defence against cannon fire. In the event there was only one military incident at this time. Two French ships came into Yarmouth roads on 30 November 1544 and tried to seize two English ships loaded with wheat for the English army at Boulogne. The townsmen recaptured the supplies and took six prisoners.[23]

In the year of the Spanish Armada, 1588, Yarmouth was defended against invasion. The walls were strengthened and earthworks built in front of them to protect them from artillery fire. This form of defence is called a *ravelin*, and Ravelin House now stands upon the earthwork. In 1596, it was ordered that all gates should be kept locked

23 *The North Gate. The gate was demolished in 1807.*

between 6 p.m. and 6 a.m. By the 17th century, flint walls were no longer seen as an adequate defence against artillery. To defend the town, parliamentarian supporters built two redoubts outside the North Gate. Major-General Ireton wanted to knock down the medieval walls and build a fort instead, but the people of the town would not allow it.

Many people have forgotten that there was once a castle in Yarmouth. It was on King Street, near Row 99. Manship tells us that it had four turrets used as watchtowers and also as beacons to warn the surrounding countryside of an enemy's approach. It was repaired several times in the 16th century, and at one time it was planned to use it as a prison, but by Manship's time it was already ruinous. In 1620, the top part was taken down and the stone used in restoring the east mount. The site was then used as a store until the 19th century when it was sold to Thomas Penrice, who set up a liquor store called the *Penrice Arms* there.

Apart from the Tolhouse, the only relic of domestic building as early as the 1208 charter lies under 50-56 Howard Street South: it is a 12th-century barrel-vaulted undercroft, or cellar, over which the hall of a private house must have stood. Still-surviving medieval brick windows in a large wall behind Northgate Street show that there was a large 14th-century property here, though nothing is known of its history.

During a period of prosperity between 1570 and 1640, the town was virtually completely rebuilt, and it survived in this form until the Second World War. Manship wrote:'No maritime town in England is better provided with fine houses than Yarmouth as anyone can see for himself better than I can describe them … . The houses are built of flint and well burnt brick and covered with tiles so the risk of fire is diminished.

24 *The Customs House: this photograph was taken during Yarmouth's oil-boom period, as shown by the number of ships at mooring.*

25 *Wooden panelling and plaster ceiling inside the Star Hotel. This is now in the Metropolitan Museum of Art in New York.*

As to their design, come and see them, save my pen the trouble of describing them, and judge for yourself.' He described the South Quay as 'the Cheapside of Yarmouth', meaning that it resembled this prosperous part of London.[24]

A century later, Daniel Defoe recorded his impression: 'In this pleasant and agreeable range of houses are some very magnificent buildings, and among the rest, the Custom House and Town-Hall, and some merchants' houses which look like little palaces, rather than the dwelling houses of private men.' One fine example is 4 South Quay, which was built by Benjamin Cooper in 1596: the date can be seen on a chimney piece in a ground-floor room. The plaster ceiling on the first floor, of the same date, is one of the finest in Britain. This is the house later owned by John Carter.

The site of the Town House on the South Quay is said to have been occupied by 'a fair, ancient and stately house', which belonged in the mid-14th century to Thomas de Drayton, Admiral of the North and one of the leading townsmen of Yarmouth. It was acquired by the Corporation in 1580, and was used for a range of purposes including as a Customs House for the collection of both royal and local customs. A public clock was erected in a turret in the roof in 1593. Part of the building was used as a chapel for the Dutch community. From 1600 this was shared with the Corporation who heard prayers and sermons there on weekdays. In the early 17th century, it became the custom for the town waits to perform on the lead roof on Sunday evenings in summer. In 1736, it was adapted as a theatre, and plays were performed there until the new Theatre opened in the 1770s.[25]

In about 1720, John Andrews, known as 'the greatest herring merchant in Europe', built his new house, now 20 South Quay. It became the Customs House in 1802 and the Port Authority Office in 1985. Behind the South Quay is the 'Old Merchant's House', with a Georgian frontage on a 17th-century building: it is now a museum.

Paul Rutledge defines the core of the town as the area bounded by St Nicholas' church and Fuller's Hill to the north, and the castle, called in documents the *kinges ston hus*, to the south. This was roughly at the southern end of Howard Street. The three main north/south streets curve gently: probably as the sea level rose, the newly-exposed land was swiftly occupied. This gradual development explains why the Rows do not run across the main streets.

Excavation at the site of the old Lacon's brewery has confirmed the gradual spread of settlement westward as the river level fell. This sense of ascent is best seen today in walking up the street called the Conge from the river to the market place. (The word 'Conge' refers to a whirlpool occurring at the bend in the river, though it is often thought to be the French word conge and to relate to the King's custom official whose house was at the bottom of the hill beside the river.) Rutledge suggests that five of the six blocks of land within the later town wall were developed before the time of the charter issued to Yarmouth in 1208, and the sixth (the area between Fuller's Hill and Rampart Street) by the later 13th century: 'by 1286 Yarmouth's settlement pattern was virtually complete'.

The town is known for its 'Rows', a unique form of urban development first recorded as early as 1198. The Rows consisted of narrow parallel passages, with houses that had only one room up and down. When more space was needed, extra rooms were added at the back so that some houses were eventually back to back with properties on neighbouring rows. Special narrow carts (known as 'troll carts') had to be used to

26 *No 5, South Quay, an 18th-century house built in header bond brickwork, with a fine Georgian doorway. Behind the frontage is the core of an earlier house.*

27 *The Conge showing the rise from the present-day river up to the earliest part of the town. The large building is Lacon's Brewery, demolished in 1974.*

28 *A typical Row: very little sunlight ever entered these windows.*

carry goods along the passages: there is one in the Tolhouse Museum. Yarmouth carts are first mentioned in an ordinance issued in 1517, where they are described as 'lately devised carts called Harry Carriers'.[26]

The Rows were largely rebuilt at the end of the 16th century. As David Dymond says, 'The characteristic house of the Rows from the 1580s onwards was a relatively small three-storeyed house of brick or flint, with one room on each floor. It often had a passage through to a backyard, a winding staircase lit by small windows against the chimney stack, and cast-iron anchors fixing joists to walls.'[27]

The most graphic description of the Rows is that given in *Household Words*, a magazine edited by Charles Dickens, although he may not have written the article himself:

> A row is a long narrow lane or alley, quite straight or as nearly so as may be, with houses on each side, both of which you can sometimes touch at once with the finger-tips of each hand, by stretching out your arms to their full extent. Now and then the houses overhang, and even join above your head, converting the row, so far, into a sort of tunnel, or tubular passage. Many and many a picturesque old bit of domestic architecture is to be hunted up amongst the rows. In some rows there is little more than a blank wall for the double boundary. In others the houses retreat into tiny courts, where washing and clear-starching are done, and wonderful nasturtiums and scarlet runners are reared from green boxes.[28]

29 *A Yarmouth cart on the South Quay.*

30 *Early photograph of a Row before paving.*

Religion

Yarmouth church was completed on its present site in 1119. It has been enlarged and altered very many times since. The spire became twisted from the effects of the fire of 1683, leading to a popular saying 'as crooked as Yarmouth steeple'. It was taken down in 1803 as it was thought to be unsafe, and replaced with a spire designed by William Wilkins.

The church was run by a group of Benedictine monks, as a cell of Norwich Cathedral priory. The earliest use of squared knapped flints in Yarmouth was in the priory. The still-surviving large 14th-century hall at the priory was probably the prior's hall, rather than the monastic dining-room as previously thought. It is now part of the Priory School. The oak-panelled ceiling dates from the early 16th century and one of the fireplaces bears the arms of the last prior, William Castleton. Panels of the arms of England and France that were originally in this Hall are now on the porch of the nearby parish church.

Small details of life in the priory can be found from its account rolls. Stocktaking at the cell in 1485 revealed 11 barrels of beer on the premises, a reasonable supply as there were only two or three monks ever in residence – but, of course, they had to cater for servants and guests as well. The prior of the cell treated the poor of the town (of whom there must have been many) to a dinner on each Christmas Day. It appears to have been a rowdy affair. In 1613, the then occupier of the parsonage, William Gostling, was asked why it was no longer held and gave as one of his reasons 'the danger of gathering together of at least a thousand people, the most of them being of the rudest and basest sort, all which meeting, there have been oftentimes danger of murder by quarrelling and fighting amongst themselves, and also breaking of windows, tables, pots, glasses, and many other disorders, which can by no means be prevented.' Gostling agreed instead to give £10 each year to the bailiffs to be quietly distributed to the needy at Christmas time!

Church income came from fees, donations, and above all from tithes. Everyone had to give 10 per cent of their income or their produce to the church. Yarmouth fishermen had to pay their tithes, too: some of the fish went straight to the priory kitchen! Other tithes in kind in the town included piglets, pigeons and poultry. A fee known as a mortuary had to be paid at a person's death, to compensate for any tithes not paid during one's lifetime. This was commonly a robe or gown, but could be an animal or a piece of plate. The church in Yarmouth received a few shillings a year from its donation boxes: the building of a chapel with an image of Henry VI led to greatly increased income for a short time, while there were regular offerings at the shrine to our Lady of Arneburgh in the church. Edward III had gone on pilgrimage to Arneburgh in thanksgiving for his great victory at Sluys, in which very many Yarmouth men had taken part, so that the shrine in Yarmouth church was 'a corporate gesture of gratitude and of civic pride'. Another source of income was from wax sales – the wax was used for candles and for moulding of images of injured body parts, placed in front of the shrine in the hope of a cure.[29]

As an important port, Yarmouth benefited from pilgrims travelling to holy places across Europe. John Paston went on pilgrimage to Santiago in Spain in 1473, beginning his journey by taking ship from Yarmouth to Calais. In 1414, the Lynn religious writer Margery Kempe took ship at Yarmouth on her pilgrimage to the Holy Land: she prayed

31 *Saint Nicholas', the mother church of Yarmouth.*

before the image of Our Lady in the church. She crossed over to Holland and travelled overland to Venice, taking ship from there to the Holy Land. The trade worked in both directions: Flemish cities had lists of approved destinations for their pilgrims, which included Walsingham and Bury St Edmunds: many travelled via Yarmouth.[30]

Wills are a good indicator of popular piety. Henry Swinden, when working on the Great Yarmouth borough archives, noted that more wills occur among these records for 1349 than in any other year, no doubt because of the Black Death described later in this chapter. He transcribed 23 of these wills. All but one left money to St Nicholas' church and 18 asked to be buried there. The testators seem more interested in their parish church than the monastic institution: almost all the money bequeathed was for the fabric of the church and only one man left money for the monks themselves. The money was often specifically for the 'new work' extending the church to the west: this would have made the building by far the largest parish church in England, but it was abandoned soon after 1349, probably because of the Black Death.

For a century, Saint Nicholas' was the only religious community in the town, but the 13th century saw the coming of the friars, whose buildings came to take up almost 20 per cent of the land inside the town walls. Friars were very different people from monks: they were dedicated to a life of poverty and originally owned nothing. They were mendicants, that is, they made their living by begging. They settled in towns where there was much poverty, Yarmouth being a prime example. They preached, heard confessions and buried the dead, and also welcomed ordinary people to their services, especially to the evening service, compline, which people were encouraged to attend after their day's work was over.

Dominican and Franciscan friars had both arrived in Yarmouth by about 1270, followed by the Carmelites in 1278. The fourth major order, the Austin friars, set up their main house in Gorleston, but they did have a cell in Yarmouth. The word Ostend in Ostend Row is a corruption of the word Austin: part of a doorway arch can still be seen in the wall of the Society of Friends' meeting house, which now occupies the site of this cell.

The value of friars to a town is controversial. W.R. Richmond wrote of the friars at Yarmouth: 'They touched with love and pity the lives of thousands of the poor and sorrowful, who but for them would have died without knowledge of the Redeemer, or without being brightened by one ray of human sympathy.' Others disagreed. One local opponent of the friars was a woman called Margery Blackster who in 1428 told off one of the Yarmouth Carmelite friars for begging: she said that he would please God better by leaving the friary and going to the plough.

Evidence of the general popularity of friars in Yarmouth can be seen in the 23 wills for 1349 already mentioned. Only two of the testators asked for a friary burial, but no fewer than 15 left money to friaries. There was an occasional precious gift: William de Motte bequeathed to the Yarmouth Carmelite Friars a silver cup with a pelican on the lid. This gift underlines the main problem with friars: their very popularity was the undoing of their original ideals. As people gave them more land and more possessions, they became almost as wealthy as the monks, and the poverty of the original founders became just a memory.

Friary sites tended to be much smaller than monastic ones but they might have space for gardens. According to C.J. Palmer, the Franciscan friary at Great Yarmouth had a 'strawberry yard' and mulberry trees: at least one of the trees was still standing in 1571, over 30 years after the friary had been dissolved. When ten-year-old Nicholas Hyndry went to Gorleston friary in about 1500 it was to gather crocus flowers (years later he was to claim that the friars held him there against his will and forced him to take their vows).

The Benedictine monastery and the friaries were all dissolved under King Henry VIII. Very little remains to be seen, apart from part of the cloister and some fragments of wall-painting within the Franciscan friary, a unique survival.

Within a century of the end of the friaries, Nonconformity was becoming a force in Yarmouth, under the leadership of William Bridge. Bridge was born in 1600 and became Rector of St Peter Hungate in Norwich in 1636. He was excommunicated for his beliefs and left for Holland, where he became pastor of the Congregational Church in Rotterdam. He returned to England in 1642 to be the first pastor of the Yarmouth Congregational Church. He died in London in 1670. Several members of this church, such as Isaac Preston, William Emperor and Daniel Shepherd, became aldermen of Yarmouth during the Commonwealth period. However, they were all dismissed at the Restoration.[31]

Records survive of other people leaving Yarmouth for Holland in the years 1637 to 1639. Some left because Protestantism was better tolerated there, returning to

32   *The cloisters of the Franciscan friary.*

Yarmouth when conditions improved. The Rayner family and James Gedney left in June 1637, but returned to Yarmouth in 1642 to help establish the Congregational Church. Barbrey Meecke, a widow, who also left in 1637, came back in 1651 to become a member of the same church. However, some of these travellers from Yarmouth went on from Holland to New England. These included Francis Lawes of Norwich and his family, who took with them their servant Samuel Lincorne, aged 18 years. The family of President Abraham Lincoln is descended from this servant.[32]

Half a century later, the Congregationalists were followed by the Quakers. The Friends' Meeting House in Howard Street was erected in 1692, and it was originally necessary to use steps to get in! There is a small and little-known cemetery to the east of the building. The only Anglican church was still St Nicholas, but there was an obvious need for a second: St George's chapel was built by John Price in 1714-6 and is loosely modelled on St Clement Danes in London.

One aspect of popular religion was the belief in witchcraft. Occasional accusations of witchcraft occur throughout the ages, but in Yarmouth, as in most towns, they were at their peak in the 16th and 17th centuries, culminating in the Great Witch Trial of 1645.

A typical case is that of Elizabeth Butcher from 1582 to 1584. In March 1582, Elizabeth and Cecilia Atkin were found guilty of witchcraft by the Yarmouth Sessions Court. They were sentenced to stand in the pillory in the Market Place every market day until they confessed their guilt. Cecilia presumably did so as she disappears from the record but Elizabeth was more obstinate: in August 1582 she was sentenced to a year in gaol, unless she confessed her guilt, and to make occasional appearances in the pillory 'as an example to others'. Even this was not the end: in April 1584 she appeared again before the judges and this time she was sentenced to be hanged, along with another woman, Joan Lingwood, found guilty of witchcraft. There were occasional cases in the years that followed such as that of Helen Gill, who was accused of practising witchcraft in the town against a certain Catherine Smythe in 1587.

However, the biggest trial was that of 1645. Yarmouth Assembly actually invited Matthew Hopkins (the well-known 'Witchfinder–General') to come to the town to 'discover and find out' witches. He later claimed to have had 16 witches hanged in the town but this seems an exaggeration. On 10 September 1645, 11 people appeared before the sessions court charged with witchcraft of various forms. Two of them were men.

First before the court was Marcus Prynne, a gardener. He was accused of bewitching a man called John Howlett as a result of which Howlett sickened and wasted away. He was also accused on two further counts which appear to be clairvoyance rather than witchcraft as such. He told Ann Cant where a cushion was that she had lost and told John Ringer where to find some silver coins he had mislaid. The jury found Prynne not guilty. He was followed by two women, Barbara Wilkinson and Elizabeth Fassett. They were both accused of 'feeding and entertaining evil spirits' but they too were found not guilty.

The fourth person to appear, Maria Vevey or Verey, faced more specific charges as well as the usual 'entertaining and feeding evil spirits'. She was accused of practising witchcraft on four named people: however, Maria was acquitted on all counts. The fifth accused was a sailor called John Sparke. He was also acquitted. Next was Alice Ceipwell, charged with 'having used practiced and exercised witchcraft, and with many evil, wicked and diabolical spirits then and there consulted and made compact and the same evil spirits with evil intention did feed and entertain'. Alice was found guilty and the judges sentenced her to hang. She was followed by three more women, each accused of 'practising witchcraft and feeding and entertaining evil spirits'. These were Brigetta Howard and Elizabeth Dudgeon, spinsters, and Maria Blackborne, widow. Each was found guilty and each was sentenced to hang.

The tenth prisoner was Elizabeth Bradwell. She too was accused not only of sorcery and witchcraft but also of specific offences, that she 'diabolically and feloniously used, practised and exercised upon and against John Moulton, the infant son of Henry Moulton, hosier, from which the said child in the greatest peril suffered and languished.' She too was found guilty and sentenced to hang. The final prisoner, Johanna Lacey, widow, was charged with similar offences and also found guilty and sentenced to death.

For some reason the sentence on Johanna Lacey was respited, but the other five women were hanged together. This presumably took place at the gallows on the boundary between Yarmouth and Caister.

After this trial, the jurors of Yarmouth seem to have been satisfied. Five further people were charged with witchcraft at the sessions court of the following April – John Smyth, Dioni Kirsp alias Avery, Dorothy Dewe, Ann Parke and Elizabeth Clark. All were acquitted. There were no witchcraft cases in September 1646 and only one in April 1647. This was Maria Verey, one of those acquitted at the great trial of 18 months earlier: she was again found not guilty. In this year Matthew Hopkins himself suffered the fate he had inflicted on so many, being publicly hanged as a sorcerer.

Health

Medieval hospitals were really hospices, looking after the sick but not operating on people. The Hospital of St Mary the Virgin on the east side of the Market Place was founded in 1278 by Thomas Fastolfe to support eight poor men and eight poor women. It was a religious foundation, like all medieval hospitals, and so it was dissolved in 1538. The site passed to Yarmouth Corporation, who used it for a Grammar School, a Workhouse and for other purposes. The boys at the Grammar School were ordered to help re-fortify the town walls in 1588 at the time of the armada and again in 1642 when the town feared attack by Cavaliers. The corporation ceased to manage the school in 1773. There were also two lazar or leper houses in the medieval town. The site of one, just outside the North Gate, is shown on some of the early maps of Great Yarmouth.[33]

The Children's Hospital was founded in 1634, also on part of St Mary's Hospital site. It was a charity school for the training of poor children. Another school, the Bluecoat Charity School, was founded by Yarmouth Corporation in 1713. The Fishermen's Hospital was founded by the Corporation in 1702. Again it was not a hospital as we know it but a block of almshouses for 'decayed' fishermen. The statue in the courtyard is of Charity.

The Borough Assembly concerned itself with health and hygiene issues very similar to those that the town faces today, issuing orders to improve the environment. Examples include orders concerning foul gutters in the town, and others that refuse was to be placed well away from the town. In 1554, people were appointed to clean the town gutters and in 1555 it was ordered that any new house or shed must have a roof of tiles and that any house that was leased out had to have a 'sufficient chimney'. Butchers' offal was to be thrown into the sea at night within 24 hours of slaughter. Refuse – 'crappes' – and ballast were not to be thrown into the harbour. The Assembly also exercised control over the common lands on the Denes, where Yarmouth people grazed their animals. To prevent over-grazing, the number of cows was restricted to one or two per household. The animals were rounded up once a year and any strays impounded.[34]

Not everything attempted by the Assembly was achieved as shown by the dispute over selling butter in 1542 and 1543. In August 1542, it was ordered that Yarmouth people could buy butter only in the Market Place, and not 'at the bridge' or anywhere else in the town. However, in June 1543, this was repealed. People could now sell butter anywhere, but people who bought two gallons or more to try to re-sell it had to pay a fine. The violent temper of the times is shown by an order threatening imprisonment for anyone who tried to 'pull or take' butter from anyone by force. Probably the most extreme effort to control the lives of the poor was made by the Assembly on 29 December 1625 when an order was issued that 'no poor people should be married' unless they first obtained the permission of the alderman or chief constable where they lived.[35]

Borough records also reveal aspects of daily life in Yarmouth, including the dire poverty – and the smells! When the goods of John of Cressingham were distrained in 1326/7 after he and his wife were accused of beating an old woman who presumably lodged with them, they were valued at just seven pence. They amounted to little more than two stools, eight trenchers (wooden plates), a barrel, two pots and a sickle. In 1465/6, Joan Comer was prosecuted for using the common well to wash 'linen clothes soiled and full of urine'. Twenty years later, according to the records, Thomas Rant 'keeps his pigs so foully on the Denne [the Denes] that passers-by take infection from the smell'.[36]

The most dramatic health event of the Middle Ages was the plague known as the Black Death, which spread across Europe from the east in the late 1340s. It is generally accepted that it first appeared in England at Melcombe Regis (now called Weymouth) in the summer of 1348, spreading to London by November. The epidemic reached Norfolk in the spring of the following year, 1349. A later 14th-century chronicle quoted by the writer William Worcester says that in Yarmouth no less than 7,000 out of a population of 10,000 died. In fact, the mortality rate can only be guessed at: 40 per cent of the population may have died. As late as 1502, it was still being said that parts of the town were empty because of the effects of the Black Death.

The Black Death did not disappear, but attacked many times over the next three hundred years. Later waves of plague were less fatal than that of 1349, but they are better recorded. Assembly orders show the kind of defensive measures that the town took:

> Apr 28 1590. Ordered that for preventing the plague lately begun every alderman shall appoint a woman in every ward to visit the house where any sickness or death may happen and to report to the alderman whether it is the plague or not, and if it should prove to be the plague the alderman shall charge every house to be watched and no person to be admitted in or out unless every person going in shall remain there a month. And that the infected house may be provided for the watchman shall take notice of their wants and inform the alderman thereof, who shall order that their wants shall be supplied, shall take care that all necessary things shall be provided, and they that are able to be provided at their own charge, and they who are not by a general collection. And that an assessment be made on the inhabitants for defraying the expenses. And every watchman at the sick house to be allowed 8 pence a day and that the alderman of wards shall every Saturday night deliver to the bailiff a list of those who die in the week and of such houses as are infected. And for avoiding God's judgement on drunkenness so common in this town, and to avoid all meetings which may spread the infection, it is ordered that no inhabitant shall resort to any alehouse to eat or drink except in the company of a stranger and for a special business under penalty of 6 pence for the first offence, 1 shilling for the second and 3 days imprisonment for the third; the ordinance to be published by the vintners. That all body clothes etc that shall come out of infected houses shall be carried near the north mill or the old haven to the south to be aired, where stakes shall be set up on pain of having their bedding etc burnt.

When Nathaniel Brent began a visitation of East Anglia on behalf of Archbishop Laud in 1635, he did not stay long in Yarmouth, recording: 'I made as much haste out of the town as I could, because the plague there was very hot.'[37]

Plague came back to Yarmouth in 1664 and remained until 1666. It probably spread from London, reaching Norfolk both by road and by sea. The first recorded victim is Mary Call, buried on 17 November 1664, followed by Margaret Holl on the following day and Margaret's husband Francis on 19 November. Two sisters of Mary Call, Margaret and Christian, were buried on 5 December.

The parish clerk, Robert Parr, kept notes of the burials at Great Yarmouth, distinguishing plague victims from other deaths. However, Parr himself died during this time and was buried on 8 September 1665: the record does not make it clear whether he himself was a victim of the plague he was so assiduously annotating. Later records were presumably kept by his successor, John Johnson, who also entered Parr's

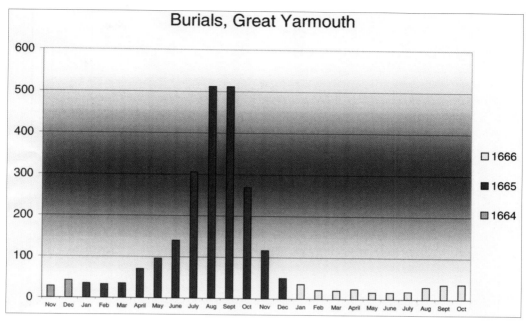

33   *The Great Plague: burials in Yarmouth, 1664-6.*

name into the burial register. Between November 1664 and October 1666, 1,410 burials of plague victims are recorded in the register, peaking in September 1665 when 116 people died of plague in the week ending 22 September. This is an under-estimate of the number of plague deaths the town. For two weeks in August 1665 no burials are recorded at all, presumably because the recording system broke down: perhaps Parr was already too ill to carry out his duties. The number of burials recorded in August is 273, so we can guess that the total number of burials in the month was at least 500, matching the 515 burials in September. After this the figures fell rapidly, 269 burials in October, 117 in November and 50 in December. These are the figures for total burials: those specifically said to be plague victims fell from a peak of 442 in September to 29 in December. By the beginning of 1666, life was back to normal, with twenty or thirty burials a month and only eight burials of plague victims in the summer.[38]

Other diseases included the sweating sickness, known all over Europe as the English Sweat. It first appeared in 1485 with further outbreaks until 1551, after which it disappeared: this could have been a form of influenza, although this is disputed. England also suffered in the European pandemic of influenza in 1501. Other influenza epidemics affecting Norfolk included those of 1537-8, 1578, 1580, 1583 and 1585.

Despite these problems, some people already saw Yarmouth as a health resort. Manship proudly wrote:

> Yarmouth is fortunate in having a place on its east side called the Denes exposed to the clean dry winds from the sea. I have myself known many people who have been sent by their doctors from Cambridge to take the sea air and have recovered their health very quickly.[39]

34   *The Fishermen's Hospital: the shape of the gables reveals the influence of Dutch architecture.*

Crime and Punishment

The gaol delivery rolls for the ten year period 1307 to 1316 have been published by the Norfolk Record Society. They give us a picture of life in a community where crimes of murder and theft were all too common. People might be arrested on suspicion alone. In 1316, Richard of Cantley was arrested by the constable of Yarmouth for 'wandering around at night with unknown sailors who were discovered with pieces of cloth and arms which they had stolen'. The jurors decided he was of good repute and he was acquitted. William of Scot(land) was arrested on suspicion 'because he is a Scot and enemy of the king'. The jury found nothing against him.

Murder cases are also recorded. In 1315, William Galt was accused of killing Alexander of Wymondham at Great Yarmouth: he was acquitted. An unnamed Yarmouth man was murdered on the road between Terrington and Clenchwarton in 1316 and robbed of over £20 in cash. A man called Ludbright was murdered in Yarmouth in the same year and Ingelhorn of Happisburgh was accused of the crime.

Most cases are very briefly recorded, but one murder case does give more detail. In 1312, Sybel Clinne and Matilda Arnald were charged with killing Godfrey atte Watles. Godfrey was found to be literally a lunatic: during the moon's crescent he was mad. He met Sybel in Middlegate, seized her by her hood and dragged her into a narrow lane called John's Row Alley. As they entered the lane, Godfrey tried to strangle Sybel with her hood: she stabbed him in the stomach and he died immediately. The jury decided that she had killed him in self defence, and she was sent back to prison to await a pardon from the king.

35 *Saint George's Chapel.*

Three cases of petty theft that came before the court on one day, 20 March 1316, are more typical. Thomas Payn and William Pykun were charged with stealing a 'maple wood vessel' from a Yarmouth house. Payne turned informer while Pykun was acquitted. Thomas of Winchelsea and Adam le White of Billockby broke down a fence near the quay and stole board and timber. The case was dismissed because the stolen property was only worth ten pence. The last case of the three had a more tragic outcome. William Asketel, his pregnant wife Catherine, and the latter's mother Joan were accused of possessing stolen property – a blue tunic and perse surcoat worth two shillings. William and Joan were acquitted but Catherine was found guilty. The only possible sentence for any criminal was death. Because she was pregnant, Catherine would not have been hanged straight away, but the respite was only temporary: after the baby had been born, she would have been hanged. Harsh treatment, many people might think, for a case of small-time receiving of stolen goods, but standard practice in the Middle Ages.

There was a more serious case in Yarmouth at the same time, however. A gang of men broke into the Leper Hospital, killed a servant there, and stole silver and cloth. At least one of the gang was probably a professional thief, as he was accused of other robberies at Felbrigg and Hardley. Two of the men claimed to be clerks (clergymen), indeed the name of one was given as 'Richard, nephew of the vicar of Hickling'. If they could prove their clerical status they would be handed over to the Bishop's court: if found guilty there, the punishment would not be execution but some form of penance.[40]

By the 18th century, newspapers are providing a source of information on crime in addition to records of the courts. These examples include theft, smuggling and murder, and reflect Yarmouth's position as a cosmopolitan town:

36   *South Quay, showing the Georgian Town Hall.*

1728: Whereas on Sunday the 28th Day of January last, John Arrold, a North Yarmouth man and Master of a Sloop (as 'twas said) came to the Blue Anchor Inn, near the Millgate of Portsmouth, and hired and rode away with a black Mare (full fourteen hands and a half high, a large switch Tail, a Wall Speck in each Eye, Pads well, and is of full Age), for Petersfield, in the road to London (as he pretended) but was seen to ride through Chichester in Sussex, and has not since been heard of. If any Person can make a Discovery, so as the Mare may be had again, all reasonable Charges, with a handsome Gratuity, shall be immediately paid by Thomas Stables, Master of the said Inn. NB The Mare has an S burnt in the near Flank.

1746, Yarmouth, Sep 15. Last night, between Eleven and Twelve o'clock, a young woman was cruelly murder'd at an Ale-House in this Town. She was violently bruis'd on her Breasts and Neck, and thrown out of a Garret Window into the Street, so that she died immediately. Two of Sir Robert Rich's Dragoons, quarter'd in this Town, were sent to Goal on Suspicion; but it is believed that the Murder was committed by two Sailors belonging to the Hazard Man of War, which sail'd for Harwich this morning. The Coroner's Inquest, after spending six Hours in taking Examinations, brought in their Verdict, Wilful Murder by Persons unknown. An Express is sent to Captain Grant, of the Hazard, for the two men.

1750, Yarmouth, July 19. On Monday last Capt. Ward, commander of the Swift Sloop of War, on the Lynn Station, cruising off the Lincolnshire Coast, saw a French Cutter, which he came up with, and took, to the Northward of Dimlington; she had on Board seven Men, all English, and some of them supposed to be outlaw'd, 300 Half Anchors of Brandy, and 400 Weight of Tea, which the Captain carried to Lynn.[41]

Life Stories

JOHN PEREBROWN

Little known today, Perebrown was the Nelson of his time. He was born in Great
Yarmouth and his house was at or near the Conge. He was Lord Admiral of the navy
north of the Thames under Edward II and Edward III. His great victory was the Battle
of Sluys in 1340: he led the English fleet which annihilated the French navy – the
French are said to have lost 160 ships and 15,000 men. Richmond tells the story of
the battle:

> To the English fleet Yarmouth supplied 43 ships on board of which were 1,075
> of our own town, and Perebroune, a burgess of Yarmouth, was entrusted with the
> supreme command. He arranged that each ship, on board of which were men-at-
> arms, should be supported in its attack on a French ship by two vessels filled with
> archers to shoot down the Frenchmen on the decks while the men-at-arms boarded.
> The plan was successful, and the French fleet were swept from the Channel. For the
> splendid services rendered by Perebroune he was raised to the rank of admiral, and
> in honour of his victory the king permitted Yarmouth to place in the municipal
> coat of arms three royal demi-lions (half-lions) in front of the tail ends of three
> appetising herrings.[42]

This, still the borough 'logo', can be seen in many places in the town, on the railings of
council flats, on waste and recycling bins, and on seats along the front, for example. Few
of those who see it ever give a thought to the origins of this unusual image.

Perebroune was a key man in pre-Black Death Yarmouth, with a finger in many
pies. He was a merchant and a ship owner, with at least seven fishing boats as well as
a fish house, and also four trading vessels. He was a major player in the wine trade.
Perebrown was MP for the borough in the 1320s, served as bailiff no fewer than 15
times, and was one of the men responsible for the collection of money to build and
maintain the town walls. In the 1330s he was being taxed at 50 per cent more than the
next wealthy Yarmouth merchant, an indication of his dominant status in the town. In
1314, he was involved in a dispute with the inhabitants of Southtown, which forced
him to take refuge for a time on one of his ships. He was involved in national politics,
taking the side of Prince Edward, later King Edward III, against his father in 1327.

Perebrown died in 1342 or 1343. He failed to establish a family dynasty in Yarmouth:
he had just one son, Farman, who died in 1348 or 1349, probably a victim of the Black
Death. He is commemorated in Yarmouth in the street named Perebrown Avenue.

MILES CORBETT

Corbett was born in 1594 or 1595, the son of Sir John Corbett of Sprowston (not
Thomas, as is claimed in many books). He studied law and became recorder of
Yarmouth in 1625 and one of its MPs in 1628, representing the borough for 37 years.
When Civil War broke out in 1642, both Yarmouth Corporation and Corbett himself
were keen supporters of Parliament against the King. He was one of the commission
that drew up charges against Archbishop Laud, which led to Laud's execution in 1645.
Corbett was Cromwell's lawyer and one of those who sat in judgement on Charles I
and signed his death warrant. In 1650, he became a civil commissioner for Ireland.

When the monarchy was restored in 1660, Corbett's life (as for all the 'regicides' who had signed Charles's death warrant) was forfeit. He fled to the continent but was eventually captured at Delft. He was brought back to England and hanged, drawn and quartered with two other regicides at Tyburn on 19 April 1662. The diarist Samuel Pepys noted the calmness that he and his fellow sufferers showed at their execution. Corbett had a wife, Mary, who survived him, and several children, including a son named John. The day before his death, Corbett wrote to John saying that he bequeathed him his cause and his faith, but no estate. His Yarmouth house off the Market Place (later the *Weavers' Arms*) has a plaque to him on the wall. [43]

THOMAS ALLISON

Allison was born in Yarmouth in 1647 and became a freeman of the borough in 1668. He was a merchant and was employed by the Russia Company, trading between London and Archangel on the Baltic Sea. The great adventure of his life took place in 1697 when, on 8 October, he embarked on his ship the *Ann* of Yarmouth for a voyage from Archangel to Gravesend.

Driven by a storm, the *Ann* became disabled and eventually saw land off North Cape, the northernmost point of Scandinavia. The ship anchored in Porsangen Fjord, and Allison and his 24 men prepared to winter in the Arctic. The *Ann* served for shelter and there was plenty of fuel available from larch and willow trees on the nearby hills. Food was the main problem. There was no animal life around and the men were forced to forage for shellfish. Christmas was celebrated with a hand-out of beer and honey which Allison had kept back for the occasion. There were thaws in the New Year, but each time the icy conditions returned and by February the rations had to be cut. In the middle of March, a ship bearing provisions finally turned up, and the ice eventually broke on 25 March 1698. The *Ann* continued on her journey to Gravesend, reaching the port on 24 April: the voyage from Archangel had taken seven months!

Allison published his story in 1699, in a book intended both for other seamen and for the general public. The book captured the imagination, especially on its republication in 1808, and is an early example of true-life travel and adventure, a genre still very popular today. He made other voyages as well: in his will made in 1704 he describes himself as 'in good health of body but being going to sea and considering the many uncertainties of this mortal life'. He died in Yarmouth in 1706, being buried there on 30 September: his will refers only to his wife Mary, probably his second wife, and to his daughter Ann, so he presumably had no surviving sons.

Chapter Three

To the Sea – Yarmouth 1759-1900

Before the mid-18th century, the prosperity of Yarmouth was built upon two foundations, fishing and trade. A third foundation began in a small way when bathing in sea water became fashionable: in 1759 the Sea Baths were opened near the beach. From this time Yarmouth began to assume its modern role as a seaside resort and the town slowly started to turn its face from the river towards the sea. The local press carried advertisements for the new facility:

> 1760: YARMOUTH BATHS
> On Monday the 19th of May next, will be opened at Great Yarmouth, in Norfolk.
> Two commodious covered Sea Baths, one for Gentlemen, and the other for Ladies, with four dressing Rooms and a large Ante-Chamber to each. The Baths will be supplied every Morning from the Sea by a continued current through them during the Bathing Time.
> NB Great Variety of convenient Lodgings in the Town.

John Preston lists the developments over the next 60 years:

> In 1788, adjoining to the north-end of the original building, a large and pleasant public room was added, and which has undergone much improvement, more particularly through the exertions of the present proprietor. Three London papers are taken here daily, and two provincial papers weekly. About two years since, the Baths and Bath-rooms were purchased by Mr Bly, who laid out a considerable sum in erecting most excellent hot and cold baths, and in making the public rooms convenient for company, where they have a full view of the ocean, and of that beautiful promenade the jetty, and may enjoy salubrious sea breezes in the most agreeable manner. Here are also occasionally balls, public breakfasts and tea-parties, and a band of music attends twice or thrice a week for the amusement of a numerous and genteel company, who assemble, more or less, every evening, from the end of May to the middle of October. Towards the south part of the building a new room has been lately made, in which is a large handsome billiard-table, which appears much to attract the notice of visitors, and is a great source of amusement, particularly in rainy weather.[1]

A Georgian holiday guide summed up the attractions of Yarmouth to the visitor, especially the wealthy:

> The town is excellently paved, well lighted, and kept uncommonly neat and clean, and the spirit of the inhabitants have spared no expense to furnish accommodation

37   *The jetty, sea front and Bath House, a painting by John Butcher now in the Town Hall.*

and comfort, to render the visitors' stay pleasant. The improvements that have been made in recent years, and are still making, are extensive, and excite astonishment in the mind of every stranger.

One circumstance occurs here which is not to be met with in any other watering place where there is an extensive population, NOT A BEGGAR TO BE SEEN, so admirably is the police conducted, and the miseries of the lower order of people so humanely attended to.[2]

As soon as a tourist trade develops, the selling of 'tripper-bait' follows. By the end of the 18th century, the souvenir market had already begun in Yarmouth: William Absalon was selling pottery decorated with images such as a Yarmouth cart and phrases like 'A Trifle From Yarmouth'.

From the later 18th century, visitors to Yarmouth have left records of their impressions. In May 1790, Parson Woodforde, the eminent diarist, decided to spend a few days in Yarmouth with his family. They took a coach from their home village of Witchingham to Norwich, and there caught the 3 p.m. coach to Yarmouth, arriving at 7 p.m. and putting up at the *Angel* in the Market Place. First impressions were favourable: 'My Brother and Wife and Mrs R. Clarke were highly pleased with Yarmouth and the Sea View.' On the following day they hired three 'Yarmouth Coaches' to take them down the sea front to the Fort: 'the sea rather rough the Wind being high and very cold we found it'. His temper was not improved by finding that were no facilities at the Fort for anything more sophisticated than a glass of porter.

Woodforde did not comment on his ride in a Yarmouth coach, but Sylas Neville was distinctly unimpressed by them: 'They are indeed vile carriages, shake one intolerably except upon carpet ground & are very weighty to the horse.'[3]

A later visitor who has left his reflections on the town is a Nonconformist minister from London, Mr Marten. He, his wife and daughter came by sea, embarking from Custom House stairs at seven in the evening on 7 September 1825. The journey was not without incident: the starboard paddle wheel suddenly came into contact with the paddle box, driving away the boards and causing panic on deck. However, the problem was soon sorted out, and the boat continued on its way, arriving at 2 p.m., having taken 17 hours for the trip. The family stayed at the *Crown and Anchor*, on the Quay near the Haven Bridge: 'as we proceeded thither we admired the pleasantness of the town – the number of ships in the Harbour – the goodness of the Houses and the apparent order and neatness of the Place. We had an Evening walk on the fine jetty extending far into the sea and to which we walked over the fine sands on the shore almost more than shoe deep and which made walking a matter of considerable labour.'[4]

Water and road were the only two ways to reach Yarmouth, but both were long, inconvenient and dangerous. The journey by river from Norwich was speeded up by the introduction of a steam packet in 1813. On Good Friday 1817, however, the boat – the *Telegraph* – blew up just as it was leaving Norwich: eight adults and a child were killed at once and a tenth person later died in hospital. The boat was replaced by one on which horses worked in machines similar to treadmills to provide power.

By 1768, there were 'flying machines' which claimed to provide a fast link to London. Sylas Neville records travelling on one. He left Bishopgate in London at 7 a.m. on 10 October and reached Newmarket for the overnight stop. Leaving there at 5 a.m. they travelled to the *Maid's Head* in Norwich, where he stayed the night before catching the 9 a.m. stagecoach to Yarmouth. The return was only a little quicker – Neville left Yarmouth at 4 a.m. on 14 October, spending the night at Bury St Edmunds. They had a second early start, leaving Bury at four in the morning and reached London at 7 p.m. In the early 19th century a coach named the Telegraph was doing the journey in 16 hours, going through Ipswich rather than via Norwich.[5]

Before 1831 the only road from Yarmouth to Norwich went north through Caister and around the low hills to the north of the marshes, crossing the river Bure at Acle. Throughout the centuries the marshes had increasingly been drained and tidied-up, so that it had at last become practical to create a new shorter road between Acle and Yarmouth. The process began with a bridge. Robert Cory owned the land west of Yarmouth and had a ferry across the Bure. He put up the Suspension Bridge in 1829 and obtained the right to charge tolls for the crossing. He was thinking ahead: he was one of the leading lights in the scheme to build the new road across the marshes, entering Yarmouth across his suspension bridge. The road – now known as the Acle Straight – opened for traffic in 1831. Communication west and south was improved when a new Haven Bridge opened in 1785, only to be replaced by an iron bridge in 1854: the latter cost £24,000, and a further £26,000 had to be spend on the land on which it was placed.

There were many proposals to expand the facilities of the town to attract even more visitors. This is a typical example:

> Mahomed's Baths. It is proposed to form an ESTABLISHMENT of BATHS consisting of S D MAHOMED'S INDIAN MEDICATED VAPOUR and SHAMPOOING BATHS, HOT and COLD SEA-WATER, SHOWER and DOUCH BATHS; under the superintendence of MR H MAHOMED of Brighton.

Above and below: **38** *The bridges of 1785 and 1854, with a variety of shipping, including Norfolk wherries, in both scenes.*

Mahomed's Indian Medicated Vapour and Shampooing Baths have long been celebrated in Brighton and London for the numerous, and almost miraculous, cures performed by them in cases of RHEUMATIC AFFECTIONS, GOUT, SCIATICA, LUMBAGO, STIFF JOINTS, SPRAINS, CUTANEOUS DISEASES etc etc.

To the Nobility, Gentry, and Medical Profession, such an Establishment must be a great acquisition; and MR H MAHOMED pledges himself to give such attention to the Patients of those Medical Gentlemen who may honor him with their support, as he trusts will gain for him the same liberal patronage that he has received in London and Brighton.

It is proposed, by a Committee of Gentlemen resident in Great Yarmouth, to erect a suitable Building adjoining the VICTORIA HOTEL, in the NEW TOWN, for the accommodation of Mr Mahomed's Establishment.

The capital required is estimated at £2600, which it is proposed to raise by Shares; and it is calculated that a handsome return will be obtained, whilst at the same time a great public benefit will be accomplished.

A meeting to promote the scheme was held at the *Victoria Hotel* on 20 July 1842.[6]

The one development that made Yarmouth the great resort that it became was the coming of the railway. Railways were privately funded with a view to making a profitable return. The prospect of a railway to Yarmouth was expected to attract many private investors:

There are perhaps few places in the Kingdom that will ultimately derive more permanent advantages from the introduction of railways than the Town of GREAT YARMOUTH.

Placed at the extreme eastern point of the Kingdom, it could only until recently be approached by a tedious journey of fourteen hours from London. Now, in point of time-distance, Great Yarmouth takes the former relative position of Brighton with the Metropolis, being accessible in less than six hours. The Midland Counties are also now placed by the same means within a few hours distance of Great Yarmouth; and this important Sea-Port, hitherto but little known, yet presenting so many attractions to those who are in pursuit of health or recreation, has now become a Bathing-Place of considerable resort.[7]

There were schemes from the late 1830s onwards to run a railway between Norwich and Yarmouth. Work finally began in 1843, with 1,500 men working on the project. The line formally opened on 30 April 1844, with regular trains beginning on the following day. The shareholders and friends of the Yarmouth and Norwich Railway gave a celebratory dinner at the *Victoria Hotel* on 1 May. The mayor, Charles Palmer, said 'they were meet together for the purpose of celebrating a new era in the history of Yarmouth. Hitherto the town had not kept pace with other towns in the kingdom; but the first step in advance was now made; and he trusted that the inhabitants would not rest satisfied until railway communications were carried out to their fullest extent.'[8]

Then, as now, the terminus of the line was at Vauxhall, on the west side of the Bure. This meant that the only way to the station from the town was via Cory's suspension bridge, which therefore had to take much more traffic. After some acrimony between Cory and the railway, the bridge was widened by adding a walkway to each side, jutting

THE
YARMOUTH & NORWICH RAILWAY

WILL BE

OPENED TO THE PUBLIC FOR THE CONVEYANCE

OF

PASSENGERS, PARCELS, AND GOODS,

On WEDNESDAY, MAY 1st, 1844.

TIME-TABLE.

FARES.
Children in arms, **Free.**
Under Ten Years of Age, **Half-price.**

Down Trains. Departure.	Miles.	DAILY MORNING		DAILY AFTERN.		SUNDAYS MORNING		SUNDAYS AFT.	First Class. s. d.	Second Class. s. d.	Third Class. s. d.
NORWICH		9	11	4	7	8	9	7	—	—	—
SURLINGHAM F.	5	9 12	11 12	4 12	7 12	8 12	9 12	7 12	1 0	0 9	0 6
BRUNDALL	6	9 15	11 15	4 15	7 15	8 15	9 15	7 15	1 0	0 9	0 6
BUCKENHAM	8	9 20	11 20	4 20	7 20	8 20	9 20	7 20	1 6	1 0	0 8
CANTLEY	10	9 25	11 25	4 25	7 25	8 25	9 25	7 25	2 0	1 6	0 10
REEDHAM	12	9 30	11 30	4 30	7 30	8 30	9 30	7 30	2 6	1 8	1 0
YARMOUTH	20¼	—							3 6	2 6	1 3

Up Trains. Departure.	Miles.	DAILY MORNING		DAILY AFTERN.		SUNDAYS MOR.	AFTERN.		First Class. s. d.	Second Class. s. d.	Third Class. s. d.
YARMOUTH		8	10	3	8	10	6	8	—	—	—
REEDHAM	8	8 15	10 15	3 15	8 15	10 15	6 15	8 15	1 6	1 0	0 8
CANTLEY	10	8 25	10 25	3 25	8 25	10 25	6 25	8 25	1 6	1 0	0 10
BUCKENHAM	12	8 30	10 30	3 30	8 30	10 30	6 30	8 30	2 6	1 8	1 0
BRUNDALL	14	8 35	10 35	3 35	8 35	10 35	6 35	8 35	3 0	2 0	1 0
SURLINGHAM F.	15	8 38	10 38	3 38	8 38	10 38	6 38	8 38	3 0	2 0	1 0
NORWICH	20¼	—							3 6	2 6	1 3

Tickets between Yarmouth and Norwich to go and return on the same day—First Class 5s Second Class 4s. Third Class 2s.

Monthly Tickets may be had on application to the Secretary.

Horses and Carriages can only be taken at Norwich and Yarmouth Stations, and will be required to be at the Station a quarter of an hour before the time of starting.

Passengers to be at the intermediate Stations ten minutes before the Trains arrive.

TO & FROM NORWICH & YARMOUTH.

HORSES.			DOGS.	CARRIAGES.	
One Horse.	Two Horses. One Property and in same box.	Three Horses.	Each.	Four Wheels.	Two Wheels.
s. d. 7 0	s. d. 10 0	s. d. 14 0	s. d. 1 0	s. d. 10 0	s. d. 7 0

An Omnibus from **Lowestoft** Daily, at half-past **8** in the Morning, to join the **10** o'clock Train to Norwich, and in the Evening at half-past **6**, to join the **8** o'clock Train; and from Yarmouth to Lowestoft on the arrival of the **Down Trains** quarter before **10**, and at quarter before **8**. FARES—Inside 1s. 6d. Outside 1s. Omnibuses to any Hotel and all parts of Norwich and Yarmouth 6d. each.

By Order,

G. N. TOOTAL, Secretary.

Norwich Office, 25th April, 1844.

39 *Railway timetable for the Yarmouth and Norwich Railway, 1844.*

40   *The fall of the suspension bridge.*

out beyond the suspension chains. This served its purpose exactly a year: then, at 5p.m. on Friday 2 May 1845, disaster struck. The *Norwich Mercury* tells the story:

> On the afternoon [of 2 May 1845] Nelson, the clown at Mr Cooke's Circus, had undertaken to swim in a tub, drawn by four geese, from the drawbridge on the Quay to the Suspension Bridge across the North river a foolish exhibition – but it was one which, from its novelty in Yarmouth, was calculated to attract the multitude. As early as 5 o'clock, when the train arrived from Norwich, although raining smartly, thousands of spectators had already assembled to witness the feat on both sides of the river. The Bridge was then comparatively clear. The Clown commenced his feat with the flood tide at the drawbridge, and had entered the North river. There were many persons on the Bridge, and as he drew near, the multitude upon it endeavoured to obtain a full view as he should pass underneath. Already he had reached Bessey's Wharf, not far from the Bridge, when one or two of the rods were observed to give way; an instant alarm was given to quit the bridge. Alas! the caution came too late. The chains broke and, quick as the passing thought, one entire side fell, and the whole mass of the human beings, whose numbers were estimated from three to four hundred, were swept into the river below.'

The final death toll was 79. A closer look at the victims underlies the nature of the tragedy. They were almost all young. Thirty-three were aged ten or under and a further 21 were aged between 11 and 15. Only 16 of the dead were over 20 years old. The tragedy was also concentrated especially on a small area within the town. No fewer than 29 of the dead had lived with 150 yards of the bridge, in houses in the area bounded by Fuller's Hill, Northgate Street and the Town Wall at Rampart Road. A further 13 came from the rows between Fuller's Hill and the Market Place. There are few reminders of the disaster in Yarmouth today, apart from one gravestone in the parish churchyard. Just inside the main entrance is the stone of George Beloe, an eight-year-old child killed in the disaster: it bears a carving of the bridge as it fell.

A new bridge replaced the one that had collapsed and a further bridge, the River Bure Railway Bridge, was built in 1848. It was an iron plate girder bridge for pedestrians and horse trams, which ran over the bridge and down the quay to the Fishmarket. In 1884, the Great Eastern Railway decided to use steam locomotives to haul the quay traffic. This meant building a new and much stronger bridge. This is the present bridge, first opened in 1887: trams stopped using it in 1928 but the pedestrian part of the bridge is still an essential link between the railway station and the town centre.

By 1846, a direct line was running between Norwich and London so that Yarmouth was linked to the national railway system. As Yarmouth grew as a holiday destination, the number of passengers increased. Day trips were soon established: on 30 June 1846, an excursion organised by Nonconformists carried 6,000 day-trippers from Attleborough and Norwich. The Norfolk novelist Mary Mann has an evocative description of children visiting Yarmouth and experiencing the seaside for the very first time in their lives:

> The first mad rush to the sea – the glistening, glittering blue-and-green-and-gold-and-silver dancing sea – more glorious than anything the children's eyes have yet beheld: and enough of it – enough for all of them! … the perils of cliff-climbing; of seaweed hunting; of paddling, and the dear delight of feeling the caressing waves, hailed with shouts of welcoming laughter, creep over grimy little toes, rise above red ankles, swirl about fat and skinny knees.[9]

Of course, day-trippers also went the other way with 1,500 people taking a trip from Yarmouth to London on one occasion. In 1883, the 'short-cut' via Acle was introduced, cutting the length of the journey between Yarmouth and Norwich by two miles. Meanwhile, links to the Midlands were established through a rival line, which terminated at a new station, Yarmouth Beach. A direct line between Yarmouth and Lowestoft was opened in 1903 terminating in another new station, Yarmouth Southtown. This line was connected to Beach station by a long railway bridge over Breydon Water, one section of which swung open to allow large ships to sail up to Norwich. At the peak of the railway era, Yarmouth thus had three passenger termini – Vauxhall, Beach and Southtown.[10]

Within twenty years of the opening of the railway, the approach by train was the norm. Nall wrote in 1866:

> The Visitor's approach to Great Yarmouth is most commonly made by the Eastern Counties Railway from Norwich. The line for the last few miles winds round the northern banks of the Breydon Water, and from this point, looking out of the carriage window across the lake, he will see stretched out before him a panorama of houses, shipping, trees, and water, all picturesquely intermingled, and extending north and south in a lengthened and imposing perspective. The eye travels from point to point, to church spires and towers, along the roofs of public buildings, warehouses and factories, to the top masts of shipping, and the sails and cappings of gigantic windmills. Each extremity of the landscape has its fitting termination, the venerable tower and spire of St Nicholas' Church defining the northern limit; the lofty and graceful proportions of the Nelson Column, with the heights of Gorleston, the extreme southern boundary.[11]

41   *Britannia Pier.*

Travel by sea was still attractive to many, but carried dangers. The wooden paddle steamer the *William Joliffe* ran between Yarmouth and London from 1854. The local press described a journey on a rough day in August 1856: 'this steam-vessel left London on Saturday evening with 300 passengers, chiefly excursionists to the races. The weather was unpropitious, and as the night came the wind freshened from the east and north east. And about 2 am of Saturday it blew very hard. On arriving off the harbour, it was considered hazardous to attempt to bring the vessel in, and the captain therefore put her back to Lowestoft, where the passengers were landed, and conveyed thence by train. Had it not been for the able conduct of the captain, the consequence might have been serious, for it was deemed necessary for the safety of some, to lash them to the vessel. We are happy to say that, beyond a drenching, no great injury occurred.'[12]

The town was continually adding features to attract the holidaymaker, and the residents also benefited from the increasing range of facilities. A pier as a memorial to the Duke of Wellington was proposed as early as 1843 and work was started in 1853: the work cost £7,000 and took four months to complete. In 1858, the Britannia Pier followed, 750 feet long and costing £6,000. It had an adventurous career: twice in the first ten years ships were driven through the pier: after the first such accident it was shortened by about 80 feet. In 1876, the Council decided to widen the Marina Drive by 60 feet along a length of 3,000 feet, from Britannia Pier to Wellington Pier, at a cost of £2,500. The first purpose-built amusement arcade, the Paradium, opened in 1887.

Outdoor recreational spaces were also developed. There had been horse racing on the South Denes since at least 1715. The first permanent structure on the site was the grandstand built in 1849. The open space known as Chapel Denes or St George's Denes was enclosed and planted by the Council in 1866, under the name of St George's

42   *'Under Britannia Pier'.*

Park. Wellesley Recreation Ground was formally opened in 1888. The original iron gates still survive at the south-west entrance, and a grandstand erected in 1891 is still in use, the oldest football grandstand in Britain.

Another attraction was the Royal Aquarium, intended to serve several functions including those of aquarium and skating rink, on the model of an establishment at Boulogne, 'at once an assembly room, a club, a winter garden, and an Exhibition of the wonders of nature and art, it will supply to the Marine visitor *the one thing always wanting* on the sands at English watering places – a place of pleasure, and refuge, and refreshment, and recreation room, whether in sunshine or storm'. Patrons included the Maharajah Duleep Singh, the Duke of Grafton and Jeremiah James Colman, the Norwich Mustard King. It opened in 1876: 'In its early days there really were fishes to be seen in tanks facing the corridor on the eastern side of the building, but they were neglected by the public, who showed a strong preference for roller skating on the floor of the main hall, which had been laid with asphalt. In due course, as in other places, the craze for skating passed away and the Aquarium became a theatre pure and simple and in the summer season the leading one in the east of England.' Oscar Wilde once gave a lecture here.

One visitor, Reverend Armstrong of Dereham, was not impressed, writing in July 1877: 'During the afternoon visited the new aquarium and thought it inferior, there being a great scarcity of fishes in the tanks – in fact, Natural History seems to take second place to the concert-room and the restaurant.'[13]

We have many first-hand accounts of Yarmouth in the later 19th century. The *Lowestoft Journal* wrote in 1889:

The rush of visitors for Yarmouth on Saturday was extraordinary in character; and it is many years since such a remarkable influx has taken place previous to the August Bank Holiday. All day during Saturday visitors were pouring into the town from every railway terminus. Before 6 o'clock two London boats had arrived in the harbour; and before 10 o'clock no less than five large passengers came in all well filled with visitors. The boats belonging to the General Steam Navigation Company were the *Laverlock, Hoboken, Swift, Halcyon,* and the *Sir Walter Raleigh.* The crush will be in some measure understood when it is mentioned that of 21 trains which arrived here at the termini of the Great Eastern Railway, 13 of them were special trains, making an addition to the population of many thousands! The scene on Saturday night was an extraordinary one, for hundreds of men, women, and children were in desperate straits for sleeping accommodation, and we should imagine that every lodging-house was crammed to excess. Early on Sunday morning, namely about 5 o'clock, a special train was run from Liverpool Street, leaving there at midnight, and this train was well filled. Before breakfast the beach was filled with people, bathing, paddling, strolling, or sitting about, and the scene on the Drive during the afternoon and evening was truly a surprising one. The popular parade was a vast nosegay of bright colours and handsome costumes, 'the brave men and fair women' fairly revelling in the glorious atmosphere for which Yarmouth is so justly celebrated.[14]

Anna Bowman Dodd visited Yarmouth in the 1890s:

The northern ocean we had expected to see … but that sea of people, the swaying, restless, ceaselessly moving mass swarming over the great quays, and blackening the yellow beaches till scarce a grain of sand was to be seen: upon no such outlook had we counted. The quiet of the stifling quays on the other side of the town was now explained. Not alone Yarmouth, but the county of Norfolk and the city of London itself, had sent their quota to swell the crowds peopling the beaches of this northern Margate.

Great as it was, it was an orderly crowd. Decorum was written all over these thousands of conforming English backs.[15]

Clement Scott, the man who promoted the Cromer area as 'Poppyland', was more condescending:

He will not find here fashionable promenades or a very select society; people do not come here to dress or to show their high-heeled boots; they come here to enjoy the air and to get healthy, to brown their skins and to bathe the baby.[16]

Watching the fishermen at work was an added attraction to tourists, although some objected to the smell of mackerel being unloaded at the jetty – perhaps fortunately, the herring season followed on after most visitors had left the town. Yarmouth – and its main product – could even be promoted as a health resort. Dr Spencer Thomson boasted: 'The air is dry and bracing and favourable to people of weakly habit.' He went on to extol the virtues of visitors inhaling the smoke of the oak chips burnt in the preparation of bloaters.[17]

A further attraction, and one inhabitants would surely say is still true today, was mentioned by the *Railroad Book of England,* whose author commented that Yarmouth was:

> Specially remarkable for the surpassing beauty of its female population of every rank of life.[18]

Late 19th-century attractions included three new forms of entertainment. The Revolving Tower was built in 1897: a revolving circular car could carry up to 200 passengers to the (fixed) viewing platform 130 feet above ground. Thompson's Gravity Switchback opened on the sands north of Britannia Pier in 1887, charging three pence for adults and two pence for children: on its first August Bank Holiday takings were in excess of £100. In 1895, the Hotchkiss Bicycle Railway was set up, two circular tracks of 250 feet in diameter, each with four to six machines, some of them tandems.

Going swimming was a very different experience in Victorian Yarmouth from the scenes on the beach today. Men and women had separate areas of beach from which to bathe, and people would undress in bathing machines, which were then pulled into the water, so that they could plunge straight from the machine into the sea. In 1899, mixed bathing was approved south of Wellington Pier, but under strict conditions. The machines for males had to be at least twenty yards from those for females, and male costume had to cover the body from the neck to the knee.

In 1892, it was decided to provide electric lighting in the streets. It was estimated that it would cost £10,000 for an Electricity Station and 4,500 lamps. The Consulting Engineer wanted to illuminate the Quays, Piers, Market Place and Fishwharf with arc lamps: 'this would convert Yarmouth into a place of beauty by night surpassing other seaside resorts.' However, the Corporation decided on normal street lighting. The lights on Regent Road and the Marine Parade were opened for the first time in 1894, in front of a large crowd.

There was more to Yarmouth than the sea front: the year 1778 saw the opening of a museum and a theatre. The former was established by Daniel Boulter, who ran a shop in Yarmouth selling jewellery, haberdashery, toys and patent medicines. In August 1778, he opened a museum of natural history and antiquities in a house on the Market Place. He charged one shilling for admission and the objects on view were very diverse, including stuffed crocodiles, seals and armadillos, shells, Roman finds and a bust of Oliver Cromwell. When Captain Cook returned from his voyage to Australia and the Pacific, Boulter spent a day on the ship and purchased more than 100 objects from members of the crew. They included feather cloaks from Hawaii, a feather helmet from the Sandwich Islands, and a rare (stuffed) bird, a hook-billed red creeper, from the same islands.

Boulter died in 1802: he was a Quaker and was buried in the Society of Friends burial ground. The museum did not survive his death and his collections have been dispersed. Yarmouth had to wait another century to see the establishment of a permanent museum.[19]

The theatre in Yarmouth, the Theatre Royal, dates from 1778 and was one of the oldest in Europe: it cost £1,600 to build. It was founded from Norwich: the Norwich Company had been visiting the town since 1710, playing first in a warehouse on Middlegate and after 1736 in the Town House. Eleven subscribers each put up £100 for the new theatre, which opened on 4 December 1778. William Wilkins spent £1,500 improving the theatre between 1815 and 1820. It had its real-life tragedies: Thomas Russell was taken ill while playing in 'The Hunchback' in 1856, dying ten minutes

43 *In Dry Dock, Yarmouth, 1897.*

later. In 1860, a clown, Thomas Algar, actually died in the arms of Harlequin on stage: his death was blamed on the cold and Algar's lack of food. Nall, writing in 1866, was unimpressed with the theatre, commenting: 'Of its exterior the less said, the better'.[20]

The Fishing

The herring season at Yarmouth lasted from the beginning of September to near the end of December. Quantities were massive. In 1828, George Errington recorded that 100 boats from Yarmouth and 70 from Lowestoft, together with 50 cobles (small, open boats), brought in almost 100,000 barrels of herrings, of which just over a quarter were exported. In 1869, there were 900 Yarmouth shipping boats, employing 4,051 men and 531 boys.

In the 1780s, de la Rochefoucauld described the process of preserving the fish:

> They don't salt their herring – only the Dutch do that: they smoke them in various kinds of drying-houses, kept entirely shut, in the bottom of which they light several fires of great pieces of oak which give out little flame and much smoke.

> As soon as the herring are unloaded, which the ship does as soon as it has a full load, in order to return to the fishing ground, as soon, I say, as the herring are unloaded, the women wash them well by putting them in a rush-basket and then plunging them into a great tank of water and shaking them about; they are then threaded on to wooden spits and suspended in the fish-house I have mentioned, where they stay for a fortnight or three weeks.[21]

In fact, his first statement is not quite correct: the herring were lightly salted as the first stage of the preserving process. There was a new development in the 19th century, the *bloater*:

> A real Yarmouth bloater is a full herring slightly salted and smoked: it should be eaten within two or three days, as it will not keep long and soon loses its flavour. The precise period at which bloaters were first manufactured is not known, but is believed to have been in or about the year 1835. It is said that the discoverer was a Yarmouth herring-curer of the name of Bishop, and that his discovery was due partly to accident and partly to a happy thought. Bishop found that, by some mischance, a small quantity of a prime parcel of fresh herrings which he had bought had been overlooked. To prevent the herrings from being spoiled he sprinkled them with salt, spitted them, and hung them up in a 'smoke-house' in which oak logs were then being burned. The next morning he was both astonished and delighted at their appearance, and with their aroma and flavour. Thenceforth he made the cure of bloaters a special pursuit; and as others soon followed his example, the fame of the bloater soon became known far and wide.[22]

By the 19th century, the majority of herring were being exported. Errington has many examples, such as these entries for January and February 1817:

> The advices received this month of the sale of fish in Leghorn [Livorno, in Northern Italy], encouraged the merchants to send out more and 3 or 4 cargoes were shipped immediately. 3 of the vessels that sailed from hence on the 1st December arrived at Naples and Leghorn on the 4th January. 3 others arrived at Leghorn on the 16th January…. One vessel arrived at Naples after a passage of 70 days; sold her cargo well at 18 ducats.
>
> 4 sail of Yarmouth ships arrived at Venice, Ancona etc about the 25th Feb. No sale for herrings at Hamburg. One cargo sold well at Cadiz. Another cargo spoiled by bad weather having been out 74 days.[23]

In the later 19th century, the export of Yarmouth herrings reached new markets in Germany and Russia.

Although the herring was always the main source of income for town, other fish were also caught in large quantities. Mackerel were caught in May and June. They were not cured but packed in ice for freshness: the ice was taken from the nearby Broads in winter, an example of how the economy of the town has always been interwoven with that of its hinterland. The coming of the railway made the transport of fish to London a much quicker process, so that the sale of fresh fish from Yarmouth at Billingsgate Market became a practical proposition. Another local product was the shrimp, caught in Breydon Water, the Harbour and along the shore by specialist small boats known as

44   *Yarmouth Harbour scene, with wherry, 1897.*

shrimpers. The season for shrimping ran from March to September, coinciding with the holiday season: a tea of freshly caught shrimps was one of the great treats of a Yarmouth holiday.

Whaling also continued throughout the 18th century: in 1758, the *Prince William* of Yarmouth was one of 17 ships lost off Greenland. The peak years for whaling were in the 1780s. Finch-Crisp records that, in 1784, two vessels were fitted out for the Greenland Whale Fishery. Two public houses in Yarmouth, one on Middlegate Street and one on Gorleston Common, changed their names to the *Greenland Whale Fishery* at this time. William Youell went on board two of the ships – *Yarmouth* and *Norfolk* – on 23 July 1786, after their return from their whaling voyage: he noted that they had caught seven whales each. In 1789, seven Yarmouth ships were engaged in whale fishing off Greenland. One of them, the *Trelawny*, embarked on a new venture in November 1789, going to the South Seas rather than the Arctic and looking for sperm whales. She did not return to Yarmouth until January 1791, and the voyage was never repeated.

Whaling continued well into the following century. Errington notes the industry in 1819, for example: 'The Whale Fishery this year is an indifferent one, 55 tons the average catch. Ten sail of ships are lost at Davis's Straits. 4 whalers belonging to the Company at Altona had only one fish in two seasons.' In 1822, 'the Whale Fishery met with heavy losses. Seven ships lost at Davis's Straits and a bad voyage to Greenland'. Three years later, he noted: '4 Whale Fishers lost at Davis Straits and no success in Greenland'.[24]

Ships and the Sea

As ships became larger, improvements were made to the Harbour. In 1763, it was announced that 'PUBLIC NOTICE is hereby given, that, by means of the Pier lately erected, there is now a very safe Channel, over Yarmouth Bar, for Ships drawing Eleven Feet Water; and that there is a very great demand for Coals in this Port'.[25]

The port continued to attract the interest of observers. De la Rochefoucauld noted that: 'The port is frequented by 400 vessels, English and foreign, every year. Each vessel pays nine pence a year on its freight to the maintenance of the jetty, the lighthouses etc, and a shilling for the ship's mooring on the quay, whatever its freight.' In 1776, Woodforde recorded his impression:

> Nothing can beat what we saw today – immense sea room, ships and boats passing and re-passing – the wind being rather high, the waves being like mountains coming into shore … . In the evening we took a walk on the quay – as fine a one as ever was seen … we got on board an English vessel and were treated with wine, gin etc. the sailors behaved very civil to us; had a difficult matter to make them take anything. She was a collier, and soon going back to Sunderland.[26]

Sixty years later, in 1838, Major Cooper was equally impressed: 'There were nearly 2,000 vessels laying wind-bound in Yarmouth Roads. They got underway on November 1, and were followed by another 1,000 from the southward; all 3,000 sail went through the Roads in five hours, so that the sea could hardly be seen for ships.'[27]

In the days of sail, the safety of the ships could be dependent on the winds. The greatest loss of life in a single ship occurred on 16 March 1801. HMS *Invincible* set off from the Yarmouth Roads bound for the Baltic, but sank after running into a shoal off Happisburgh: almost 200 men were saved by a fishing vessel, but 800 men including the captain were drowned.

The Yarmouth authorities were used to caring for shipwrecked mariners. Readers of *Robinson Crusoe* will recall that Crusoe was shipwrecked off Winterton. He and his friends were taken to Yarmouth, where they were provided with a night's lodging and given money to travel home to Hull or on to London. In 1860, the Shipwrecked Sailors Home opened on Yarmouth seafront. In its first 25 years nearly 4,000 sailors stayed there. Closed in 1964, it became the Maritime Museum for East Anglia for almost forty years, and is now the Tourist Information Centre.

Sailors were heavily involved in the many riots that occurred in Georgian Yarmouth. There was serious rioting in 1792 because of the price of provisions. The rioters tried to break into the prison, seizing wooden palings from a fence in front of the gaol as weapons. The establishment tried to defend the gaol. One of the defenders, a surgeon called Francis Turner, was hit on the head by a rioter: he never recovered from his injury, lingering for four years until he died. The military were eventually called and the riot quelled.[28]

In 1796, the radical orator John Thelwall began a series of lectures in Yarmouth, using a warehouse owned by Samuel Hurry. At the second lecture, about 90 sailors rushed in and tried to seize Thelwall. They did manage to capture him, but he was freed by local supporters, including members of the Preston and Hurry families, and was able to escape. Thelwall said of Yarmouth society: 'there are no overpowering fortunes

45 *Looking from the beach out to the Roads: this photograph, taken in 1907, shows both steam and sail.*

on the one hand, and but little want or abject wretchedness on the other; and there is a good body of decent substantial families filling up the intermediate space between the merchants and the mechanics.'[29]

The diarist William Youell recorded a naval mutiny in the following year: '24 May 1797. For some time past the sailors on board admiral Duncan's ships in the roads have been in a state of mutiny. They come on shore every day and behave very violently, breaking windows etc.' On 29 May, the *Lion, Standard* and *Belliquex* men-of-war came into Yarmouth Roads flying the red flag of rebellion. The *Nassau* and other ships already there followed suit. On the following day the whole fleet sailed for the Nore, thus averting the crisis as far as Yarmouth was concerned.

In any case, the ultimate loyalty of the navy was never in serious doubt. Just four months later, on 11 October 1797, the British fleet defeated the Dutch navy off the coast of Holland at the Battle of Camperdown. The victorious fleet sailed into Yarmouth bringing back seven Dutch ships as prizes. Wounded men from both sides were taken to Yarmouth Barracks: it took three days to land all the men onto the beach. Several later died of their wounds, including the Dutch Captain Gysbert Jan van Rysoart: they are buried in St Nicholas' church.

Because of the danger of invasion by Napoleon, a semaphore system was set up in 1808 between Yarmouth and London, using already existing buildings such as church towers and windmills where possible. The Yarmouth semaphore was on the South Gate and can be seen in illustration 22. There were a total of 19 stations (the next was at Strumpshaw) and, in fine weather, a message could be sent in just 17 minutes. The system was closed down in 1814, after Napoleon had been captured and the danger was over.

Half a century later, in 1851, a sailors' strike in Yarmouth over wages led to a riot on the Quay on 22 February: several people were injured. The Yarmouth authorities had to call in soldiers from Norwich. They came by railway, taking 30 minutes for a journey which would have taken several hours by coach just seven years earlier. By 15 March the strike ended in a victory for the sailors.

Trade and Industry

Yarmouth's role as a port was still a flourishing one. Goods were offloaded to be transported upriver by *wherries*. R.H. Mottram describes these craft, unique to the rivers of east Norfolk:

> Its length is 45 to 50 feet, beam 16 feet, draft when loaded 5 feet. The 45-foot single mast, right forward, swings on a bolt pivot, fixed in a tabernacle, and has two or three hundred-weight of lead strapped to its stump, so that it can readily be lowered by a winch at the frequent bridges or when quanting. On this mast is swung the great boomless mainsail with its 30-foot gaff, giving a spread of 500 square feet of canvas. The hold, covered by twelve wooden overlapping hatches, extends from the mast back to the tiny cuddy under the monstrous tiller against which the helmsman would lean…. While time was no object, large quantities of timber, coal, grain and other goods were carried by these means, the timber cargoes especially picturesque, as the hatches were entirely removed, and the load scientifically built up above the gangways, so that the quanting was done from the edges of a floating timber stack, overlapping the actual beam of the wherry.[30]

However, the trade was dependent upon the weather. Parson Woodforde noted in his diary on 7 February 1799 that no coals could come up the river from Yarmouth: 'all bound fast by the Frost on the River.'

Like any town of its size, Yarmouth developed banks and breweries in the 18th century. Gurney and Co opened a bank in 1781, in partnership with John Turner. It was on South Quay. Later partners included members of the Brightwen and Orde families. The bank became part of Barclays when the latter was founded in 1896. Lacons, the brewing family, founded a bank on Hall Quay in 1791. The bank was bought out by Capital and Counties, who were themselves taken over by Lloyd's in 1918. Two more banks opened in 1839, branches of the National Provincial and East of England Bank opened a branch in the town: the latter lasted until 1918 when it became part of Barclays.[31]

The two largest breweries were Pagets and Lacons. Steward and Patteson bought up Samuel Paget, the Yarmouth brewers in 1845: the firm had 25 public houses in the town. The largest brewer, Lacons, had 38 pubs in Yarmouth at this date.[32]

46 *The Market Place, as painted by John Butcher. Note the Market Cross and the twisted spire of the parish church.*

It had medical practitioners, too. Sylas Neville thought of becoming a doctor in the town but decided against it, writing in 1776:

> The climate is exceedingly cold & bad in the winter & great part of the spring & therefore against a man with a bad state of health. There are few people of family or education in the town; the greater part of the principal inhabitants have gotten their fortunes by commerce without education & are from that circumstance distinguished for a kind of low pride & illiberal spirit which would agree but ill with mine; add to this that I greatly expect the majority would be against me; a great number are very high-Church & much attached to the Court party and Tory interest.[33]

The heart of the town remained the Market Place, which must have been very noisy and smelly for most of its existence. Beatniffe wrote about it in 1776: 'It is shocking to see butchers daily slaughtering calves, sheep etc. in the centre of such an opulent town, resorted to by crowds of genteel company from almost every part of England.' It was only in the later 19th century that the *Shambles*, or animal slaughtering area, was moved out of the Market Place.

Later visitors were more impressed by the market. A Colchester newspaper commented: 'Yarmouth provision market is the best in East Anglia. Even that of Norwich is very inferior to it, both for the extent of space occupied and the quality of the provisions on sale. At Yarmouth the provisions – fish, flesh, fowl and vegetables – are superb, and it is a treat to see the long files of residents carrying them home on a Saturday, with the super addition of bouquets of flowers and dried and coloured grasses.'[34]

White's *Eastern England* was also full of praise:

> What with the unusually large area, the great gathering of rustic folk and town folk,
> their words and ways, and peculiar appliances, the Market Place presents a spectacle
> full of interest. Long rows of stalls stretch from end to end, and you pass from peas
> and potatoes, mushrooms as large as dinner plates, very fine raspberries, luscious
> strawberries, and other fruits and vegetables, to a display of meat and poultry not to
> be seen elsewhere, beyond which are baskets, bedding, boxes, shoes, frippery, old iron,
> new hardware, and second-hand books. Here sits a busy knife-grinder, whirling off a
> stream of sparks, amid an admiring group. Yonder stands Cheap Jack, within a circle
> of crockery, vociferating after his manner and keeping the crowd in good humour by
> his jokes. In another place we see what becomes of the rushes with which the broads
> abound; for here are hassocks, cushions, matting and horse collars, all made of them.

Wind power was still being harnessed in the town. There were a large number of
windmills on the Denes between the town walls and the sea: several can be seen on
the 1588 map. As the town expanded, these were in the way of building developments
and gradually disappeared in the 19th century. One of the mill buildings was moved
to North Common in 1850-1 by John Baverley, where it became known as Greengrass
Mill after the family who occupied it from 1865 to 1904. The distance is about 1.5 miles.
In 1948, Gerald Bure recalled the move: 'it was brought through the town on rollers by
the bold apprentice millwrights of the Stolworthy's from between Southampton Place
and Middle Market Road and re-erected on the North Denes. We learned too that for
many years after its removal to the site, the Trinity Brethren had kept the mill painted
white to serve as a day mark for vessels entering the Cockle Gat'. The mill was the last
standing in Yarmouth: it was demolished in 1907.[35]

Health and Housing

The earliest 'real' hospitals in Yarmouth were built for the Admiralty. The first was
where Sainsbury's now stands – the wounded from the Battle of Copenhagen were
brought here. This was replaced by the building now known as the Naval Hospital,
constructed for sailors wounded in the Napoleonic Wars. It was completed in 1811,
and in 1815 as many as 600 wounded soldiers from the Battle of Waterloo were lodged
here. After the war ended, it became a barracks until 1846 when it became a military
lunatic asylum. The Admiralty claimed it once more when the Crimean War broke
out in 1854, and in 1863 the building became a naval lunatic asylum. In 1958, it was
transferred to the National Health Service, becoming a civilian mental hospital. It
closed as part of the *'Care in the Community'* programme and the site was sold in 1993.
It has since been converted into apartments.

Yarmouth Corporation had a Workhouse on the site of St Mary's Hospital from the
16th century. A much larger Workhouse to the north of the town was built in 1839.
Although originally intended to house the healthy poor, workhouses inevitably had to
look after the sick poor of all kinds, both the physically and mentally ill, and also the
elderly and infirm, orphans and unmarried mothers. Not surprisingly the infirmary
wards of many workhouses developed into Hospitals: the Workhouse in Yarmouth
became the Northgate Hospital.

47   *North Common Mill. This is a typical East Anglian post mill: the entire body of the building moves so that the sails are in the wind. It rests on an immensely strong post, here hidden within the roundhouse. The fantail moves the mill round to face the right direction.*

Yarmouth General Hospital was opened on Deneside in 1840 (a small hospital with accommodation for only three or four in-patients had opened in a house in Queen Street in 1838). The Corporation gave the site and the Hospital was funded by voluntary contributions. It was rebuilt on a larger scale in 1888 and further enlarged in 1896, 1910 and 1928.

The most-feared disease in Victorian times was cholera. S.S. Manning, a Yarmouth chemist and druggist, offered an anti-cholera specific in 1849, under the heading 'Important To All: Cholera Cured for 1s. 1½ d.' The text of his advertisements read:

> At this season of the year when Cholera and Bowel Complaints are so prevalent, and prove so frequently fatal in a few hours, it is advisable for every family to have in their possession a remedy which can be had recourse to immediately unpleasant symptoms arise.
>
> This preparation has been successfully resorted to in many severe cases without failure, is so safe and simple that it may be given to children of three months without the least danger, provided the printed directions are carefully attended to.
>
> To Mothers Suckling their Infants this medicine will be invaluable, as it will not only afford immediate relief to the mother, but through the medium of her milk will soothe and secure the child.

All Children, whether at home or at school, during the fruit season, are subject to a disordered state of bowels, which, if not speedily relieved, very often goes on to Cholera in its worst form. It is therefore actually necessary that everyone having the care or management of children should always keep in the house this valuable specific, especially those in the country who are at a long distance from a medical gentleman.

The reasonable price at which it is offered places it within the reach of the poor as well as the rich, and at the same time adapts it for gratuitous distribution by clergymen and other benevolent individuals who are accustomed to bestow medicine to their poorer neighbours.

Symptoms of the Disease – Uncomfortable feeling about the bowels, sometimes attended with griping pains and sensation of sickness at the stomach, and flushes of heat over the system, diarrhoea or looseness of bowels, with cramp and cold sweats, great loss of strength, vomiting etc.[36]

In 1973, the then Chief Public Health Inspector, F.T. Porter, described the history of environmental health in the town:

The first Public Health act of 1848 resulted in an inspection of the town by W Lee, who, in 1849, made an Enquiry into the Sanitary Condition of the Borough. The enquiry was directed towards the state of the houses, the extent of any sewerage and the supply of water. Many witnesses were called to give evidence, amongst them a Doctor William Burgess, the medical officer for the Northern District. He considered that the inhabitants would not use more than 3 or 4 pails of water a day even if a piped supply were to be provided. The Inspector hazarded the opinion that the inhabitants 'must be either very idle or very dirty people' – to which Dr Burgess replied 'They are both I assure you'. Dr Burgess was himself dead of Typhus within a few months of giving his evidence.

The worthy citizens of the town, through their elected representatives, fought hard to avoid the necessity of complying with the requirements of the Act (to install a proper water supply and sewerage system) and proceeded in turn to air their own views of the healthiness of the town in general and Mr Lee's report in particular. One paragraph I give below:

The extraordinary percentage of deaths among children under one year old, stated to be 'no less than 22.5 per cent of all born in Yarmouth', is to be attributed to the very extensive use of laudanum, Godfrey's Cordial, and similar deleterious drugs, a due allowance for which would greatly reduce the amount of preventable disease, and consequently tend to raise, in a like proportion, the average age of death of those who die from natural disease, age etc.

The Great Yarmouth Waterworks Company was formed in 1853 and was authorised to take water from Ormesby Broad, using powerful steam engines to lift the water. A water pipe was laid from Ormesby to an open reservoir in Caister, and from there to Yarmouth: the main pipe was over eight miles long, and the total cost of the works was over £80,000. Nall was impressed with this example of Victorian sanitary engineering, telling visitors to the town that the works were well worth a visit.

In 1859, a water pipe was laid under the Yare to supply water to Southtown and Gorleston, and a service reservoir built in Gorleston. In 1910 a tunnel under the Yare was built, seven feet in diameter, containing two steel pipes to supply the increasing demand for water west of the river. A further supply point in the River Bure was opened up in 1903, and new plant installed at Ormesby in 1930.[37]

Although water was now supplied, the treatment of sewage was still a major concern. Dr Airey reported on the sanitary condition of the town in 1875:

WATER-CLOSETS

In the sea-side quarter of the town, water-closets have been adopted to please visitors, and even in many of the poorer houses of that neighbourhood the facility offered by the main sewer has induced landlords to provide water-closets, usually of simple construction, and requiring to be flushed by hand. The Yarmouth Water Company has introduced, in connexion with a constant water-service, a very simple and safe arrangement of water-closet fittings, which at once secures the water from contamination and from waste. About 2,000 water closets are thus furnished. The more general adoption of this arrangement in the well-sewered parts of the town is much to be desired.

PRIVIES

With the above exceptions, privies of the ordinary type are universal, having a single seat, without provision for children, over a small shallow pit of porous brick without cement; to be emptied when full, either by a trap in the floor or by an outside door about 12 inches square, opening into a back-yard or passage, or into the public footway, according to situation. In the Rows these square, strong-hinged, iron-clamped doors are a constant feature on either side of the path, and are generally so placed that any leakage or overthrow from them trickles into the open gutter.[38]

In 1890, there were 18 deaths from typhoid fever in the town. The Rows still had an open drain in the middle of each one, and earth closets at the back or side of the houses. Many people thought this arrangement was more healthy than sewers, and they were supported by a Doctor Wyllys, who said that sewer gas actually caused typhoid fever and that the disease was especially common among 'the better class of people' who had installed flush toilets!

The early 19th century saw the beginnings of town planning, as we now know it. The town gates were now seen as in the way of traffic, and also as preventing the proper circulation of air: they were pulled down. A new road – Regent Street – was cut through the Rows in 1813 to allow a direct link between the Quay and the centre of town suitable for carriages.

Before the 19th century, all the housing in Yarmouth was within the town walls. The century saw the spread of the town eastwards towards the new sea front. The Corporation tried to impose conditions on house-building on the Denes. For example, a set of regulations was issued in 1842. 'First, second and third class' houses had to have fronts of white brick, fourth-class houses were to have fronts of red brick. All privies had to have common pans and stench traps 'to prevent the stench from escaping from bin or cesspool, to the annoyance of the adjoining lots.'[39]

Religion

Methodism came to Yarmouth five years before swimming baths. The first Methodist to preach in the town was Thomas Olivers in 1754. He met with opposition. On his venturing into one of the Rows, 'the women ranged themselves in their doorways on both sides, with basins of water, and dirt, and filth in their hands the contents of which they darted at him as he passed along'. Emerging onto the open street, 'he was assailed with such a shower of sticks, stones, turnips, apples, potatoes, etc as he never witnessed before or since'.

Fortunately, Howell Harris, a Welsh Methodist officer, came to Yarmouth with his regiment: under his protection a preacher spoke in the Market Place for several days in 1760, converting many. Wesley himself recorded these developments in his diary: 'I enquired concerning Yarmouth, a large and populous town, and as eminent both for wickedness and ignorance as ever any seaport in England. Some had endeavoured to call them to repentance; but it was at the hazard of their lives. What could be done more? Why, last summer God sent thither the regiment in which Howell Harris was an officer. He preached every night, none daring to oppose him; and hereby a seed was sown. Many were stirred up to seek God; and some of them now earnestly invited me to come over. I went this afternoon, and preached in the evening. The house was presently more than filled; and, instead of the tumult which was expected, all was quiet, as at London. Indeed the word of God was quick and powerful among them.'

Wesley was back in Yarmouth for the opening of the Wesleyan chapel in Ferry Boat Row in 1783, and visited the town on several more occasions, the last in 1790, just five months before his death. He wrote concerning this last visit: 'I went to Yarmouth, and at length found a society in peace, and much united together. In the evening, the congregation was much too large to get into the preaching-house; but they were far less noisy than usual. After supper, a little company went to prayer; and the power of God fell upon us, especially when a young woman broke out in prayer, to the surprise and comfort of us all.'[40]

Other groups of Methodists became established in the town as the movement fragmented – the Primitive Methodists who began in a hayloft on Priory Plain, built a 'Temple' on the same site in 1876. The United Methodists had a chapel in Regent Road and another in Northgate Street.[41]

The rapid growth of the town in the 19th century led to a need for more churches for all branches of Christianity. For the Anglicans, St Peter's came first in 1831-3, followed by St Andrew's in 1857-60. St John's in York Road was built especially for fishermen in 1858, and was followed by St James' in Queen's Road, built slowly because of money problems: it was begun in 1869 and not finished until 1908. In contrast, St Paul's in Salisbury Road was built in 1897-8 at a cost of just £1,000. The other churches included the Roman Catholic Church in Regent Road, built at a cost of £10,000 in 1848-50, and the Congregational Churches on Deneside, 1854, and Middlegate (now Greyfriars Way), 1870.

The Religious Census of 1851 gives us a snapshot of church-going in Victorian Yarmouth. Ministers were asked how many people had attended their services in the morning, afternoon and evening of Sunday 30 March, and how many did so on average. Unfortunately there is no way of knowing how many people went to just one service and how many went to two or even to all three, so figures cannot be exact. The census was conducted because many people in authority thought that the nation was becoming 'godless' but today the census tells us something very different; just what an enormous number of people were attending church. The parish church of St Nicholas',

48 *King Street and St George's Chapel, 1860s.*

49 *Interior of parish church, 1860s.*

for example had a total of 6,000 people at its three services as well as 1,500 scholars – and the rector added a note saying that the numbers were unusually low because of the dreadful weather on 30 March. The two other Anglican churches also had large attendances: St George's with 800 adults and 200 scholars and St Peter's with 1,000 adults and 400 scholars.

The many Nonconformist churches were also well attended. There were 1,200 Wesleyan Methodists, 2,000 Primitive Methodists, and 600 attending the Methodist New Connexion, which had recently split from the Wesleyans. A further 300 people attended the Chapel of the Countess of Huntingdon's Connexion. These Methodist groups had over 700 children in attendance as scholars.

The Baptists had three groups: 200 attended services of the General Baptists, 700 those of the Particular Baptists and 150 the services at the Zoar Baptist Chapel. The Independent Church was flourishing, with 1,000 worshippers. There were also two mariners' missionary churches attracting about 250 people. The Unitarian Church was attended by 250, the Society of Friends by just 27 in a Room that could take 255 seated and 1243 standing. The Roman Catholic Church had opened the previous year in Regent Road, but it made no return.

Putting the figures broadly, almost 8,000 people attended a Church of England service, and about 6,500 a Nonconformist service in Great Yarmouth on 30 March 1851. As the population of the town was 26,870, including children, the percentage of adults attending church was clearly very high by the standards of any later period.

The Dissenters' Burial Ground was established in 1828 when a group of trustees bought Market Garden, also known as Lampet's Garden, for £100. It was bought in the names of William Bath, a former mayor, and John Messent, the minister of the Countess of Huntingdon's chapel in Fish Street. It was open to all denominations: like all cemeteries within towns it was closed under the Burial Act of 1855. However, people who had already purchased the right continued to be buried here: the last was William Budds in 1892. By 1918/9 the burial ground was overgrown and used as a rubbish dump by nearby shops. William de Castre wrote of it: 'The graveyard is a place to make a good man shudder and a saint afraid to die.' The trustees sold the land to the Corporation in 1929. The intention was to use it as an open space: sadly, over the last few years it has had to be kept locked.[42]

There was a small Jewish community in Yarmouth at this time: according to the 1851 religious census, the Jewish synagogue had an attendance of 26 people. In April 1801, the Assembly granted a petition by Simon Hart for a cemetery in the town: a piece of land formerly used as a place to lay masts was assigned to him for a rent of 10s. 6d. a year. The cemetery contains just 18 graves in two rows. Many come from two families, the Isaacs (fruiterers of Market and Broad Rows) and the Mayers. The latter were jewellers and also millers, owning a windmill on the North Denes. The cemetery closed in 1855, and was replaced by a Jewish cemetery at Kitchener Road.

Schools in Victorian Yarmouth were funded by religious groupings, whether Anglican or Nonconformist. The Church of England Priory Schools were opened in 1853 in the medieval priory building. There were often clashes between boys of different schools. The logbook for Priory school includes this entry in 1874: 'Boys from Hospital School and Primitive Methodist cause great annoyance. Colts – ie knotted ropes – freely used this morning on the Church Plain by several boys.' This

50   *Town Hall and Town Hall Plain during the First World War.*

school was home to a well-known Yarmouth ghost story. A nasty smell began to be noticeable in the Commercial Room: the floorboards were taken up and a receptacle found containing an Egyptian mummy, which had begun to decay. The mummy was buried in the adjoining churchyard at night. This was followed by ghostly tappings at night on the church door and that of the nearby vicarage. The smell started up again in the classroom, and it was found that a leg of the mummy had been left behind: this was buried with the rest of the mummy and no more tappings were heard.

School Boards were set up under the Education Act of 1870 to build schools where there were insufficient places in the church schools for every child. The Yarmouth School Board was established in 1875 and within its first eight years spent over £14,000 on building schools, including those at Cobholm, St George's, Northgate and Gorleston. However, some church schools were founded even after 1875, such as the Roman Catholic Elementary School, which opened on Albion Road in 1881. Under the 1902 Education Act, the Boards were abolished and responsibility for education passed to the Borough Council. The issue of religious teaching within schools remained a very controversial one, however – and one which still causes strong feeling over a century later.

Schools were not free, the usual charge being two or three pence a week. In 1889, the Yarmouth School Board adopted a new set of fees for Northgate School, for example – two pence a week for infants, three pence a week for the older children. Consideration was given to those with large families: the third and subsequent children from each family were to pay just one penny a week. This school covered the children living in the poorest area of town and was also attended by children from the Union Workhouse nearby. The teachers were making extra efforts to care for their pupils in the 1880s, such as bringing in coffee and bread for their breakfasts or making arrangements for them to have a cheap or free lunch at the school.[43]

In 1891, all children became entitled to a free elementary education for the first time. In the early 1890s, Arthur Patterson, acting in his role as attendance officer to the School Board, found that up to a quarter of boys in the town were living in the heaps of herring barrels and selling stolen fish to shops. The School Board issued a notice reminding parents that boys between five and 13 years old must go to school and must not be sent to sea![44]

Crime and Punishment

Yarmouth Quarter Sessions had the power to sentence convicted criminals to death. This right was abolished in 1835, but was in fact very rarely exercised in the 19th century. In 1813, 70-year-old John Hannah was convicted of murdering his wife, by strangling. According to the local newspaper: 'After the murder he washed the woman's face, laid the corpse out, and was found sitting by the fire smoking his pipe with the body near.' On the appointed day, he was marched in procession with the dignitaries of the town and publicly hanged at the customary place, at Whitegates on the Caister Road.

In 1825, 18-year-old William Neal, his mother Mary and his sister Susan were convicted of attempted murder. The two women had bought arsenic, which William had taken to the workshop in Howard Street where he was employed as an apprentice to a shoemaker, William Hales. He added this to a meal that Hales' wife had on the stove there: the shoemaker, his wife, their small children and the daily servant, a young girl called Elizabeth Fenn, ate this meal and all became ill, although in fact all survived. The trial took place in Yarmouth on 27 April. William tried to put the blame on Elizabeth. However, the prosecution was able to produce the shopkeeper who had sold the Neals the arsenic – they had even signed for it using their own names. The Neals were found guilty and all were sentenced to death, but they did not hang: their sentence was commuted to transportation. Nothing is known of their subsequent fate. John Hannah was thus the last person actually to be hanged in Great Yarmouth.

Yarmouth magistrates also had to deal with a body-snatching case. Until recent times, the cutting up of a dead body was viewed with distaste. This meant that it was very difficult for doctors to obtain bodies that they could dissect in order to see how the body actually worked. Some doctors were prepared to buy bodies and ask no questions. In 1827, Thomas Vaughan rented a house in Boulter's Row, across the road from St Nicholas' church, under the name of Thomas Smith. He obtained a supply of boxes 2 feet 3 inches in length, 14 inches wide and 14 inches deep and began robbing graves in the nearby churchyard, filling them in afterwards so that the thefts would not be discovered. However, rumours of grave-robbing soon spread and a local baker, George Beck, uncovered the coffin of his wife Elizabeth to find that the body had gone. Searches of recent burials revealed that more than twenty bodies had been taken. Vaughan had fled to London, but he was arrested and brought back to Norfolk. He was sentenced to six months' imprisonment. In Yarmouth, high iron fences were put around the churchyard to deter such crimes: these can still be seen today.[45]

Transportation of convicts to Australia was also an option for the Yarmouth magistrates. The first transportation cases occur in 1786, the last in 1852: although transportation continued as a possible punishment until 1868, no Yarmouth magistrate employed it after this date. During this period, 179 people were sentenced to transportation, nearly all male: the figure includes just 21 females. The crimes usually involved petty theft of clothing, purses or handkerchiefs. A few incidents relate specifically to Yarmouth as a coastal town – stealing from navy stores or boats, stealing rope etc. One man stands out as committing a different sort of crime, perhaps suggesting a higher social status: Francis Clarke was transported in 1828 for failure to surrender to a commission in bankruptcy. Transportation was for seven, ten of 14 years, except for three people who each received a sentence of transportation for life: John Bowles and Lewis Goodwin in 1837 for stealing a horse, and Robert Thaxter in 1843, for stealing a cart. Thaxter had a former conviction, though Bowles and Goodwin did not: by the 1840s the majority of people who

51 *A large number of the Rows began with an archway under a larger building.*

were transported were indeed repeat offenders (recidivists, as we would say today), although this was by no means always the case.

The highest court with jurisdiction over Yarmouth was the Assizes: after 1835, all cases involving the death penalty were tried before this court, which was held in Norwich. The most sensational case to come before the Assizes was the murder of Harriet Candler. Harriet had a shop on the corner of Row 152 fronting Howard Street. At two o'clock in the morning of 19 November 1844 the police found her body there: she had been beaten over the head with a hammer, and her throat cut with a knife. Her till had been robbed. A neighbour, Samuel Yarham, was immediately suspected. At first he denied knowing anything about it. Later he turned King's Evidence, saying that he was part of a gang that had committed the crime and naming the other gang members as three local men, Robert Royal, James Mapes and James Hall. In April 1845, the three men were tried for murder at Norwich Assizes, with Yarham as prosecution witness. The men had alibis, however, or so they claimed – Royal was

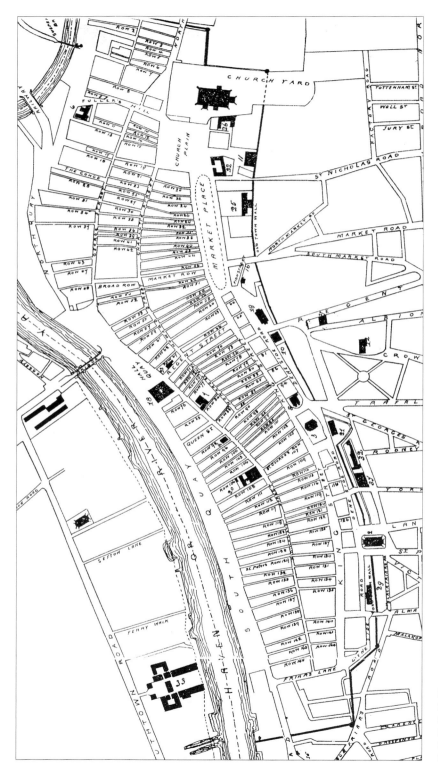

52 One of the few maps of Yarmouth to give the numbers of the Rows.

drinking in the *Half Moon* inn, Hall in his father's pub, the *Feather Tap* and Mapes was in a Yarmouth stew, or brothel! The alibis were not especially convincing as the exact time of the murder was not known, but it was basically their word against that of Yarham. The three were found not guilty. As they left Norwich Castle they were acclaimed by the mob while Yarham was hunted through the city by angry crowds: he managed to escape unharmed.

Yarham seems to have thought that as he had acted as witness he could not be accused of murder himself, and he made some very rash statements about the crime. Eventually he was arrested and charged. He was found guilty, sentenced to death and hanged outside Norwich Castle on 11 April 1846. This was the same day as the Tombland Fair so that the city was crowded, and a public hanging was an additional entertainment. The crowd watching the execution was estimated at more than 30,000 people. The *Norfolk Chronicle* described the scene: 'After the execution, gongs, drums and other instruments commenced their uproar, mountebanks and clowns their antics, the vendors of wares and exhibitors of prodigies their cries, while the whirligigs and ups-and-downs were soon in full swing. The public houses around the Hill were crowded, and hundreds finished the day in riot and intoxication.'

A minor Victorian case is interesting because it involves a marvellous example of local speech, well transcribed by the historian C.J. Palmer. In 1866, a woman was prosecuted for leaving her child alone all day in her house on Globe Row. The main prosecution witness, a bricklayer named Money, gave a statement in good Yarmouth dialect. The following is an extract: 'Vell you must know as how I vos axed to go and do a little job of bricklayerin to two or tree houses vot are in the Globe Row, don't you see. Vell I went airly in the mornin, it might be a little afore or it might be a little arter six, but it vornt much either way.' Money ignored the baby's cries for several hours, but eventually he and a friend took action: 'Vell, I bust the door open, if you'd a seen the sight that ve did you'd never a forgorit; I never shall, I do think. Ven we bust open the door there laid the poor little thing a kinder soshin on the bed, and kivered with filfth.'[46]

53 *The Priory School.*

54   *Outside the Priory School, 1860s.*

Local Government

The Municipal Corporations Act of 1835 changed the way in which towns were governed. They were now to be run by councillors, elected every three years, and aldermen, elected by the councillors for six years. For the first time, a borough could raise a general rate: previously a rate was only levied for a specific purpose such as maintaining the poor, or paving or lighting a town. Under the Act, Yarmouth – which now included Gorleston for the first time – was divided into six wards, governed by a mayor, 12 aldermen and 36 councillors. One of the first acts of this new body was to pull down the Market Cross in 1836! In 1904, the town was re-divided into 12 wards.

Before 1867 the borough returned two members to Parliament, but it was then disfranchised for corrupt election practices and remained without a representative until 1880, after which it returned one member.

After 1835, the Assembly no longer met in Guildhall: the latter was pulled down in 1850, opening up the view of the church from Church Plain and the Market Place. In 1878, after much discussion, it was decided to build a new Sessions Court and Corporate Offices on the site of the Town Hall, which would be pulled down. The council estimated the cost to be between £17,000 and £20,000, and invited architects to submit plans. Forty-one were received and Edward Boardman, the Norwich architect, was appointed to choose the best. He chose that by J.B. Pearce and in 1879 builders were invited to submit tenders: a bid of £26,200 from Lacey and Lacey of Norwich was accepted. Problems quickly arose: in March 1881 the architect wrote 'there is not the least fear that the slight settlement or strain in the

GREAT YARMOUTH
SCHOOL BOARD
CAUTION
TO
PARENTS
SENDING
CHILDREN TO SEA

Notice is Hereby Given, that the Parent of any Child between the ages of 5 and 13, sending such Child to Sea, during the time it should be at School, is liable to a **Fine of 5s.** for every offence, and the Board have resolved to direct a Prosecution in all cases occurring after this Notice.

C. H. WILTSHIRE,
31st May, 1878. Clerk to the Board.

J. BUCKLE, Machine Printer, King Street, Yarmouth.

55 'Children at Sea' poster issued by the School Board.

West front is at all serious'. However, in 1886 the west wall of the Town Hall started to slip towards the river and cracks began to appear in the building. One idea was to pull down the west wall, put in new foundations and rebuild it: this would cost £12,600. A more drastic plan was to pull down the entire Hall and build a new one on more stable ground by St George's Park: this option would cost £17,000. Fortunately, F.E. Duckham, the engineer for the docks at Millwall, came to the rescue. He in effect put the west wall of the building on a raft of concrete: the total cost of the work, which was completed in 1888, was £13,000.

The Tolhouse was no longer needed as a civic building and some councillors wanted it pulled down: C.J. Palmer led the successful opposition to this. In 1885, the Council finally decided to adopt the Libraries Act of thirty years earlier, which permitted councils to spend ratepayers' money on running a public library. Part of the building was adapted for this purpose, and the Tolhouse Museum itself opened ten years later.

Runham Vauxhall

This is the area bounded by the parish of Runham, the river Bure and Breydon Water. It is now largely occupied by the railway station and a supermarket. Until 1890 it was part of the parish of Runham: in that year it was separated from Runham and brought into the Borough of Great Yarmouth. At the same time it became an ecclesiastical parish of its own. Before the railway was built, it was the site of a pleasure garden. John Bilby, a Norwich publican enjoying a few days at the Yarmouth races in August 1836, recorded in his diary: 'Attended at the Vauxhall Gardens in the evening and I was highly satisfied: 2,000 persons present.'[47]

In spite of its small size, Runham Vauxhall had its own School Board, and built a school in 1877: the designer was J.W. Cockrill. It cost just over £1,000. The problem for the children was getting to it. The only access was along a footpath frequently flooded with effluent from overflowing cesspools of nearby houses. In 1882 the Schools Inspector reported, 'the Infants have frequently to be carried to school, and except in very dry weather, it is very difficult if not impossible for any child to reach school with dry feet unless remarkably well shod.' The school tried to provide a bridge over the ditch but its owner, James Royal, would not give his permission – even though he was on the School Board himself! The footpath was finally completed in 1884, but the whole area was unhealthy: 'night soil' from the privies of Yarmouth was dumped there by the scavenger contracted by the Borough Council. The Board became part of Great Yarmouth School Board in 1890.[48]

Nelson and Yarmouth

Nelson is forever associated with Yarmouth, a town he visited on several occasions, most notably on his return to England after the Battle of the Nile. He hired a ship at Cuxhaven and after five days England was sighted. Nelson landed at Gorleston Quay. He was borne in a horse-drawn carriage along the Southtown Road to Haven Bridge. The horses were left behind and the crowd pulled the carriage to the *Wrestlers* inn. The landlady, Sarah Suckling, was a relation of Nelson. She asked him she could rename her inn the *Nelson Arms*. 'That would be absurd,' said Nelson, 'seeing that I have but one.' The Mayor and Corporation came to the inn to give Nelson the freedom of the borough. The clerk produced a bible on which the oath was to be made. Nelson put his left hand on the book and the clerk interposed, 'Your *right* hand, my Lord'. 'That', replied Nelson, 'is at Tenerife.' The clerk's *faux pas* was never forgotten in Yarmouth.[49]

Nelson then went to an upper window in the inn. It was pouring with rain but an enormous crowd waited outside for Nelson to speak. He did so, and his remarks included the famous phrase, 'I am myself a Norfolk man, and glory in being so'. This was followed by a service at St Nicholas' church just across the road. As Nelson walked down the nave, the organist played 'See the Conquering Hero Comes'. After the service there were parades and salutes. In the evening the town was illuminated.

In March 1801, the British Fleet gathered in Yarmouth Roads. Nelson joined the Fleet at Yarmouth and sailed to the Baltic, winning the Battle of Copenhagen on 1 April 1801. On his return, the Corporation wanted to wine and dine Nelson once more. He refused and went instead to visit his sick and wounded men in the (old) naval hospital. One piece of repartee is still remembered:

> Nelson: Well Jack, what's the matter with you?
> Sailor: Lost my arm, your honour.
> Nelson (looking down at his own empty sleeve): Well, Jack, then you and I are spoiled for fishermen![50]

Nelson, of course, died at the Battle of Trafalgar in October 1805. It was decided to erect a monument to him to be paid for by the whole county. In 1815, the Committee resolved that the Monument should be erected on the sea coast. They then thought

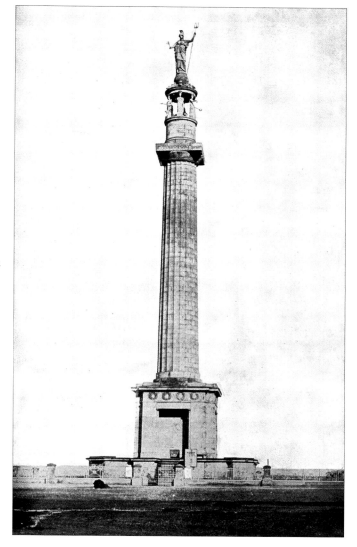

56   *The Norfolk Pillar.*

about alternatives and asked the architect William Wilkins to examine four other possible locations: in Scratby or Caister parish; on Mousehold Hill near Norwich; on Norwich Castle Hill; at the junction of the two London roads near the Norfolk and Norwich Hospital, Norwich. In the end, Yarmouth was chosen and the monument erected. It is made from stone brought from Cullalo in Scotland, not (as is often said) from Killaloe in Ireland. The monument is 144 feet high, just one foot shorter than the better-known column in Trafalgar Square in London. Indeed it was intended to be twenty feet taller than it is, but the expense of the foundations prevented this – it is, like all of Yarmouth, built upon sand.[51]

The keeper of the monument was James Sharman, a native of Yarmouth who had been on the *Victory* and had helped carry the dying Nelson from the deck. Armstrong records a conversation with him in 1856:

57 *Yarmouth seen from Gorleston, with the Norfolk Pillar on the right.*

Walked to the Nelson Column to chat with the old Trafalgar man. He approved of a steam Navy, which we thought that he would consider an innovation, on the grounds that it would 'finish off a battle in half the time'. At Trafalgar half the ships could not get into action as there was no breeze. He said that Nelson was always of a delicate constitution. He had never seen Lady Hamilton. Nelson's daughter Horatia once visited him at the Column and gave him five shillings and a bottle of wine. He seems an honest and seriously disposed old fellow. He says that there is plenty of smuggling going on in tobacco but not in spirits, and that a large quantity of the former was taken by the Coastguard at Lowestoft a few nights back.

Sharman died in 1867 at the age of 82.

Life Stories

MARIA COOPER (BRANSBY) AND ASTLEY COOPER

Maria was born in Shotesham in 1737, the daughter of James and Anna Bransby. She married Samuel Cooper, a clergyman, in 1761. The family moved to Yarmouth when Cooper became curate in 1781: they lived in the Parsonage House beside St Nicholas' church. He died in 1800 and Maria continued to live in the town for a further six years before moving to Dursley, Gloucestershire. Maria's fame is as a writer of novels, each of which was written in the form of a series of letters. The first was *Letters between Emilia and Harriet*, published in 1762. *The Exemplary Mother, or Letters between Mrs Villars and her Family* was her best-known book, first published in 1769 and reissued during her time in Yarmouth, in 1784. All her books were published anonymously.

Maria thought writing was an especially appropriate role for women, commenting in *An Exemplary Mother* that writing was 'a more rational employ' than other pastimes, and that men 'will scarcely be afraid of women, because they are capable of being agreeable companions, and useful friends'.

Maria combined writing with her traditional roles of wife and mother. She had no fewer than ten children, including five daughters all of whom died young from consumption. Mary died in Dursley in 1807.

Astley Cooper, their son, was born in Brooke in 1764, moving with his parents to Yarmouth in 1781. He acquired a reputation as a wild youth, once climbing the spire of St Nicholas' church with two of his mother's pillows and scattering the feathers inside them into the air. He studied medicine in Yarmouth under a relative, Francis Turner, but moved to London in 1784. He became the most highly-paid physician of his day and a lecturer in anatomy. His interest in the latter made him a customer of Thomas Vaughan, the Yarmouth body snatcher, and he gave financial support to Vaughan when he was in prison. Cooper acted as consulting surgeon for Guy's Hospital from 1825.

Cooper married Anne Cock in 1791: their only child, a daughter, died in infancy. Anne died in 1827 and in the following year Cooper married Catherine Jones and, at the age of 60, retired to a farm near Hemel Hempstead, where, according to Arthur Mee, 'he would buy up old and worn-out horses, feed them, doctor them, and make them into new and healthy creatures'. Cooper died in 1841 and, at his own request, was buried beneath the floor of Guy's Hospital chapel. There is a statue of him in St Paul's Cathedral in London.

JEMIMA KINDERSLEY (WICKSTEED)

Jemima Wicksteed was born in Yarmouth in October 1741. Of humble origins, she grew to be a renowned beauty and at the age of 20 she married Lieutenant Nathaniel Kindersley of the Royal Artillery: in true Jane Austen fashion, they met at a ball. The family went to India in 1764 where Kindersley worked as an artillery captain. In 1769 Jemima and her son returned to England because of sickness: Nicholas remained in India where he died a year later.

In 1777, Jemima published the book that made her famous: *Letters from the Island of Teneriffe, Brazil, the Cape of Good Hope and the East Indies*. It is one of the first travel books ever to be written by a woman. She took a keen interest in the role of women in India, and looked into the practice of suttee, where a wife commits suicide on the death of her husband. She also gives an account of the life and customs of Moslem women in India, one of the first to appear in Western Europe.

Jemima took an interest in the role of women in society, translating the *Essay on the Character, Manners and Understanding of Women in Different Ages*, written in French by Antoine Thomas. She added two essays of her own on the subject to the book, one suggesting that the power of women was directly inverse to their sexual attractiveness to men, so that Indian men limited the rights of their women while the Dutch, being less prey to jealousy, allowed their women much more influence. The other essay called for improved education for women.

Jemima died in Middlesex in April 1809.

DAWSON TURNER

Dawson Turner was born at Middlegate in 1775. It was not the family home – his mother was paying a visit to her mother's uncle when she gave birth! He followed in his father's profession as a banker: the bank was on Hall Plain, between Rows 53 and 55. It was replaced in 1854 by a new building designed by Anthony Salvin.

Turner is best known for his leisure activities, being a keen botanist, collector of antiquities and patron of the arts. He published several books on mosses and fungi. His major single achievement was his work on Blomefield's *Norfolk*. This had originally been published in 11 volumes: Turner collected over 7,000 illustrations and expanded the work to fifty-six volumes. Part of this fantastic resource is now in the British Library, having been purchased for the nation after Turner's death at a cost of £460.

Turner employed many helpers in his search for specimens. One was Lilly Wigg, the son of a Smallburgh shoemaker who kept a small school in Fighting Cock Row in Yarmouth. He was interested in birds and fishes found along the Yarmouth coastline, but most of all in seaweeds. In 1801, when Wigg was in his fifties, Turner gave him a job as a clerk in his bank. Wigg was an early exponent of eating a diet from nature: he worked for 20 years on a book about edible wild plants. Unfortunately it was never published and Wigg himself died in 1828: parts of his manuscript still survive.

Turner was a great lover of paintings. He was a patron to John Crome and John Sell Cotman, the Norwich artists. In 1814 he bought Bellini's *Madonna and Child Enthroned with St Peter and St Paul and a Donor* and this graced the drawing room of his house in South Quay for many years. He paid just £54 for this painting; now worth millions of pounds, it is in the Birmingham Museum and Art Gallery.

Turner married Mary Palgrave in 1796: they had 11 children, three of whom died in infancy. Mary died in 1850. Turner then married Rosamund Duff, a widow 35 years his junior. This created a local scandal and the couple moved to London. Turner died on 20 June 1858 and is buried in Brompton cemetery. There is a plaque to him on the bank on Hall Plain.

MARY AND ANNA SEWELL

Mary Sewell was born Mary Wright in 1797 in Felthorpe. She married Isaac Sewell at Lamas Meeting House (they were both Quakers) and moved to Yarmouth, where Isaac owned a grocer's shop. They lived in the house on Church Plain Yarmouth now known as Anna Sewell House: their daughter Anna was born here in 1820. The family moved to London in 1822, and did not return to Norfolk until 1867 when they settled in Catton.

Mary published several books: they were ballads with a strong moral content. The most famous was *Mother's Last Words*, about two orphaned chimney-sweeps. It was published by Jarrold's of Norwich and sold more than a million copies. The follow-up, *Our Father's Care*, about an orphaned water-cress girl sold almost as well.

Anna led the life of an invalid following a fall when she was 14 years old. She and her brother Philip frequently spent their summers at their grandparents' farm at Buxton: this was where she learned to love horses. They would often visit Sewell relatives in Yarmouth while in Norfolk: their grandfather's brothers ran a grocery shop at 28, Market Place. Anna was frequently too ill to make the most of these visits to the town of her birth. In September 1835, she wrote to her mother, 'on first day I woke with a obstropolus cold and sore throat which so increased in the evening that I felt quite poorly and went to bed early and found it worse in the morning so that I had not much pleasure in Yarmouth.'[52]

Anna wrote only one book, *Black Beauty*: this was also published by Jarrold's. It took her six years to write, being finally published in November 1877, and has become one of the best-selling and most-loved children's stories of all time. Anna did not live to see its full success, dying in 1878. Mary died in 1884 and both women are buried in the Quaker graveyard at Lamas.

The house where Anna was born still exists although Anna might not recognise its exterior – local historian Harry Johnson created the present front from old timber, brick and glass in 1932, and the mullioned window was brought here from a house in Row 51. Behind it, however, is timber-framing, almost the only example now remaining in central Yarmouth.

SIR JAMES PAGET

Paget was born in Yarmouth in 1814, at 59, South Quay, the home of his father, Samuel, a brewer and shipowner. He went to a local school in a room over the Greyfriars cloister and became apprentice to a Yarmouth doctor, Charles Costerton, who was mayor of Yarmouth in 1825. Paget was interested in botany, his brother Charles (who followed his father in the brewery business) in insects. Together they wrote *Sketch of the Natural History of Yarmouth and its Neighbourhood*, published in 1834.

In the same year, Paget moved to London, enrolling at St Bartholomew's Hospital. After qualifying, he continued to work at the Hospital. He was also on the council of the Royal College of Surgeons for 15 years and vice-chancellor of the University of London between 1884 and 1895. Paget wrote almost two hundred books and papers, and his name has become attached to several medical discoveries, such as 'Paget's disease of the bone' and 'Paget's abscess'. Paget's Test is used to distinguish between solid and cystic tumours.

Paget became the leading surgeon in London, with a practice worth £10,000 a year. In 1858, he was appointed Surgeon-in-Ordinary to Queen Victoria, and in 1863 to the Prince of Wales. He returned many times to his native Yarmouth. He wrote that the town, 'once a busy place of commerce and shipbuilding is now a fishing port and seaside watering place'. He regretted the changes to the South Quay: 'Good housing becoming counting houses and handsome frontages built out as shops and all signs of active foreign commerce gone. Now scarcely a house on the Quay appears to be a private residence.'[53]

Paget died on 30 December 1899 and is buried in Finchley Cemetery. Today his name is honoured in the 'Sir James Paget Hospital', serving the people of his native Yarmouth as well as many others in Norfolk and north-east Suffolk.

Chapter Four

Great Yarmouth 1900-1974

T he early 20th century was a boom time for Yarmouth, with both the holiday business and the fishing industry at their peak. In 1900, the town was summed up:

> Yarmouth stands near the top of the list of the most popular seaside resorts of this country, very few towns having a larger aggregate of pleasure and health seekers. It has been a pleasure resort since the early days of the last century, and gradually the good people have come to recognise the substantial advantages to be derived from the summer visitor. It is safe to say that no town is so solicitous for the comfort of its guests – no expense is spared by the municipal authorities to make the town healthy and attractive; and their efforts are fully appreciated by the large numbers who are drawn hither, increasing year by year. During the summer of 1900 it was calculated that during the month of August there was a weekly average of over 60,000 visitors staying in the town, and to these must be added the excursionists, of whom as many as 20,000 are poured in by the railways and steamers in one day. Large as these numbers may seem there is ample accommodation for all; although it must be confessed that numbers of people on the night before August Bank Holiday have had to sleep on the sandhills and the beach for want of room. During August the beach in the daytime is literally black with the long line of people sitting and lying down, extending from some distance south of the Wellington or Corporation Pier to the rifle Butts, a distance of considerably over a mile. The visitor is monarch of all he surveys. The whole town is given up to him and his pleasures.[1]

The town was not content to rest on its laurels, constantly seeking new attractions. In 1903, the Australian convict ship *Success* was on view for the summer season. In the same year, the Borough Surveyor told the Council that he had received an offer to take the Winter Gardens from Torquay for £1,300. The original cost of the building had been £12,358. He said that the building could take 2,000 people and could be put up north of the Wellington Pier. It would cost £1,200 to £1,300 to take the building down, transport it to Yarmouth and re-erect it. He went down to Torquay and was impressed: 'For Yarmouth, I consider the building would be of immense service; in such a season as last it would have turned the small loss made on the gardens into a profit. I have no doubt that its acquisition would tend to lengthen the season with better class visitors, and on wet days to be able to provide for 2,000 more persons under cover, should be the means of adding to the popularity of the town. The building is of such a size, that if it is desired a good swimming bath of quite the usual proportions could be put in it, and not occupy more than one-third its floor space.'

58   *Belle steamers at the Quay.*

59   *A crowded Central Parade in the heyday of the tourist business.*

60 *The Winter Gardens, exterior.*

60a *Wedding Reception inside the Winter Gardens in 1924. The bride is Evelyn Aitken, daughter of the Vicar of Yarmouth, the groom John Thornhill, formerly a curate in the town. They are surrounded by six bridesmaids and a page.*

61 *The Cobholm, heading downstream past the Norfolk Pillar.*

The structure was larger than he expected and he now estimated the cost of removal and re-erection at £2,000. The Council voted 15-0 in favour of buying the structure and invited tenders for the work. They were lucky: the lower of the two tenders they received, from Messrs Crabtree & Co, was for £1,115 10s. 0d., and this naturally was accepted.[2]

Five years later, there were new attractions. In June 1908, the *Hippodrome* advertised 'the Australian Woodcutters – the felling and axemanship of Jackson and Maclaren – actual trees transported from the Australian Bush felled in the Arena by these skilled experts in the use of Axe and Saw'. In the same year, the cinema made its first appearance in the town:

> With the opening of the handsome building recently erected on the Marine Parade South, there will be added another place of amusement in the Town. THE GEM, for that is the name given to the new hall which will be run by a syndicate of gentlemen well known in the music hall world, who will provide entertainment consisting chiefly of the display of bioscope pictures. A unique feature is that the entertainment is proceeding all day. For a small payment, ranging from 2d to 6d, visitors can enter when they please, stay as long as they like and go out when they like. On Sunday a series of colour moving Tableaux, depicting sacred subjects, will be on view all day, including incidents in the life of Christ.[3]

When the *Gem* first opened, the authorities insisted that men and women sit on separate sides of the auditorium! Other cinemas followed: the *Empire* in 1911, the *Regent* in 1914, and the *Central* in the Market Place. The latter was the least successful, running only between 1915 and 1922. It re-opened as the *Plaza* in 1928 but closed for good in 1939: the site is now occupied by Woolworth's.

Some Midlands firms sent their entire workforce on holiday:

All Saturday morning trippers were pouring into Yarmouth, a number of heavy trains arriving from London and the Midland districts. The Londoners came from Southtown station in a festive mood several of them singing and cake-walking as the fancy moved them. In the evening they returned to their trains in the same good humour, many of them heavily freighted with the local specialities, boxes of bloaters and 'Yarmouth Rock'. Two trains at the Beach station brought the Humber Company's employees from Beeston, Nottinghamshire. Breakfast was served on the train en route to Yarmouth, where headquarters had been secured at the Queen's Hotel, opposite the Britannia Pier. At five o'clock the staff dinner was held at the Norfolk Artillery men's hotel and just before midnight the return train started for Beeston, taking tired but still happy holiday makers home.[4]

Some people were becoming concerned with the way animals were treated on the beach. In 1911, the Council decided that they would no longer issue licences for goat carts. Two years later they discussed the rights of donkeys; it was suggested that nobody over 16 should be allowed to ride on them, and that the donkeys should have a minimum of an hour's rest without their saddles each day.

These were good years for the fishing business, too. The year 1900 saw a record catch, with 375 million herring brought back to Yarmouth: the ships blocked the river from its mouth up to the Town Hall and it was possible to cross the river by leaping from boat to boat. Patterson estimates the 1902 catch at 600,000 cran, which he equates to an almost unbelievable 631,578,800 fish. By 1913, there were more than a thousand fishing boats, and in 1914 there was a new record catch of 840,299 cran – about 900 million fish! This was to be the highest catch of all time.

62   *The* Yarmouth Belle *enters the river.*

The shipping trade flourished, too, with the occasional disaster. The proverb about 'rats leaving a sinking ship' was proved all too true in November 1905, when the sailing-barque *Erna* was driven ashore beside the North Pier. 'Then came the amazing sight, which witnesses say they will never forget. As the ship fell apart, hundreds of rats scuttled out from hiding in her, and plunged into the sea. In droves they swam ashore – big rats, little rats, old rats, young rats, all frantically making for the safety of the beach. Some were clinging to spars and deck furniture washed from the ship, while others were clinging to upturned boxes and crates like 'little old men' on rafts. Most of them reached the safety of the shore, and in their mad rush to get away, few, if any, of the spectators were inclined to stand in their path – at one time a patch of the beach was black with them.'[5]

The other trades in the town saw their ups and downs. Grouts went bankrupt in 1890. Money was raised to set up a new firm, and the business

63 *The Town Hall, with sailing ship and railway trucks.*

flourished once more in the 20th century. In 1907 a new artificial silk called rayon was made, the first commercial manufacture of this yarn in England.[6]

Unemployment was a problem, especially in the slack period between the end of the fishing season and the start of the holiday season. By March 1905, 600 unemployed men were working on improvements north of the Jetty. A soup kitchen was set up in the Market Place and almost 5,000 portions were distributed.

There was a social revolution on 1 January 1909 in Yarmouth and everywhere else in Britain: old age pensions were paid out for the first time. The shop next to the Post Office in Regent Street was opened for the purpose. The first pensioner in Yarmouth to receive the money was Robert Walters, who was given four shillings a week to supplement his meagre naval pension.

With the new century came a new form of public transport within the borough. The Corporation began running electric trams from 19 June 1902: 'On that day two of the new tramcars, gaily decorated with flags and bunting, clattered their way from the Town Hall to the 'car shed' at Caister Road, through the crowds lining Regent Street and the Market Place, and carrying civic leaders and corporation officials. At the depot, the then mayor (Col W. Diver) declared the service open.' Fares were 1d. and 2d., and 72,540 passengers were carried in the first fortnight.

64   *A Yarmouth herring drifter: YH 105, Wydale.*

In 1904, extra routes were laid to Queen's Road and the Fish Wharf, and in the same year the route to Gorleston was taken over by the Corporation and converted to electricity. In 1906 the services were extended to cover Caister, the North Quay and the Marine Parade: trams could run at up to 10mph on the flat Parade but speeds fell to 3 mph over the 'hump' of Fuller's Hill.[7]

In 1913, the Corporation and the Port and Haven Commissioners decided to promote a new Haven Bridge with a double tram track. This would cost £80,000, with each body contributing half: the Corporation would raise theirs by selling off the Fish Wharf. In the following year, they held a referendum about the new bridge: out of a 12,530 electorate, 2,342 voted in favour and 4,327 against, so the scheme was abandoned.

J.W. Cockrill became Borough Surveyor in 1882 and continued in office for over 40 years. In 1907, he submitted plans for a garden suburb on land north of Hamilton Road that the Corporation had bought from Mr Greengrass for £350. Proposed streets were named in January 1908 – Sandringham, Balmoral, Windsor, Royal, Alexandra and Osborne Avenues. Unemployed labour was used to level the land and also to build a bridge over the railway. Barnard Bridge cost £1,050 and the ornamental detail in the concrete of its columns reminds us of the surveyor's nickname of 'Concrete Cockrill'.

Yarmouth hit the headlines for the wrong reasons in 1900: on the morning of 23 September, a local boy found the body of a young woman on the beach with a bootlace knotted tightly around her throat. Identification took some time as she had been staying in lodgings under the name of Mrs Hood, but it was eventually found that she was Mary Bennett, the wife of Herbert Bennett, a labourer living in Woolwich.

65 *Primitive Methodists celebrating the centenary of their movement on 21 July 1907. The three standing gentlemen are W.M. Buddery, T.W. Swindell and the Rev. Arthur Wood.*

Bennett was arrested on 7 November and tried at the Old Bailey in February 1901: it was felt that there was so much local feeling against him that a fair trial could not be had in Norwich. The evidence was contradictory, with some witnesses saying that Bennett was in Yarmouth on the night of the murder but one man being sure that he had been with him in London. However, he was found guilty, brought to Norwich prison and hanged there on 21 March. He maintained his innocence to the end: when the flagpole bearing the black flag that was raised on execution days snapped, some saw it as a sign that an innocent man was being executed.

Most crime, of course, was at a much more petty level, and sometimes a result of desperation, as in the case of Samuel Beckett, seen walking down Frederick Road carrying a sack at 4.45 on a June morning in 1907. A policeman opened the sack, which contained oranges. At first Beckett claimed he had bought them but he eventually admitted he had stolen them from a stall in the Market Place, saying, 'I was hungry and when in the market saw a stall with canvas around it, I tore the canvas and took some oranges and grapes'. Beckett had only left the Workhouse the previous morning, so was presumably homeless as well as hungry, but the law had to take its course: he was sentenced to seven days in prison with hard labour.[8]

The early 20th century witnessed an intensification of the struggle for women's rights, and Yarmouth played its part. The town saw an arson campaign by militant suffragettes. On 27 September 1913, one of the largest fires ever seen in Yarmouth broke out. At 2 o'clock in the morning the Southtown timber yard of W. Palgrave Brown was found to be ablaze. The firemen took 24 hours to control the blaze. In October, the suffragettes' own newspaper announced: 'GIGANTIC FIRE AT YARMOUTH – Timber Yards a Sea of Flames. Damage estimated at over £40,000.' On the following day, three greens on Yarmouth golf links were damaged: cards in favour of the suffragettes were left on the course. A postcard was received by the local newspaper office which read: 'The Timber Yard was fired by Suffragettes. There is no mystery. Votes for Women.'

66 *A tram passing through Yarmouth Market Place.*

67 *Public meeting in the Market Place, 1907, showing the square cleared of all stalls.*

On 17 April 1914, the pavilion on the Britannia Pier in Yarmouth was destroyed by fire. According to *The Suffragette*, which carried a photograph of the blazing building, suffragette messages were found on the beach nearby:

VOTES FOR WOMEN. MR McKENNA HAS NEARLY KILLED MRS
PANKHURST. WE CAN SHOW NO MERCY UNTIL WOMEN ARE
ENFRANCHISED.

It was the charisma of the Pankhursts that attracted younger women. In 1910 Christabel Pankhurst spoke at Great Yarmouth, creating an impression that 21-year

68   *The first air-raid in Britain: St Peter's Plain, Yarmouth, 19 January 1915.*

old Henrietta Grenville was to remember over 60 years later: 'I was so impressed by
her elegance, the way she put things. I was convinced by what she had to say and after
hearing her, wrote to headquarters to ask what I could do.'[9]

The First World War

The role of Yarmouth between 1914 and 1918 has been discussed in my book *Norfolk
in the First World War* (Phillimore 2004). Its position so close to the Continent exposed
the town to direct attack, and the fear of invasion was also very real.

The night of 19 January 1915 saw the first-ever air raids on Britain, when Zeppelins
dropped bombs on Yarmouth and Lynn: the Yarmouth raid was the earlier of the two.
The Zeppelin L3, piloted by Peter Strasser, crossed the Norfolk coast at about 8 p.m.:
dropping a parachute flare, the pilot was able to identify where he was, and then headed
south. The first bomb fell on a farm at Little Ormesby, followed by bombs at 6, Albemarle
Road and at the rear of 78, Crown Road. The fourth bomb fell on St Peter's Plain and
this was the one that killed two people. It badly damaged St Peter's Villa, occupied by
Mr Ellis, a fishworker. He was very lucky to survive, having gone into his kitchen just two
minutes before the bomb fell: he was cut by glass as the kitchen window shattered. His
family were even more fortunate as they were on holiday in Cornwall at the time.

However, two neighbours were not so lucky. The body of Samuel Smith, a 53-year-old
shoemaker, was found near his shop, with part of his head blown away. That of Martha
Taylor, 72 years old, was found in the street with a large wound in her body: part of one
of her arms had been blown off. Martha lived with her sister at 2, St Peter's Plain. Further
bombs were dropped as the Zeppelin moved south. There was considerable damage to
the Fishwharf, especially to the Restaurant Rooms, but there were no more casualties. By
9.30p.m., the Zeppelin was on its journey across the North Sea and back home.

Martha was buried in Gorleston, Sam Smith in Kitchener Road cemetery, next to the grave of his sister Agnes Hutt. Teacher Mark Coller has taken an interest in these graves, and placed flowers on Martha's grave on the 90th anniversary of her death. He commented: 'Martha and her twin sister, Jane Eliza, had been together all their lives. Martha was a canvas beater and they had both worked as domestic servants.' He gave a powerful assessment of the significance of these deaths: 'The loss of a poor old woman from Great Yarmouth has been largely forgotten. However, I believe her loss was important. She symbolises the point at which this country descended into total war. The point at which civilians became legitimate targets for zeppelins, air raids and suicide bombers.'[10]

There was no defence against this first air raid, but the British were able to use planes to attack later raiders. A Zeppelin, L 21, was shot down by pilots from Yarmouth ten miles off Lowestoft on 28 November 1916. As well as being the first town attacked by a Zeppelin during the war, Yarmouth was also the last town – and the captain was once again Peter Strasser. The raid was on the night of 5/6 August 1918. Egbert Cadbury led an attack on the Zeppelin from Yarmouth airfield: the machine was brought down and Strasser was killed. In 1986, a cigarette lighter made from the wreckage and signed by Cadbury was presented to the Maritime Museum.

There had been a bombardment of the town by German navy ships in November 1914, but no damage was done as no shells came even as far as the beach. Later bombardments were rather more serious. Yarmouth was bombarded on the night of 14 January 1916. Damaged buildings included St Nicholas' and St James' schools. One hundred boys at the former were moved to the Primitive Methodist Sunday School building while repairs were carried out, while some classes at St James' were closed until the shattered window panes could be repaired. There was another bombardment on 25 April 1916, which began at 4.15 in the morning and lasted 55 minutes.[11]

Fear of invasion led to some panic in the town, as the writer Henry Rider Haggard recorded in his diary:

> Presently there arose murmurs from the esplanade without, which I should explain is plunged in the most intense darkness in these dark and moonless nights and yet seems to be the haunt of hundreds who wander about in the gloom, feeling their way from post to post. Next the landlady's daughter arrived saying that soldiers and police had called explaining that light was escaping from the window; that the esplanade was filled from side to side with a mob who swore that signalling to the Germans was going on from the house and that there was much excitement … the whole thing is madness for how could anyone signal with a lamp or candle over the Yarmouth roads filled with mine sweepers to the deep water miles away? In Yarmouth I am informed this spy hunting has become an absolute mania, so much that the unfortunate landlady … thinks she will have to leave the house.[12]

Physical evidence for the threat of invasion can be seen on both sides of the Acle Straight just west of the Vauxhall holiday camp: two pill boxes of First World War vintage still stand beside the road.

Yarmouth men fought in the army and in the navy, and left many memories. One man told his tale to the *Yarmouth Mercury* in October 1918. Private B. Storey, from Row 48, was in the Surrey Regiment. On 3 May 1917 after going over the top, he was

69 *Edward, Prince of Wales, in Yarmouth, 1918.*

wounded with a bullet in the knee and captured. He was sent as a prisoner of war to Hamburg and then to Limburg. He recalled life in the camp for the local press:

> The food he describes as mainly consisting of swede water and cabbage water, or so-called soup, and it was only the parcels they received through the Red Cross that kept them alive. The German guards were angry at their prisoners receiving parcels, and he recalls one occasion when the food they had received had been placed on the tea table that the guard knocked over the table in an attempt to spoil the food. No doubt, he says, the Germans are very badly off for food, the bread often containing potato peelings and sawdust. Their guards would ask them frequently to give them some of the bread they received, but they declined, preferring to give it to the Russian and Italian prisoners, who, he says, suffered terribly, more so indeed than the British. The Germans also made bodged attempts to remove the bullet from Storey's knee, as a result of which he expected to be lame for life.[13]

Between the Wars

Many recollections survive of holidays in Yarmouth in the days between the wars, the writer often looking back to an idyllic childhood. Here are three accounts from different sources, which together give a clear picture of the town at this period:

> Just as the ancient pier and harbour, the shipping, the cliffs, the red roofs clustering on the hill over-looking Gorleston's beautiful bay and silken sands, are the chief glory of that resort, so Yarmouth's greatest is its miles of varied sea front. Many strangers, thinking of this borough only in terms of fish, have marvelled to discover the size of this marine pleasaunce and the lure of its many attributes. Gardens, promenades, boating lakes, garden canals, model yacht ponds, bowling greens, swimming pool, tennis courts, piers and a pleasure beach alternate along its five miles or so of fascinating sea front.

Beyond this line of colour and animation lie the sands and the sea-shore. It is characteristic of the East Anglian sea-board that its beaches are spacious, soft and kindly. At Yarmouth they attain their best and afford a magnificent playground for old and young. On the central beach gather the majority who love the company of their fellows; to the north or to the south are large tracts of sand and marram hill as secluded as any Cornish bay, ideal for family picnics and bathing parties. Sea bathing and sun bathing fill the long health-giving days. And there is no more pleasant sight than the hosts of brown-legged kiddies splashing happily in the little waves and building wondrous moated castles.

Both Yarmouth and Gorleston are a paradise for children.[14]

We would go on to the jetty and jump from there on to the sand, daring each other to jump from a greater height until we came to a point where it was too steep to jump and then we would decide that we had had enough of that particular form of entertainment.

By this time, what with all the fresh air and exercise, we would be getting hungry. So we would decide to return by the 'front' after fortifying ourselves with an ice wafer or a cornet which cost a half-penny. The Marine parade was, in its own way, as exciting as the beach, for there was the Hippodrome with the pictures outside of the 'artistes' to look at and, if we went round to the back, the chance of seeing some ponies or an elephant being taken from one entrance to another.[15]

The most popular, as Cromer is the most fashionable, of East Anglian watering-places. It affords everything for which people visit the East Coast. It has a sea front of over two miles, and its port is the principal fishing port of Norfolk. The most famous of its ancient houses is the 'Star' Hotel, and Elizabethan building whose hall is now used as a bar. The South Quay is one of the most delightful in the country; the ships lie on one side, and opposite stretches an avenue of lime trees backed by quaint old houses. In a street parallel with the South Quay stands the Old Toll House, one of the oldest municipal buildings in the country. It existed in 1362, and is approached by an external staircase which leads to a fine doorway decorated with dog-tooth moulding. The old streets of Yarmouth have a singular charm and repay a visit with camera or sketch book.[16]

The most popular form of entertainment in Yarmouth between the wars was the cinema – many young people went several times a week. In the 1930s a cinema ticket cost sixpence, the price of a pint of beer – and Saturday morning matinees were even cheaper. As always, proprietors were in search of the sensational. In July 1919, for example, *The Hippodrome* was showing the film of Henrik Ibsen's *The Ghosts*, stressing that it was based on a play banned by the censor. As a result 'hundreds are being turned away nightly through being unable to secure seats … the picture has caused a sensation'. Not to be outdone, the *Gem* offered a series of films under the title *Adventures Among the Cannibals*. These were made at great personal risk by Martin Johnson who – accompanied by 'his plucky wife' as the promoters put it – explored the islands of the South Pacific with a camera: 'Penetrating – sometimes in the face of urgent warnings – thick jungle, wild mountain forests … the intrepid explorers have brought back pictures which unveil the life of a new and strange world.'[17]

The success of the fishing industry meant that there was pressure for space on the South Denes. It was decided to move the racecourse to the North Denes: the first meeting at the new course was held on 15 September 1920, before a crowd of 25,000

70 *Typical postcard sent from Yarmouth in the 1920s. The message on the back begins: 'Dear Geraldine – hope Daddy got the bloaters'.*

people. Two grandstands were moved from the old course to the new one: they are still in use today.[18]

Sunday amusements were not allowed, but attitudes were gradually changing. In 1931, according to A.W. Ecclestone, 'two girls clad in shorts on Sunday afternoon created a sensation among the more respectably clad citizens'. Two years later, however, an application to open the Pleasure Beach on Sundays was not rejected but adjourned until the following year. In 1935, the Council approved Sunday opening for the Bathing Pool, Waterways, Bowling Greens and Tennis Courts. After the war, on 18 July 1946, the Borough held a referendum, asking whether 'cinematographic entertainments' should be allowed to open on Sundays. The voters decided in favour of Sunday opening by 4,084 to 1,342 votes.

Many people have memories of the Scots in Yarmouth during the herring season. Maurice Smith recalls:

> The fishermen slept on the boats but the girls were accommodated in lodgings. Not all the boarding houses would take them because of the odour of fish which they brought indoors. Many of the landladies were glad of the extra cash outside the holiday season and prepared for the herring season by stripping the room of all but the essential furnishings such as bed and washstand. Before entering the house the girls used to leave their oilskins and boots outside.
>
> You could smell them coming in the street and hear them too, for their tongues were never still and the strange sound of their Gaelic speech used to fascinate me. They usually wore dark clothes: thick long skirts with navy woollen seamen's jerseys. Scarves were tied round their heads and a shawl, if the wind was bitter, completed

71 *'The end of the trams, 9 May 1931'.*

72 *Arnold's store on fire, 1919, photograph taken by Judith Ferrier.*

the outfit. With long knitting needles tucked under their arms and balls of wool in their apron pockets, they knitted with incredible speed as they walked along.

The Scotsmen would not engage in fishing on the Sabbath, so none of their boats left their moorings. It was a remarkable sight to walk along the riverside and see the drifters packed, side by side, so that very little of the river could be seen. It was an eerie feeling to experience the silence and lack of movement in contrast and hubbub of activity that came from the quays on weekdays.

Father told me that the Scotch fisher folk would go into his shop at the beginning of the herring season and put down a deposit on articles of furniture. As many of them came from remote parts of Scotland it was their opportunity of setting up their homes. Many of them would return to the shop week by week just to look at their chosen pieces so father had to store them so they were readily available for their scrutiny. About the middle of December, at the end of the season, the furniture was carefully stowed on the vessels for their homeward journey to Scotland.[19]

Other sea-borne trade continued to be important. Chief commodities between the wars – apart from herrings – were grain, coal, and timber. The coal trade increased when coal-fired power stations opened by the river at Norwich in 1926 and at Yarmouth itself in 1929.

The sea, as ever, was a dangerous place on which to ply one's trade. The RNLI had a lifeboat station in Yarmouth from 1857, operating from the Lifeboat Shed on the Marine Parade. In 1919, however, the station closed and the Gorleston lifeboats assumed responsibility for the whole coastline of this area. One spectacular example of a shipwreck occurred when the *Porthcawl*, laden with 2,000 tons of esparto grass, caught fire near the Happisburgh Lightship in September 1933. The Captain decided to try to run the ship onto the beach at Yarmouth, but the fire took hold too quickly: Gorleston lifeboat took off the crew. The blazing ship made a dramatic spectacle for the many holidaymakers watching from the beach, and boat trips were run to give a better view. The *Porthcawl* blazed for a week and at one point threatened to run up against the Britannia Pier, but she just cleared it. A tug then pushed her onto the beach. Eventually she was towed to Hull by two salvage tugs, but it was found to be too expensive to repair her and she was broken up. Her image must survive among the photographs of many trippers who were fortunate enough to be on holiday in Yarmouth in September 1933![20]

Unemployment was a great problem in the years between the wars, made worse by the collapse of the Russian market which had been taking up to 90 per cent of the herring catch. In 1922, it was said that 800 of the 1,300 fishermen in the town had had no work since 1920. As they were paid by a share of the profits from the catch rather than by a weekly wage, they could not even claim unemployment benefit. By July 1922, there were 3,443 unemployed in the town. They held an open-air meeting in the Market Place, and marched to the Town Hall carrying banners with the words: 'They fought for you, can they work for you?' A contingent of 30 went by boat from Hall Quay to London as part of a national protest. The season of 1922 was not as bad as feared, however, with between 700 and 800 boats landing over 342,000 cran. There was a decline by 1939 to 303,083 cran.

Works for the unemployed in 1926 included the construction of roads and sewers on the Barrack estate, and building a new sea wall from Sandown Road to Beaconsfield Road.

73 *The Porthcawl stranded and on fire, September 1933.*

The era of the trams did not last long. The system was running at a loss by the early 1920s and the Corporation turned to buses, starting with three open-top buses bought second-hand from the London General Omnibus Company. They were used at first to supplement the trams, but in 1926 another seven buses were bought, this time single-deckers, and they replaced the trams on the route between the Fish Wharf and Newtown. The great day of the tram was over. In 1930, the line from Haven Bridge to Gorleston was replaced by buses. These continued across the bridge up to Theatre Plain: for the first time it was not necessary for passengers to change vehicle and walk over the bridge in order to cross the river. The last tram ran in 1933, with the same ceremonies that had seen their first running just 31 years earlier.[21]

The new Haven Bridge was opened in 1930, the Prince of Wales performing the ceremony. The opening spans are 45 feet long and raised by electric power, with provision for raising and lowering by hand if necessary. The bridge cost £200,000, of which the Ministry of Transport bore 65 per cent and the Corporation and the Port and Haven Commissioners 17.5 per cent each.[22]

We have seen that plague was the most feared disease of the Middle Ages, cholera in the Victorian period. In the 20th century, it was flu. The influenza pandemic of 1918-19 killed over 15 million people worldwide, especially focusing on young adults. It arrived in England in the spring of 1918, with further peaks in autumn 1918 and in the spring of 1919: about 150,000 people in England and Wales succumbed. In Yarmouth, 5,000 leaflets offering advice were delivered in October 1918:

> Advice to the Public:
> The occurrence of epidemic catarrhs would be greatly decreased by continuous flushing with air of each occupied bedroom and living-room. This implies the need

for adequate warm clothing, especially for persons engaged in sedentary occupations and for children and old people.

Overcrowding in dwellings, or in unventilated assembly rooms and places of entertainment, should be avoided. The aggregation of large numbers of persons in one room, especially for sleeping, is dangerous when catarrhs are prevalent.

Dirtiness, whether personal or of living or working rooms, and dusty conditions favour infection. Indiscriminate expectoration is always a source of risk of infection, and is especially dangerous during the prevalence of Influenza.

Gargling the throat with a solution of 1 in 5000 permanganate of potassium, in water containing 0.8 per cent of common salt night and morning is to be recommended. In addition, this solution should be poured into the palm of the hand, snuffed up through the nostrils, and expelled through the mouth.

Prolonged mental strain or over-fatigue, and, still more, alcoholism, favour infection, and complication by pneumonia is especially fatal among immoderate drinkers. Persons with septic conditions of the mouth, teeth, nose or throat are especially prone to catarrhal attacks. The treatment of these conditions is important.

It is particularly important that sick persons and old people should be protected against exposure to Influenza.[23]

The epidemic shows up in the school logbooks for the town. At Cobholm Boys' School, the headmaster noted a considerable drop in attendance due to 'Spanish Influenza' on 8 July 1918. The disease returned in October: 133 children were off sick on the 18th. The school was closed until 28 October, and this was then extended to 4 November; there were still 134 children absent on that day. There was another spell of sickness in the last week of February and the first week of March 1919, with many absences from school. At Church Road school, 52 boys were absent on 8 July 1918 and this rose to 77 four days later. Influenza returned to the school in February-March 1919, effecting pupils and also several staff members, including the headmaster.

Because of the war, the Borough Medical Officer was only issuing summary annual reports. He noted that the outstanding features of 1918 were the epidemics of influenza in July and October, with the resultant increase in death rates, but did not give actual figures: 'Owing to the shortage of nurses, little could be done beyond distribution of pamphlets giving advice. School closure was tried in the second epidemic, together with the shutting of cinemas to children, but there was no evidence that these measures had any effect.' In the year 1919 he reported that 83 people had died of influenza, nearly three times the average for the past ten years, 'owing to the final wave of the great epidemic of 1918-9'. By the late spring of 1919, the epidemic was over: public health regulations were rescinded at the end of May. In 1920, just seven people died of influenza in the borough.[24]

The period between the wars saw considerable improvements in the living conditions of most people, especially in housing. There was a new atmosphere: it was time to build homes for heroes. As early as June 1919, plans were announced to build many new council houses – 162 on North Denes, 102 in Southtown and 163 in Gorleston. These were followed by 46 semi-detached houses along Royal Square (now Onslow Avenue) and Barnard Avenue. These houses cost about £1,000 each to build, and were let at 11 shillings a week. More council houses on the North Denes followed – 24 in

74 *Aerial view, showing Breydon Railway Bridge and the Revolving Tower, 1930s.*

Raleigh and Drake Avenues in 1925 and 48 in Beresford Road and Perebrown Avenue in 1927. The increasing population of the area was reflected in the opening of a new railway station – Newtown Halt – in 1933. In 1926 work started on 120 houses on the Barracks estate at the south end of the town: it was decided to name the new roads after Dickens' characters. In the following year, the Housing Committee decided to build 56 houses on the Barracks estate and 48 houses on Southtown Common.[25]

The inter-war period saw a great spread in the domestic use of electricity. Only one home in 17 had an electricity supply in 1920. The figure rose to one home in three by 1930, and to two in three by 1939: however, in the 1930s, three-quarters of the population still used gas to cook. Great Yarmouth was one of the first towns to set up its own electricity generating station, on the South Denes in the 1880s. By 1928, the number of customers supplied by the undertaking was over 20,000 within the urban area, and some 40 villages were also being supplied.[26]

Fridges were becoming common among the rich by the 1930s, but few of the middle class and none of the working class had them before the war. This meant that fresh food had to be purchased far more frequently than today. Meat, fish and greengroceries might be delivered two or three times a week to those who could afford to pay for the service, milk twice a day. Elspeth McAdam remembered the struggle to keep milk from going off:

Milk bottles appeared in Yarmouth in about 1920 but most milkmen still brought milk round in churns, driving a 'milk-float' looking rather like a Roman chariot. The milk was in brass-bound churns, with dippers hanging on the side. You took your jug to the door, the milkman took it to his 'chariot', took the lid off the churn, put in the pint or half pint dipper, poured the milk into the jug and returned it to you. Cream was brought in miniature cans, similar to the churns. In summer, Mother boiled the milk at once, bringing it to the point where bubbles just began to appear around the edge of the pan, then poured the hot milk into a jug, which was stood in a large bowl of cold water. It was sometimes my job, if I was available, to stir the milk with a silver spoon until it was cool. This was to help it cool quickly and to prevent a skim forming. We had no fridge until after we moved to London, so we had to use wet muslin and wet porous pots to put butter and milk in when the weather was hot. It was not very successful but better than nothing.[27]

New schools were built such as Greenacre Elementary School, opened in 1929:

The senior boys' school comprises five classrooms accommodating 40 scholars in each, a science room, handwork room, cloakrooms, offices and stores. The senior girls have a similar number of classrooms, with a domestic science room, and a cookery and laundry centre. The junior and infants departments have six classrooms, each accommodating fifty scholars. Each block has a head teacher's study and teachers' common room on the first floor. Heating is on the low pressure system from a central boiler-house.

The main features of the school are the lighting and ventilation. All classrooms have a continuous north light, and are approached by covered ways to the south, with doors opening direct into them, thus converting these classrooms into open-air rooms during the summer. There are also inter-communicating doors to enable the classrooms to be cleared during inclement weather. Each department has its own entrance and playground, and the offices [toilets] are approached by covered ways.

The general scheme for decoration consists of coloured glazed brick dadoes, cream walls and white frieze and ceiling. The forecourts are laid out as lawns and flower-beds, and a portion of the site has been reserved for netball for the girls.

The total cost of the school (including furniture, £1,679) was £33,891, or £31.4 per scholar. This does not include cost of land.[28]

The disposal of waste was becoming an issue in the town. A 'refuse destructor' was built in 1902, designed by Cockrill. It was on the outskirts of town but by the 1920s the houses had grown out to it, leading to many complaints about the smell. There was no provision for salvage: everything was burnt. In 1931, the building was completely remodelled. As the refuse passed along a conveyor belt, two men removed any material worth salvaging. The firebrick lining of the 216-feet-high chimney was rebuilt to allow for the much-increased heat of the new processes. The chimney was destroyed during the war, to the relief of many who thought that German bombers used it as a sight-line.[29]

The Second World War

Many aspects of the war in Yarmouth are covered in my *Norfolk in the Second World War* (Phillimore 2006). Dorothy Calvert recalled the early days:

We waited a long time for the 'phoney war' to end and the real one to start, but once it got going we spent our nights in our Boulton and Paul's shelter, which Mum had erected, in the front downstairs room, and there Mum, my two younger sisters, and occasional friends that had dropped in, spent the night, with the bottle of 'hard stuff', the tin of biscuits, water, a torch, an axe, the first aid kit, and a whistle. We would somehow settle down to rest, or sit and talk, and in a funny way, find no end to laugh at.[30]

As in the First World War, women moved into jobs normally done by men. A historian of the bus company writes:

The Second World War faced the Department with the most serious period in its history. With Yarmouth declared a defence evacuation area, the service was reduced to 'skeleton' proportions. Most of the buses were laid up and employees left in answer to the Service's call, and the 'clippies', Yarmouth's first women bus conductors, did a splendid job.

Humour and fortitude were qualities which sustained those who were left to carry on through the dark days of war, particularly during the savagery of Yarmouth's ordeals by bomb and fire. One driver saw a bomb plummet into the road ahead of him, but coolly negotiated his heavy bus round the crater and continued his journey. Many others faced trying tests as they went about their daily task with the ever-present risk of death or injury. But the buses kept moving.

In 1942 the Caister Road depot received a direct hit, much damage being caused to the building and to the buses parked there. Many buses were sent to Coventry where they helped to carry factory workers, and for a time some were engaged on daily runs to Norwich with building workers needed to repair bomb damage.[31]

Some 217 civilians were killed in air raids on the town between 1940 and 1943: the number would have been far higher if children and other civilians had not been

75 *Wartime clippie: the first Yarmouth bus conductress, Emily Leggett, with the acting transport manager, F.W. Sharman, and the Mayor, E.R. Herman, October 1941.*

evacuated from the town. There was an extremely severe raid on the night of 7-8 April 1941, another on 9 July 1941, and a third on 25 July 1942: it was in the last of these that the parish church was destroyed.

In two incidents just two months apart, 34 young servicewomen died in Yarmouth. On 18 March 1943, eight Wrens were killed as result of an air raid on 8, Nelson Street South. They were based at HMS *Midge*, a coastal forces base responsible for maintaining Motor Torpedo Boats, Motor Gun Boats and Mine Layers. They were:

NAME	AGE	WHERE FROM	WHERE BURIED
Ann Jago-Brown	33	Middlesbrough	Caister
Muriel Rainton	19	Ealing	Ealing
Anne Drummond	25	Crieff, Scotland	Caister
Joan Hughes	20	Birmingham	Caister
Violet Powell	21	London	London
Ellen Regan	34	Ilford	Caister
Aileen Kilburn	19	Chesham, Bucks	Chesham
Rita Turner	19	Maldon, Essex	Maldon

A plaque on the site commemorates their heroism. On 11 May, 26 ATS girls were killed in another raid. These young girls also came from all over Britain, and their names are given here, apparently for the first time:

Doris Travers	21	Northampton	Caister
Isobel Norah James	24	Rolleston, Staffs	Rolleston
Lilian Maud Grimmer	18	Yarmouth	Caister
Jessie Sharp	22	Hessle, Yorkshire	Hessle
May Johnson	20	South Lincs	Caister
Bernice Bell	22	Manchester	Manchester
Jessica Margaret Patricia Lewis	22	Bournemouth	[not known]
Hannah Macleod	23	Stornoway	Stornoway
Elizabeth Mackay	27	Nigg, Scotland	Nigg
Viola Wells	23	Fulstow, Lincs	Caister
Marjorie Sutton	20	Fulstow, Lincs	Caister
Louisa Agnes Maxwell	22	Gosforth	Gosforth
Jean Copley	21	Aston, Sheffield	Aston
Louisa Farnes	22	Stockton-on-Tees	Stockton
Jean Macauley	32	Glasgow	Caister
Eileen Hunt	21	Easthorpe, Newark	[not known]
Molly Carter	21	Sheffield	Sheffield
Enid Line	23	Crouch End, London	London
Vera Mann	25	Leeds	Leeds
Doris Wimbush	28	Doncaster	Caister
Dorothy Ann Fawkes	25	West Woodburn	Corsenside
Margaret F Galbraith	23	Birchvale, Cheshire	Caister Cemetery
Kathleen Gaunt	20	Bingley, Yorkshire	Bingley
Ivy Moore	24	Grimsby	Grimsby
Joan Roma Pearson	25	Grimsby	Grimsby
Jeannie Dewar Scougall	21	Edinburgh	Edinburgh

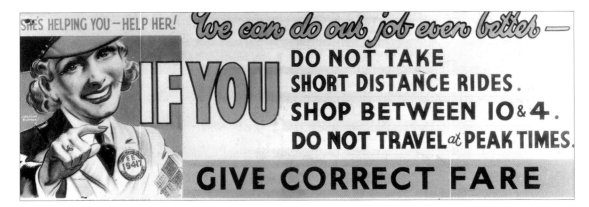

SHE'S HELPING YOU – HELP HER! *We can do our job even better –*
IF YOU DO NOT TAKE SHORT DISTANCE RIDES. SHOP BETWEEN 10&4. DO NOT TRAVEL *at* PEAK TIMES.
GIVE CORRECT FARE

76   *Wartime bus advertisement.*

The girls were living in a billet near Wellesley Park: their bodies were laid out in the Park and their possessions listed, usually just a small amount of cash, a lipstick and in several cases a – sadly ineffective – good luck charm.

Grout's played an important role in the war. From 1932, the firm supplied the silk used by the Ministry of Aviation to make parachutes. In the Second World War this process was moved to Leek in Staffordshire and Leigh in Lancashire because of the fear of invasion. In 1941 the South Mill was destroyed by bombing; the boiler man, George Green, was killed. When Japan entered the war in 1941, it ceased to supply Britain and America with the raw silk that was used to make parachutes. This led to the use of nylon, an artificial material invented just before the war in New York and London, hence its name. It was used in America for making stockings, but this was not permitted in wartime Britain: instead it was used by Grout's for making parachutes from 1942 onwards.[32]

Dorothy Calvert described her memories of working at Grout's:

> I was sweet seventeen when the war started, a happy ordinary girl, working in our silk factory as a weaver of beautiful silk, out of which the 'perks' were sheer pure silk stockings at sixpence a pair, and bundles of pure silk remnants for half a crown, out of which I had pretty undies made. As soon as the war started, we had to start weaving parachute silk and bandages. The monotony of this work was rotten at the best of times, but after the factory was bombed, and one part was demolished, we spent the best part of the time keeping the 'dust and muck' off the work, and when it rained, the water, which dripped through the obliging, well-placed holes in the roof. This was all going on between the air-raid warnings, which gave us a few seconds to run over two tennis courts into our submarine-like shelters, as the 'Germans' flew overhead, trying to hit us with machine gun bullets.[33]

There were of course many dramatic events in the North Sea during the war. Here we can take just two examples that show that at sea there was no phoney war. In January 1940, the Trinity House vessel *Reculver* was relieving lightship crews when she was attacked without warning by a German bomber. An officer was killed and 30 men badly injured: they were taken ashore by the Gorleston lifeboat and two other vessels and rushed to hospital. In April, HMS *Dunoon* was struck by a mine 25 miles off Yarmouth: the captain and two officers were killed. Commander Donald Swift made sure that all 52 survivors, including seven badly-injured men, were put into boats or on life rafts. He searched the ship while it was rapidly sinking to check that nobody was left on board, before diving into the water. He was picked up by one of the ship's boats, and eventually a destroyer came to the rescue.[34]

Not everyone behaved well in wartime: thieving and looting was not unknown. Cases before the local courts in January 1943 show the kind of crimes committed. The most serious was that of William Bee, a corporal in the RAF, who had climbed into the *Aquarium Theatre* after a window had been blown out in an air raid. He helped himself to spirits and also stole alcohol, cigarettes and money, including some that had been collected in aid of prisoners of war. He admitted several similar offences and was sentenced to 18 months in prison. Leonard Wright broke into an empty house: when a suspicious neighbour called the police, Wright was eventually found hiding in the Anderson shelter in the garden with his spoils: he was sent to prison for nine months. Wright clearly had a difficult war: he had joined the army but been dismissed as unfit for military service.

By far the most common crime in wartime was that of showing a light during blackout: one Yarmouth man was prosecuted for striking a match in a telephone box so that his girlfriend could read the numbers on the dial! The case of Rosa Littlewood shows the psychological strains the war could create. Accused of showing a light at her home in Irongate Square, she said that it was the very first night that she had dared to sleep upstairs, previously she had slept downstairs for safety. She was fined £1, the standard punishment for this extremely common offence.[35]

For other people, the war had its pleasant side as well as its painful one. Olive Swift (later Partridge), a Wren serving in Great Yarmouth, recalled:

> We had a very good social life which helped us through the dark days. We went to the cinema a lot, the pictures we called it, and danced wherever we were invited. A favourite place was across the river, to Gorleston on Sea. It was called the Floral Hall, and a lot of fun was had there. Of course we took our turn of night duty, but whenever we were free, there was somewhere nice to go. If we had an off duty weekend, we would borrow a dinghy from an MGB

77   *Rosebay willowherb grows in a bombed-out St Nicholas' church.*

and row or sail up the Norfolk Broads. Other times we would ride our bikes into the country, and explore old churches. One Sunday we were in time for a service, and about six of us sat in a pew together. Unfortunately one of us got the giggles and set the others off. I think the vicar forgave us though, as he took us on a tour of the church and grounds afterwards.

In the evenings, we would often go to a fair on Britannia pier, with a glass of Babycham, and a cigarette in a long holder, we felt as girls do, war or peace, it was ultimate enjoyment.[36]

1945-1974

Yarmouth was soon back in business as a holiday town, but more people were coming by road rather than by railway. At summer weekends, about 750 coaches arrived at Beach Station every day! An official report noted that: 'Every year the car parking problem is becoming more acute.' Between 1952 and 1960, five acres of ground had been laid out as car parks, providing about 600 car spaces. The local bus service reached the peak of popularity after the war: in 1945-6, ten million passengers were carried for the first time. By 1952, the Department employed 230 people full-time, with a further 60 in the holiday season. Fares were raised by a halfpenny in 1951, the first rise since before the war. In 1960, it was estimated that there were 750,000 staying visitors in an average season [37]

Top-class entertainment was the order of the day. *Gorleston Pavilion* saw the acting debut in 1955 of Bill Pertwee, later a star of 'Dad's Army', and several Minstrels shows. In 1962, an Old Time Music Hall ran successfully throughout the summer. Attractions at the House of Wax in the 1960s included the Beatles, James Bond, and Ilya Kuryakin the heartthrob in the TV series 'Man from U.N.C.L.E.'

The quality of entertainment in the town in the 1960s can be seen by the names of those appearing in the 1967 season, which included Morecambe and Wise, Val Doonican, Mike and Bernie Winters and Freddie and the Dreamers. The Beatles appeared at the ABC on two Sundays in 1963: on 30 June and 28 July. Some of the 1960s rock bands went on to become stadium rock megastars, such as the Rolling Stones, who played two shows at the *ABC* on 25 July 1965, and Pink Floyd, who performed at the *Floral Hall* on 19 July 1966. Local journalist Keith Skipper was not impressed with the latter, describing them as 'Pink Fraud'![38]

Facilities were developing all the time. The coastguard station on the sea front was demolished in 1964, to be replaced by the Tower Complex, a hotel with 72 bedrooms, restaurant, ballrooms and discotheque. It had a large ice-skating rink on the ground floor, but this closed after only 19 months due to lack of support and was replaced by small shopping units.

Yarmouth stadium on the Caister Road was built in 1940, but did not open until 1946. It featured greyhound racing. A new form of spectator entertainment, motor-cycle speedway, opened in 1948. The crowd in the first season averaged 8,000, and one meeting in the early 1950s saw a record crowd of 11,000. Sadly, there were two fatal accidents in the first season – Reg Craven was killed riding for Yarmouth at Poole and the Australian Max Pearce died in a crash at Yarmouth. The most famous rider was Billy Bales, who went on to ride for England and become a finalist at the world championship. He was only 19 when he first rode and looked younger: when he went

78   *Yarmouth Beach coach station.*

79   *Entertainment at the* Royal Aquarium, *1964.*

80   *Punch and Judy on the beach, 1955.*

to the clubhouse for a drink after one ride, the attendant refused to let him in! By the early 1960s, the attendances had declined and the last league meeting was held in August 1961. Yarmouth Town football club achieved its greatest success on 21 November 1953, beating Crystal Palace 1-0 in the FA Cup at the Wellesley. Just fewer than 9,000 spectators saw the match and the gate receipts were just over £900, so that the average cost of a ticket is a straightforward calculation.[39]

John Seymour summed up Yarmouth in 1970:

> The A47 runs straight as a ruler across the flat marshes to Great Yarmouth. Yarmouth is supposed by many people to be nothing but fat cockney women in funny paper hats jostling each other along the crowded prom. It is that, but many other things too. To the sailor it is an exciting harbour entrance, and many a good ship has smashed herself against the South Pier, or missed the harbour and rammed the beach to north or south of it, or – in sailing ship days – been forced to beach herself on the 'spending ground' round the bend of the harbour in desperation. To the Broads pleasure sailor Yarmouth is a long 'marina' where the Bure meets the Yare, where he can tie up preparatory to making the (to him) perilous crossing of Breydon Water. To the lover of ancient places it is a big town of narrow streets and 'rows', old buildings and much history – which is nearly all connected with herrings.[40]

In fact the herring was rapidly becoming part of the town's history. In 1913, there were 742 Scottish boats and 264 English boats, catching a total of 824,000 cran. By the 1920s, the herring industry was in decline and by the 1950s it was obvious that the North Sea had been over-fished. In 1970, there were no English boats at all and just five Scottish ones, gathering a catch of just 60 cran. The North Sea stock of the fish was falling, and

81   *Concern with one's weight is nothing new: 'Jockey Scales', 1955.*

in 1977 a ban on herring fishing from the East Coast was introduced. It lasted for four years, and fishing has been strictly regulated ever since, with the UK quota decided by the Council of Europe. The trade in other types of fish was also in terminal decline: from 17,000 packages in 1945, trade died to nothing at all just ten years later.[41]

Fortunately, Yarmouth was able to adapt: Shell-Mex opened an enlarged oil depot in the town in 1947. In 1959, the new power station was opened, using oil instead of coal. Its tower, 360 feet high, became the tallest building in Norfolk but had a relatively short life, being demolished in 1998. By 1960, revenues from the oil trade accounted for a third of the port's revenue. The changes were summed up by the Borough Council:

> There have been far reaching changes in the local industrial structure. For example, since the war the herring industry has declined in importance, but food processing has greatly increased, particularly by the introduction of frozen foods. The manufacture of shoes has virtually ceased, but the engineering industry now employs a large number of people on the electrical side. Textile manufacture, timber and joinery trades and moulded paper products also provide more employment.
>
> Since 1952 over 75 acres have been brought into use for industrial purposes. Most of the land on the South Denes has now been built upon or leased for industry.[42]

North Sea oil and gas provided the town's salvation. As C.R. Temple memorably phrased it: 'By a quirk of fate the North Sea provides not only fish but also the wherewithal to cook it – namely gas.' Unfortunately, by the time the fuel came along, the fish had largely disappeared! (Incidentally, local tradition insists that the fish finger was developed first in Great Yarmouth!)

By the summer of 1967, nine out of 11 exploration rigs operating in the British sector were serviced through Great Yarmouth. Rig supply bases covered 25 acres of the port. Large-scale employers included BP, with a staff of 150 in Yarmouth and the International Drilling Company with 250 local employees. Brown and Root's pipe-processing yard opened in 1966 and employed about 200 people. By the end of the decade, South and East Quays in Yarmouth and Bollard Quay in Gorleston were given over to supply ships, pipe carriers and tugs serving the North Sea Gas operations.

The local press painted a rosy picture: 'The most noticeable changes in the port are physical. Over 2000 feet of rotting derelict quays have been reconstructed; acres of rough land, much of which was never used before, have been brought into use, and divided into compartments where olive green, blue and grey warehouses and sheds, and cedar wood office units, have sprung up; land has been levelled and laid out as storage areas for pipes and huge castings, machinery and stacks of bagged chemicals.'[43]

In 1973, the authorities were optimistic:

> The port is of national importance and capable of accommodating ships of a maximum length of 300 feet…. It is known as 'the Gateway to the broads'. Ships of up to 500 gross tons can proceed up the river to the Norwich power station, and ships up to 300 tons to Norwich City. The port facilities include about 23,000 feet run, deep draught berthage, ample wharfage and covered storage, cranes with lifting capacity of up to 23 tons and a quayside railhead and dry docks. It is linked by road and rail to the Midlands and London.
>
> The fishing industry has virtually ceased to exist and there is no longer a fishing fleet; but this industry has happily been replaced by the development of a very virile light industry.
>
> The South Denes, once a very large open area used exclusively by the former fishing industry for net drying is now more or less completely developed by other industries and most of the buildings formerly used by the fishing industry have been converted for these industrial purposes too.
>
> The town's main industries come within the following categories: – electrical, general and marine engineering, ship building, processing of foods, weaving, box manufacture, paper pulp industry, milling, agricultural industry, holiday industry, and more recently Great Yarmouth has become an important base for gas and oil exploration and development in the North Sea.[44]

The Development Plan promised a 'substantial change' in the housing situation in the borough. The clearance of slums and war-damaged houses would reduce the population of the area east of the river from 33,100 to 20,700, and that at Cobholm and Southtown by 700 to 5,200. Where would they go? The answer, the borough planners decided, was to Gorleston, on the west bank of the Yare. The population of Gorleston was predicted to rise from 14,100 to 27,200 in just ten years. A temporary bungalow estate of 700 houses was already under way at Shrublands, and four main estates would be built: Claydon, Magdalen College, Cliff Park and a permanent estate at Shrublands. Naturally this would mean a huge shift of the school population and a £1 million programme of capital expenditure for new schools was planned from 1947/8 to 1957/8.[45]

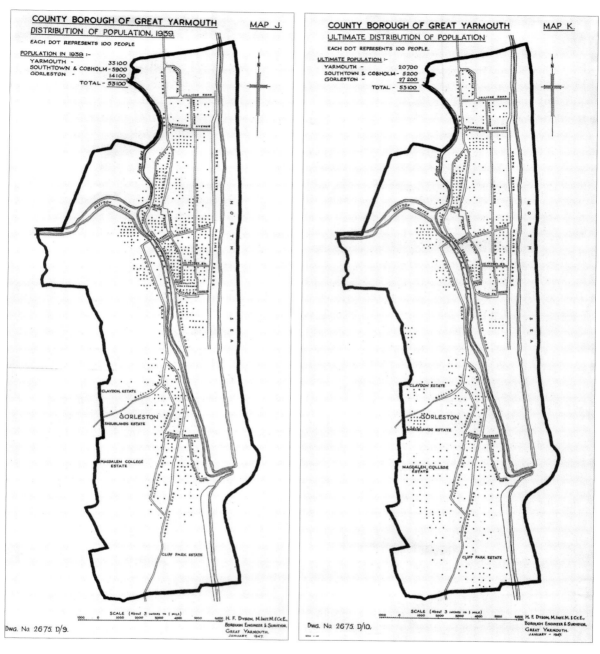

82 *Maps to show the movement of population to the West Bank after the Second World War.*

To cope with emergency needs, temporary housing was erected at Shrublands, work beginning in January 1946. Other needs were considered: a plan to put up a children's playground on the corner of Crab Lane and Cemetery Road at a cost of £2,500 came to nothing because it would have been in the way of proposed road widening, but £200 was spent on putting up two Nissan huts for use as a temporary social centre. In June 1947, the Council supplied each bungalow with a refrigerator, clearly now regarded as an essential domestic item. By 1960, nine public houses had been built or rebuilt to serve the new residential areas. Some were built or rebuilt on the east side of the river, too, such as the *Mariners*, built in 1955-7 to a design by A.W. Ecclestone.[46]

The first major estate to be built was the Magdalen College estate. Site development was at first done by German prisoners of war, but these were withdrawn in February 1946. The first development was of 120 houses, soon followed by a further 28. Of these first 148 houses, 102 were to have three bedrooms, 30 to have four bedrooms, and 16 were to be two-bedroom houses. Estimates were sought and those of three builders accepted – Comben and Wakeling (28 houses for £39,476), H A Holmes (25 for £34,237), and J. Cooper (12 for £16,398). This came to a total of £90,111, but the Ministry of Health thought that this was too expensive and the designs were pared down so that the houses could be built for £81,989. The cooking was by gas – the Council borrowed £10,000 from the Ministry for the cookers – and everything else was electric. In April 1947, 30 street names with college connections were chosen, such as Oriel Avenue, Peterhouse Avenue and Sidney Sussex Way.[47]

Under the Town and Country Planning Act of 1947, a 20-year development plan was developed to start in 1952. In 1962, a Progress report was published. Three major aspects of the infrastructure were assessed – roads, housing and schools. About 3,300 houses were built in the borough between 1951 and 1960. The number of the families on the waiting list was over 2,000 in 1952. By 1962, this had been cut to 800, some 34 per cent of whom were waiting for 'Old Persons' Dwellings'. To make space for the housing, 100 acres of farmland in Gorleston had been lost. A further 87 acres were available within the borough for residential development, but it was clear that this would not be enough to cope with future demands.[48]

The Local Education Authority took control of the Grammar school in 1944. It became co-educational in 1970 and fully comprehensive in 1981. Grant maintained status was acquired in 1993 and Technology College status was achieved in 1997. Four new secondary schools and two primary schools were quickly built: all the new schools were west of the river, three on the Magdalen College estate (Peterhouse Infants and Junior, and Herman primary), and a mixed secondary school on the Cliff Park estate.

The education authorities were already having to look for space beyond the boundaries of Great Yarmouth. A new Technical School and the Girls' High School were built outside the borough, in Bradwell. In all, about 90 acres of land were laid out for new schools and their playing fields, of which 34 acres were outside the Borough boundary. Some schools were still needed east of the river of course. By 1962, the original plan to close the Hospital school was given up, and a new mixed secondary school for children of the North Denes area (Styles Secondary Modern) was proposed.[49]

St Nicholas' church was rebuilt by Stephen Dykes Bower between 1957 and 1960. The architectural historian, Nikolaus Pevsner, writing in 1962, thought the result was a great disappointment: 'The story is this. The church was, as we have seen, gutted in 1942.

83 *Buy your bloaters here: Regent Fish Stores, Regent Road, 1955.*

84 *Lydia Eva, South Quay. She was the last herring drifter ever built and has been preserved and restored.*

85 *Form II, Greenacre School, 1947-8.*

86 *Junior Football team, Greenacre School, 1962-3.*

87 The Mariners' Arms, *showing the striking 'random work' of the gable; the architect was A.W. Ecclestone.*

Of course it could have been reconstructed as it was at the time, largely original and partly Victorian. Nothing would have been wrong with that. What Mr Dykes Bower did instead is not to copy but to make up his own Transitional and Gothic. What an opportunity was lost thereby! What thrilling things might have been done inside! A modern interior, airy, noble, of fine materials could have arisen to affirm the vitality of 20th-century church architecture inside the 13th-century walls. How defeatist does the imitation-Gothic interior appear, once this has been realised.' However, the second edition of the book, as revised by Bill Wilson, took a more tolerant view, explaining that the War Damage Commission gave a grant of just £315,000, a quarter of that given to Coventry, and also that the parochial church council insisted on a traditional design – 'given the paucity of the funding, what Dykes Bower produced is a competent, if not particularly imaginative, reworking of the existing building with much more open space than before'.[50]

Major road programmes between 1952 and 1960 included widening the A47 at the borough boundary and at Fuller's Hill, reconstructing Hall Quay, and building two new roads (Yarmouth Way and Nottingham Way) between South Quay and King Street. In Gorleston, Cemetery Road had been reconstructed, widened and renamed Oriel Way, and Cemetery Lane widened and renamed Shrublands Way ('Way' was clearly the buzz word among Yarmouth planners in the 1950s). Future plans included a

88 *The South Quay and the Bridge, 6.15pm, Tuesday 2 August 1966.*

89 *The Victoria Arcade. Why do the clocks appear to show different times?*

90 *Havenbridge House and the two Yare crossings, Haven Bridge and Breydon Bridge.*

new link road from Acle New Road to the sea front, the widening and improvement of Howard Street North and South, and a new link road from St Nicholas' Road to South Market Road. The provision of a second crossing of the Yare was under consideration.[51]

A new river crossing between Gorleston and the southern end of the Yarmouth peninsula was indeed part of the post-war plan for the Borough. A report of 1947 recommended a bridge as being much cheaper than a tunnel, but how high it would have to be was a matter of dispute. The Port and Haven Commissioners were insisting on a clearance of 140 feet above the river, but the engineers pointed out that only two or three ships needing this sort of clearance had gone up the river in the seven years before the war. They proposed a clearance of 100 feet. The estimated cost, excluding the price of land, was £500,000, one-third the cost of a tunnel, and the building work would take two or three years. The project fell through, but in 1967, the idea of a new river crossing was reconsidered with the Council putting forward a plan for a high-level bridge between the South Denes and Church Road in Gorleston: the cost would have been £2 million, not counting the necessary purchase of land. The Port and Haven Commissioners now insisted on a clearance of 100 feet which the Council thought was too high, pointing out that it was 20 feet higher than over the Manchester Ship Canal!

The railway system began to shrink in the 1950s. The Breydon Bridge was closed for repairs in September 1953 and never re-opened. The line to the Midlands closed in 1959, which meant the end of Newtown and Yarmouth Beach stations: the new methods of public transport showed up when the latter was converted into a bus and coach station. Southtown station closed in 1970. Expansion of the port required improved transport facilities, but this now meant roads. In 1961, the frozen food plant was sending 50 to 100 tons of produce a day by rail, but by 1968 this traffic was going by lorry. The freight lines along the Quay closed on 1 January 1976.[52]

Gorleston had no fewer than three stations on the line between Yarmouth and Lowestoft – Gorleston North, Gorleston-on-Sea and Gorleston golf links. These all closed when the line was shut down in May 1970. The only line remaining is that first opened, from Yarmouth Vauxhall to Norwich, and from there to London and the Midlands.[53]

The 1953 Floods

January 1953 saw one of the greatest storm surges ever in the North Sea. Water began to rise in the streets of Yarmouth at about 9.30 on 31 January, an hour before high tide. Meanwhile, at Gorleston the usual Saturday dance was going on in the *Floral Hall* while floodwater was gradually creeping up the steps outside. High tide was at 10 p.m., but this was not the end of the crisis. At about 11 p.m. the defending walls around Breydon Water gave way: 'a sheet of water poured ceaselessly through at least three huge breaches, and high walls of spray broke over what was left of the wall.' The walls were made of clay – 'too low, too steep and too weak'. It proved very difficult to repair the breaches under flood conditions: at first people rowed out in small boats with sandbags to try to block up the holes in the walls.

Many people have recorded their recollections of the floods of 1953:

Father was finally persuaded to leave around 10:30 am on the Monday when the tide was relatively low, and we got out the same way as my sister had on the day before. Through the front door with father standing between the stairs and the prow of the boat. Off up Crittens Road we were rowed until we grounded then there were men to carry or piggyback to dry land. The cat was left upstairs and survived until my parents were eventually to return to feed him a week later. We were directed to the Salvation Army Citadel in Middlegate, walking there and were given hot food and clothes if we needed them, some people were wet through having waded out of their homes.[54]

Jack Loveday, living in Lichfield Road, was just one of many who were trapped in their homes: 'We began to take portable items of furniture upstairs, as well as food and water. Then the electricity failed, but we continued to work by the light of an oil lamp and candles. Soon the water was in all the downstairs and the fire hissed out. The water, due to the fact that the house was built at the highest part of the street, eventually stopped at the third stair tread.'

The Loveday family were evacuated at 6.30 p.m. on 1 February: 'Eventually, I waded out to a lorry, my wife and baby being carried out, together with the lady from whom we rented the rooms. The lorry took us to the town hall, a very cold ride on an open vehicle. The passengers' ages ranged from Anita, our baby of five months, to a lady of ninety who sat huddled in a corner of the lorry clutching a small lamp.'[55]

Ten Yarmouth people died during the flood. Three of the victims were drowned during the rapid inrush of water, the other seven were elderly people trapped in their homes: three were drowned, four died from shock and exposure. More than 1,000 houses in Gorleston were flooded, some to a depth of six feet. Fireman Frederick Sadd became a local hero, using a boat to help 27 people to safety during the night. He was awarded the George Medal. Over 10,000 people had to be evacuated from their homes.

Life Stories

ETHEL LEACH

The late 19th- and early 20th-centuries saw women beginning to achieve positions of power in local government for the first time in history. Ethel Leach achieved very many firsts for women within Yarmouth. In 1881, Ethel stood as the first woman candidate for Yarmouth School Board: 'She faced contumely and almost insult. Her election meeting was stormy, but she won through.' She was on the Board until it was abolished in 1902, and was then co-opted onto the Education Committee that replaced it. She remained on the Committee until her death: during her time, no fewer than 15 schools were established in the borough. She was also one of the first women to serve on the Yarmouth Board of Guardians.

In 1920, Ethel became Yarmouth's first female Justice of the Peace. On her appointment, she stressed that she was interested not in punishment but in reform and in preventative work. She 'recalled a most interesting experience she had in visiting a State prison in Rhode Island Mass., where the building was fine and healthy and the cells well-lighted, ventilated and warm. Reading, drawing and painting were allowed in leisure hours, and many of the cells were decorated with water-colours and drawings – the labour of the prisoners. The men were given opportunities of learning

91 *The Lower Ferry.*

trades and she was struck with the human look in their faces and the fact that they looked as if they still had some interest in life and their past life had not altogether crushed them.'

Ethel became Yarmouth's first woman mayor in 1924 and first woman alderman in 1929. When she was elected mayor, she quoted a line from the poet Alfred Tennyson: 'woman's cause is man's, they rise or sink together, bond or free.' In 1932, a new school was opened in Gorleston and named the Ethel Leach School in her honour. In the following year, Ethel's portrait was unveiled at Stradbroke Grove Senior Girls' School. At the unveiling, Ethel said that she could not bear corporal punishment and that she was proud to hear teachers boast now that they had not a cane in their school.

Ethel was born Mary Ethel Johnson in 1851 in Yarmouth: she married John Leach, a Yarmouth hardware merchant, in 1869. They had one son, Bruce. John Leach died in 1902. Ethel died in April 1936 after 54 years of public service: she is buried in Gorleston cemetery.[56]

KENNETH COLYER

Colyer was born in Great Yarmouth on 18 April 1928: his mother, Ruby, was staying with relatives in the town at the time. The family home was a flat in Fitzroy Square in London: his father, also Kenneth, was a chauffeur and butler, and his mother worked as a housemaid and cook. Colyer joined the merchant navy just after the war and learned to play the trumpet while at sea. He played jazz in New Orleans style and spent three months there in 1952-3. In fact, he overstayed his visitor's visa and spent over a month in prison before being deported: he came to fame through a series of letters written from prison, which were published in the *Melody Maker*. On his return he formed a band that included Chris Barber on trombone and Lonnie Donegan on banjo.

It was while he was in New Orleans that Colyer discovered 'skiffle' – good-time music played by people who could not afford real musical instruments and used jugs, washboards and anything else that came to hand. This became the most popular part of Colyer's stage act: Bill Wyman of the Rolling Stones recalled that it was the energy and rhythm of skiffle that led boys of his generation to take up music, leading to the rock explosion of the 1960s. In fact Colyer played a direct part in the rise of the Stones: their regular appearances in his club in London in 1963 were one springboard to their later fame.

Colyer formed other bands, one of which included Acker Bilk on clarinet, and went on to play a major part in the revival of New Orleans jazz in Europe. In 1987 he was forced to give up playing through ill-health. Colyer spent the last years of his life in France, dying there on 8 March 1988: his ashes were scattered in the English Channel.[57]

KENNETH MACMILLAN

MacMillan was the son of William MacMillan, a labourer who met his wife Edith Shreeve in Ormesby when his regiment was posted there. He was born in Dunfermline on 11 December 1929, the family moving to Yarmouth shortly after his birth. MacMillan was evacuated to Broughton in Nottinghamshire as a schoolboy in June 1940, but very soon came back because he was homesick there, returning just as Yarmouth itself was coming under frequent air raid attack. He then won a scholarship to Great Yarmouth Grammar School: the school spent their war in Retford, Nottinghamshire, but allowed its pupils to return home in the holidays. MacMillan's family life was blighted by personal tragedy: one sibling died in infancy, his mother died when he was twelve and his father just four years later.

MacMillan already knew Scottish and tap dancing: while at Retford he was introduced to ballet by Jean Thomas, a local dance teacher. He said later: 'I was transported into a world which seemed so exotic to me, living at a time when death and destruction was an everyday occurrence.' On his return to Yarmouth he was taught by a local ballet teacher, Phyllis Adams, who helped him to go on to Sadler's Wells Ballet School.

MacMillan began as a dancer but made his name as a writer of ballet. He brought the art form into the 20th century with his plots and settings. His ballets included 'The Burrow' (1958) which was based on a short story by Franz Kafka and dealt with a group of oppressed people living in terror; 'The Invitation' (1960), with a graphic depiction of the rape of a young girl; and 'The Judas Tree' (1992), set on the Canary Wharf construction site in London, and including a gang rape and a lynching. 'Playground' was set in a lunatic asylum, and 'Valley of Shadows' included scenes in a Nazi concentration camp. His personal life and his wartime experiences in Yarmouth no doubt contributed to these themes. He himself wrote: 'The more I look at my work, the more it seems that, unwittingly, I choose the lonely, outcast, rejected figure.'

MacMillan was knighted in 1983. He died of a heart attack backstage at the Royal Opera House on 19 October 1992, and was cremated in London.[58]

Chapter Five

The West Bank – Gorleston, Southtown and Cobholm

GORLESTON WAS GORLESTON ERE YARMOUTH BEGUN
AND WILL BE GORLESTON WHEN YARMOUTH IS GONE

GORLESTON GREAT ONE DAY WILL BE;
YARMOUTH BURIED IN THE SEA

These traditional rhymes express a basic truth: the central part of Gorleston is several metres above present sea level. It was inhabited before the sandbank on which Yarmouth stands emerged from the sea, and, if sea levels continue to rise, will still be inhabited when Yarmouth itself has disappeared: perhaps the post-war planners were wiser than they knew when they moved the former inhabitants of the Rows in Yarmouth to new housing estates in Gorleston.

The name 'Gorleston' comes from the old spelling for the river Yare (Gerne), and so simply means 'to[w]n on the Yare'. Both J.G. Nall and R.H. Teasdel refer to a prehistoric stone circle in Gorleston: Nall says that the stones were ten feet high and were taken down in 1768 (a century before he was writing). Teasdel says that the stones were recycled – they were used to strengthen the harbour. Both writers say that their existence was preserved in the place name of the field in which they stood: Stone Close or Stone Piece, and Teasdel gives us the precise location by informing us that Gorleston-on-Sea station was later built on the site. If the story is anything more than a myth, it would be fascinating to know from where the stones were carried: there is no suitable building stone anywhere in East Anglia. Perhaps archaeological work on the harbour will bring these stones to light one day.

There is plenty of evidence for Roman occupation of Gorleston. According to C.J. Palmer, a fine Roman vase was found in Gorleston in 1770, and several burial urns and some javelin heads were discovered in 1817. Teasdel records that Roman coins have been found, including one of a Roman soldier, with a figure of victory in his right hand, and the Christian symbol, the *Chi-Rho*, in his left hand. Other skeletons are assigned by Nall to Saxon and Danish times: 'The number of skeletons and bones turned up from time to time authenticate current tradition that Gorleston was the scene of various engagements during the successive invasions of Saxons and Danes.'[1]

Domesday Book says that, in 1066, the manor of Gorleston was held by Earl Guert, the brother of King Harold, and like him killed at the Battle of Hastings in 1066. It had 20 villagers, with 300 sheep and a small number of cattle, and produced salt using three salt-houses on the seashore: it also had 24 fishermen, who were based across the

92 *New band enclosure, Gorleston.*

river at Yarmouth. The village appears to have declined over the next 20 years – by 1086, the number of villagers had fallen to 12, the number of ploughs had gone down from seven to four, and the five cattle enumerated in 1066 had disappeared.

The ownership of the manor passed through several families over the centuries. In 1255, it was granted to John Baliol but his estates were forfeited to the Crown when he became King of Scotland and renounced his allegiance to King Edward I. In 1386, Richard II gave the manor to Michael de la Pole, Earl of Suffolk, and it passed down several generations of the family before becoming forfeit to the Crown once more just over a century later. In 1510, the manor was granted to Edmund Jernegan or Jerningham. Sir Robert Paston was Lord of the Manor in 1664, and Samuel Morton Peto, the railway king, in the 19th century. There was a sub-manor called Gorleston Bacons, which passed through many hands over the centuries.

Gorleston and Little Yarmouth (Southtown) were in the hundred of Lothingland. When, under the charter of 1208, Yarmouth began charging ships eight pence to moor and unload, the king's warden in Lothingland, Roger FitzOsbert, tried to undercut the town by charging just four pence! This led to an Inquiry, at which the men of Yarmouth said that they had 'nothing but the four winds and the sea' to pay their fee farm to the king, meaning that they had no income from land ownership, but only from charges on trading vessels. The Inquiry decided that ships that moored within a rod's length of Gorleston need not pay dues to Yarmouth, but that all other ships did have to pay. Basic articles such as corn, salt, cheese and coal could be landed at Gorleston.

The disputes continued and a further decision in favour of Yarmouth was decreed in a royal charter of 1306. Yarmouth was a borough, the charter made clear, whereas Gorleston and Southtown were not: therefore everything had to go through Yarmouth. A royal charter of 1333 favoured Yarmouth even further. Only the ships actually belonging to the town of Gorleston could load or unload there, and, even then, cargoes of wool and hides would have to pay customs dues to Yarmouth.[2]

Very little is known of medieval Gorleston, and only one secular building survives, a fragment of a once much larger 15th-century hall house in Baker Street. The village had two other indications of its prosperity, a weekly market and an annual fair. The market was set up by Roger FitzOsbert: it was held on the Lord's Day (Sunday). The fair was held every year at Whitsun. It survived well beyond the Middle Ages but only by losing the character of a general fair – Teasdel says it had become a fair for toys. Sylas Neville in 1770 recorded in his diary that he 'was persuaded to go to Gorleston Fair, much frequented by the low people, particularly the more profligate'. There was a lazar house in Gorleston, but all that is known about it is a bequest made in a will of 1372.[3]

The medieval village was centred on the parish church. It still contains a 15th-century seven sacrament font: the eighth panel is the Last Judgement. The church also has a very early brass, known as the Bacon Brass, and probably a monument to Sir John Bacon, mentioned in the Inquisition Rolls of 1292. The brass was taken out of the church many centuries ago and was in the collection of Craven Orde in 1830 – it was bought by John Rokewood Gage who restored it to the church.[4]

There was one religious house in Gorleston, an Augustinian friary founded by William Woderove and his wife Margaret in the later thirteenth century. It was a high-status institution and many famous people chose to be buried in its cemetery, including Richard, Earl of Gloucester (died 1261) and William de Ufford, Earl of Suffolk, who died in 1382. Teasdel comments that: 'The great glory of the Priory was its library, collected by a former Prior, John Brome, who died in the reign of Henry VI, 1449. In 1492 a new library had to be made; it was 100 feet long, 30 feet wide, wainscoted and furnished with desks and settles. It contained, *inter alia*, a missal beautifully bound in vellum by a Brother of the Hospital, Smithfield.'[5]

Another medieval illuminated manuscript associated with the town is the Gorleston Psalter, 'one of the masterpieces of English Gothic Art and a cornerstone of the so-called East Anglian school of manuscript illumination'. We know that the psalter is directly connected to Gorleston because it includes a calendar that mentions the feast of the dedication of Gorleston Church, 8 March. The initial letters of each section of the book are illuminated, with coloured drawings around the letter, but the psalter is especially famous for the grotesque and highly imaginative coloured drawings in the margins of the pages. Some are pure works of imagination: on one page a funeral procession is conducted by rabbits who have pressed two hounds into service as pallbearers, and on another a monster with a head at each end is eating a human being who is wearing only a pair of black slippers! The Warenne arms occur on almost 130 line endings: many other coats of arms appear, but none so frequently, so that Sir John de Warenne could well have ordered the manuscript.[6]

The friary was dissolved in 1538, and by the later 16th century it was in ruins. These were the most prominent feature of the village. Camden noted 'a small ruinous religious House, which is of some use to the Sea men'. The Chorography of Suffolk describes Gorleston as 'a town by Yarmouth where yet is seen a tower the remnant of an ancient monasterye'. John Kirby wrote in 1735: 'Gorleston is a tolerable well built Village about four furlongs in length, in which is nothing observable, but the Ruins of an old Building, supposed by Mr Camden to be the remains of some Religious House.'[7]

The 17th century saw plague and civil war and both impacted on Gorleston. In 1604, plague was brought by a Scottish vessel from Edinburgh, and in 1667 three people were reported to have died from plague in the village. In 1643, the trained bands of Lothingland were ordered to assemble once every week at eight in the morning 'at the house of William Killett the elder, at Gorleston, with their arms complete, there to be exercised. Every man to bring with him powder, match and bullets'. Killet's house was probably in the High Street.[8]

In 1734, a pack of hounds was established at Gorleston, 'William Roote, innkeeper, undertaking for £30 a year to kennel and maintain twelve couple, and to hunt the same, and provide himself with one horse, able and fit to pursue the chase of the fox and hare. Also, to breed, train and keep a sufficient number of young hounds.'[9]

The village played an important part in the naval wars of the later 18th century. A fort to defend the harbour was erected at the top of Cliff Hill in 1782, and was armed with six 24-pounder and nine 18-pounder guns. A well was sunk at the foot of White Lion steps in 1797 to supply water for naval vessels: it is still there today. Samuel Paget was the victualling contractor for the navy, and Admiral Duncan once said of him: 'That's the man who won the Battle of Camperdown.'

By the 19th century, Gorleston was becoming a desirable place to live, especially for navy men. One example that is still prominent in the town is the house called Koolunga, which was originally called Hill House. It was built in 1826 – it has a datestone to say so. The builder was John Garnham, who was born in 1789 and joined the Royal Navy in 1805, on the day before his 16th birthday. Garnham married in 1824 and lived in Hill House from 1826 until his death in 1872. In 1898 the house was bought by Commander Charles Williamson, who worked for the P & O Line, for whom he travelled the world. He had visited Australia, and indeed had a relative there and it was presumably as a memento of this that he renamed the house Koolunga (the name of a small settlement in Australia).[10]

Being on the west bank of the river, Gorleston was in the county of Suffolk. From 1832 it became part of Great Yarmouth for electoral purposes, and in 1835 it became part of the borough of Great Yarmouth. Yarmouth maintained its poor as a Union under the Poor Law Act of 1834. The parish of Gorleston (including the hamlet of Southtown) was not part of this Union. It was in the Mutford and Lothingland Hundred, which was incorporated for the maintenance of the poor in 1763, and established a workhouse at Oulton.

The inmates in Oulton Workhouse in 1881 included 15 who had been born in Gorleston and three born in Southtown. William Balls, a 'boat fireman' by occupation, was there together with his three children, Thomas, William and Maryann, all aged between eight and eleven. An example of a single-parent family in distress was that of 33-year-old Martha Becket, with her four children aged between three and eleven: Walter, William, Maudie and Emma. All five were born in Gorleston. Other Gorleston children in the Workhouse were orphans or abandoned children, like Charles and Robert Bircham, aged nine and thirteen.

The Gorleston parish registers give us an idea of the patterns of mortality in the 19th-century village. Ages at burial are given from the beginning of 1813. Of the first 100 burials, no fewer than 26 are of babies under one year old, and a further 29 are under nine years old. This enormous rate of infant and child mortality is an obvious

93 *Shipbuilding at Hewett's Yard 1 'Blessing the keel'.*

key difference between Gorleston two hundred years ago and life today. Once past childhood, there was a reasonable chance of survival: of the 100 burials, 12 were of people aged 70 or upwards, including two in their eighties.[11]

From the 18th century, Nonconformist churches were beginning to emerge. A Methodist preacher, Mr Boon, tried to establish a following in 1791, describing the village as 'dark as any under heaven'. Thomas Dawson hired a schoolroom for services in 1794, and built a small chapel in 1798 at a cost of £300. A Methodist chapel was opened in the High Street in 1840. A schoolroom was built in Lowestoft road in 1866, and the present chapel adjoining it was erected in 1899. It contains the original pulpit from which John Wesley preached on his five visits to Yarmouth in the 1780s; the pulpit was brought here from the Deneside Methodist church when the latter was demolished. The Primitive Methodists arrived in Gorleston in 1833, using an old chapel in Burnt Lane. They built a new chapel and schoolroom on Beccles road in 1868. The Baptists opened a church in Lowestoft Road in 1875; it had a meeting hall and a Sunday school.[12]

An important 19th-century industry was shipbuilding. The Hewett family originally began building ships in Barking in 1764: by 1833 the fleet had 133 vessels. It was known as the 'Short Blue Fleet' from the square blue flag flown on all the ships. One of the family, Samuel Hewett, opened a base at Yarmouth in 1865 and two years later they created a dock and an icehouse at Gorleston, which expanded until by 1890 most of the Short Blue Fleet had moved to Gorleston. However, its success there was short-lived, suffering from the introduction of steam trawlers. The dock and buildings were sold in 1905 and the fleet sold to a Grimsby concern.[13]

Gorleston had its own brewery: John Sayer Bell had 22 tied houses, eight in Gorleston itself. From 1845, they were leased to the Norwich brewers, Steward and Patteson and the latter completed their purchase in 1866.[14]

By the 19th century, visitors to Yarmouth were taking in Gorleston, too. Mr Marten, staying at a Yarmouth inn, wrote in 1825:

94   *Shipbuilding at Hewett's Yard 2.*

Somewhat beyond Gorleston ... there are heights of much verdure affording a
distant view over the land and along the coast to the westward and a wide expanse of
sea. Here we sat for some time enjoying the sight of a young party seated and taking
their refreshments: the ships and boats under sail and at anchor – those nearer
within the long piers and up the river – the Pillar erected on Yare-mouth Denes in
memory of the gallant Nelson – the Jetty and the distant town of Yarmouth with
the numerous ships in the Roads the more distant then getting under weigh on the
turning of the Tide.

The Pier is a fine long walk well taken care of and is an inviting promenade
having nothing in the way of the pedestrian to whom the sea view is wide open
and under whose Eye the Fishers – Men and Boys – sit on a lower part – are
watching their floats or occasionally drawing up their little captives .... We thought
Gorleston a very quiet and pleasant retreat for those who in their relaxation would
prefer abstraction from the bustle of business – while from the circumstance of this
being the outlet and inlet for all the numerous ships of Yarmouth every tide must
present sufficient novelty to remove from fear of overmuch solitude.[15]

In 1867, the *Illustrated London News* said of Gorleston, 'the place is entirely inhabited by
fishermen, boatmen and other seafaring people'. Cliff Hill was occupied by beachmen
until the later 19th century and some of their lifeboat houses still survive on Brush
Quay: they made their living by rescuing ships in distress and by salvage.

There were many fatalities among the beachmen. In January 1866, the *Rescuer*
capsized while crossing the Harbour bar on its way to assist a ship in distress. The 16
men on board were thrown into the water: 12 drowned. In December 1867, the *Rescuer*
was involved in an even greater tragedy. She spotted a long boat off Scroby Sands
containing 23 men: they were from the *George Kendall*, which had been abandoned as
she was drifting towards Cross Sands. Some of the men climbed into the *Rescuer*, which
took the rest in tow in their boat and headed back to harbour. As they reached the bar
they were involved in a collision with a Yarmouth fishing boat, the *James and Ellen*. The
crew and the men from the *George Kendall* were all hurled into the water: 25 people
died, six of the crew of the *Rescuer* and 19 men from the *George Kendall*. The inquest

jury returned a verdict of accidental death. However, many thought the *James and Ellen* was to blame. One of those drowned was 20-year old James Leggett. His tombstone can still be seen in Gorleston churchyard. It reads:

> Whose life was cruelly taken away by the lugger of Yarmouth on Tuesday 3rd Dec 1867 when bringing into harbour in the lifeboat Rescuer twenty two of the shipwrecked crew of the George Kendall of Hull of whom nineteen perished at the same time.[16]

The RNLI established its first lifeboat station at Gorleston in 1866: by 1897 there were four! The citizens of Leicester raised the money for the first RNLI lifeboat at Gorleston, and for the lifeboat shed as well: not surprisingly, the first lifeboat was named the *Leicester* in honour of their generosity, as were the next two lifeboats: the three *Leicesters* saved over 200 lives between them. The lighthouse on Quay Road was built in 1887 as a guide into the harbour entrance that could be seen by ships several miles out to sea. Private lifeboats continued, however. One, the *Refuge*, was driven onto a sandbank in

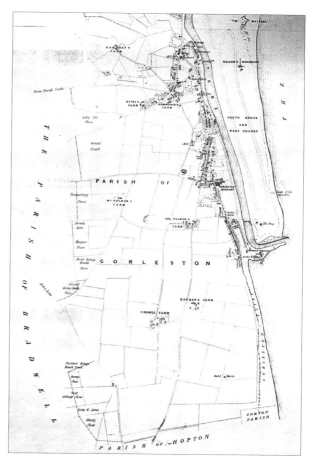

95   *Gorleston in 1842: apart from houses along the main road, the village is made up of a few farms.*

1888, with the loss of four of her crew. Elizabeth Simpson Stone of Norwich was a witness of the tragedy: she paid for the replacement vessel, which was built in Yarmouth by James Beeching at a cost of £300. The *Elizabeth Simpson* gave grand service for over half a century until her retirement in 1939: she had saved 441 lives.

Sydney Harris, coxswain of Gorleston lifeboat, is the only man to have received the silver medal five times. His first award followed an incident in January 1905. The *James Stevens No. 3* lifeboat took the six-man crew off the Lowestoft brig *Celerity* at 6 p.m. on 15 January: it was impossible to get back across the bar because of the low tide, and the crew had to anchor outside in the storm until 2 a.m. After three further instances of heroic behaviour, Harris' final award came in 1916. On 29 March, the *Dart* sank off Lowestoft in blinding snow and a storm of almost unprecedented violence. The four-man crew took to the rigging. Harris held the lifeboat steady in the storm while another lifeboat man, Edward Bensley, jumped into the rigging and rescued the four men, now helpless from exposure.[17]

96   *The first electric tram in Gorleston, 25 June 1905.*

After 1880, terrace houses began to go up behind Cliff Hill, mainly occupied by fishermen. Holiday development began with the launching of the Cliff Park estate in 1883, sold as building plots, and the laying out of Marine Drive in 1890. Two large hotels opened in the 1890s, the *Pier* and the *Cliff*. The latter was by Norwich architect George Skipper, but his building was destroyed by fire in 1915. Further seaside developments followed: gardens and a bandstand were erected in 1896. The town was always concerned that its image should be that of a more genteel resort than Yarmouth: in 1890, regulations prohibited puppet shows, noisy or dangerous games, walking or lying on the slopes of the Cliffs – and bad language!

Meanwhile, Gorleston was developing as a town. The population, which had been only 1,788 in 1801, more than doubled by 1851 to 3,999. A National school was erected in High Street in 1840, on the site of a small piece of open green. Social facilities developed throughout the 19th century. Saint Andrew's Hall was built in 1874 and used for concerts and exhibitions: however, it was sold in 1900. There were many clubs and societies in the Victorian town, such as the Cricket Club formed in 1885 and a Bicycle Club, which had more members than any other in Eastern England. A Quoits Club opened at the *White Lion* in 1880, launching itself with an onion and lettuce tea and concert, and Gorleston Recreation Ground opened in 1889.[18]

The parish church was restored in 1872, the thatched roof being replaced with tiles. Gorleston Cottage Hospital opened in 1889. Lacon's set up a branch of their bank in the town in 1894. The town was always anxious to protect itself against its bigger rival across the river. In 1891 a proposal to close Gorleston Library led to a public meeting of protest. It was decided to keep it open and to allocate to it 20 per cent of the new books bought by the Borough. The Carnegie Library in Gorleston opened in 1907 with 4,000 books.[19]

A closer link between the two towns was forged when the tramway was opened in March 1875. It began at Haven Bridge, ran along the Southtown Road and the High Street, and on to England's Lane, ending at the *William IV* above the harbour. The trams were pulled by two horses: the road was so steep at England's Lane that ponies had to be attached to help pull each tramcar. The fare was two pence, but first-class passengers paid three pence, for which they were provided with straw to keep their feet warm! After 1887 the trams only ran as far as Baker Street. Yarmouth Corporation bought the tramway for £13,400, and the horse trams came to an end in April 1905, to be replaced by electric cars from 25 June.[20]

At the turn of the century, the Yarmouth Borough Surveyor was instructed to prepare a plan to build a hall in Gorleston to seat 750 people, with a subsidiary hall for 250, the total cost not to exceed £6,000. Like the Millennium Dome in London a century later, it was much delayed. In August 1900, the *Yarmouth Mercury* wrote: 'not yet completed, notwithstanding that the contract time had long since expired, the Gorleston Pavilion was hurried pell mell into use without pomp or ceremony on Monday evening, when the first concert took place. Gorleston people are annoyed. Their compliments are of a negative kind when thinking and speaking of the [delays] displayed in putting the finishing touches to this, the first substantial indication of the town fathers' paternal solicitude for the welfare of this end of the Borough, and the failure to effect a good advertisement for this rising and ambitious township, by having an imposing opening ceremony performed by some celebrity, Royalty has been hinted at.' It opened for the 1901 season, even though on the first night 'workmen were still hammering about in the building'. In 1908, George Gilbert took over, changing the name to the Gorleston Palace and showing films.[21]

In 1903, the Corporation extended the Marine Parade and cut the ravine through the cliffs. In the following year, Uncle Walter's Pierrots opened on Gorleston cliffs, but a proposal to have a Singers' Ring on the beach was abandoned because it aroused so much opposition. In 1906, the *Ward Lock* Guide said: 'few places have grown so rapidly or been so improved as Gorleston. The sands are fine and broad, the air pure and bracing.'

The 1901 census returns provide a snapshot of Gorleston life as it faced the new century. It was a town of contrasts, as we can see by comparing a page of entries for Bulls Lane with a page for the High Street. In Bulls Lane, every adult was a worker, the only man described as 'working on his own account' being Christopher Leggett,

97 *The Pier gardens and beyond, June 1967.*

a shrimp fisherman. Other employments included fishermen, bricklayers and general labourers, and also three market gardeners, showing how rural Gorleston still was. Only two women were in work, a charwoman and a sweet-maker. Twenty-three of the 31 residents had been born in Gorleston, and every person had been born in either Norfolk or Suffolk.

The feel of High Street was very different. Three people are described as 'living on their own means' and they had come from a long way away to live in Gorleston: two from London and one from Edinburgh. In fact, 11 of the 26 people on the sample page were born beyond the confines of Norfolk and Suffolk. The only 'workers' are the three apprentice sons of boat builder and ship owner Henry Darby, and the son of Emmeline Souster who was an architect's pupil. However, these were the upwardly mobile middle class rather than the aristocrats of society: only one family had a live–in servant, for example. She was 18-year-old Gertrude Fiske, and like so many domestic servants had come in from the countryside nearby, in Gertrude's case, from Beccles.

In 1905 it was announced that 'Belle Steamers now stop at Gorleston'. On one occasion, in August 1938, the *Queen of the Channel* had left Yarmouth bound for Ostend with more than 1,000 passengers when she was caught by the strong tide at Gorleston and ploughed into the South Pier. The passengers were thrown onto the deck and at least eleven needed hospital treatment. The ship returned to Fish Quay and the passengers were given back their money.

Some of the day boats were quite large, such as the *New Skylark* run by three Gorleston men, James Sutton, George Shreeve and Arthur Beckett, which was licensed to hold well over 100 passengers. The boat was involved in a disaster on 1 September 1903: fortunately there were only eight trippers on board on this occasion, together with two musicians who regularly entertained the passengers on the trip. Despite clear weather and a calm sea, the *New Skylark* was run down by the *F E Webb*, a steel collier, off Scroby Sands and everyone on board pitched into the water. Three Lowestoft fishing vessels were close at hand and able to pick up six survivors, while a seventh was rescued by a boat lowered from the *F E Webb*: three passengers and all three crewmen were drowned. According to one of the minstrels, the two women on board were kept afloat by the air in their voluminous clothing: modesty can have its rewards!

Gorleston's first purpose-built cinema, the *Coliseum* in the High Street, opened in 1913. It was a large cinema, with 964 seats. The cinema was run by the Attree family. In the days of silent films, Miss Shaw organised back-stage sound effects to give realism to the screen pictures! The *Coliseum* closed in 1970, and was demolished to make way for shops and a car park. A rival cinema, *Filmland*, also opened in 1913: this was in Beach Road.[22]

The East Anglian School for Blind and Deaf Children opened in Gorleston in 1912: it cost £11,000 to build and was jointly operated by eight local authorities. It had both classrooms and workshops. In 1936, a kindergarten and a swimming pool were added, on land given by the Borough Council.

The effect of the First World War on a Gorleston family can be illustrated by the Stewards. Walter Steward was a fisherman. He and his wife, Ellen, had four sons and three daughters: they lost two sons and a son-in-law in the war. Their eldest son, Walter, fought in Gallipoli. He was in the troop transport the *Royal Edward*, which was torpedoed in the Mediterranean. Many soldiers were killed but Walter was rescued

98 *Gorleston Quay, with lighthouse and tram.*

after several hours in the water, only to be killed at Suvla Bay after just two weeks in action: he was 24 years old. His youngest brother, John, served in the *Edwardian*: he was drowned off Scotland in October 1917 while attempting to save the life of another man. After John's death, Ellen Steward dressed herself in black: she never again wore any other colour.

Their brother-in-law was Frederick Lake, husband of their sister Ellen. Like so many men of Gorleston he too served at sea. He was in the *First Prize*, a sailing ship captured from the Germans on the first day of the war (hence her name). In 1916, she was fitted out as a Q-ship, a decoy ship to attract German submarines and then attack them. After an adventurous career, she was finally sunk in August 1917: all the crew, including Lake, died.[23]

Gorleston church has memorials to choirboys killed in the war, including Herbert Lowther, who died of his wounds at Etaples, and Bertie Wilkinson, killed in the Battle of the Somme.

The years between the wars saw significant developments in the holiday business in the town. Gorleston Holiday Camp was founded in the 1930s. Many people arrived by train and the camp had its own path from the railway station, as well as a main entrance off the A12. The camp was run by Lin and Grace Thrower. Gary Seeley recalled visits to the camp as a child in the 1960s: 'every day was packed with entertainment whatever the weather. Swimming, Putting, Snooker, Table Tennis, Tennis, Cricket, Football, Bowls, silly games with a very large ball, Donkey Derby, Bingo, Film Show, Competitions, Campers Show, Dancing, Sports Day including the egg and spoon race, the sack race, the 3-legged race, Tug-of-War (both on the grass and across the pool), rambles down to the beach … the list goes on and on!'

The holiday camp was used by the Army during the war. After 1953, the Norfolk Association for the Handicapped began to run holidays for the disabled at the Camp: the whole camp was put at their disposal for the last two weeks of the summer season. Stars performing in Yarmouth often gave their services as judges at competitions, such as the fancy hat competition, including Harry Worth and Bob Monkhouse. The Camp finally closed in 1974 and the site was then built on: it is now the Elmhurst Court Housing Estate.[24]

Further developments between the wars included the Winter Gardens in 1929 to the design of A.W. Ecclestone, and the *Floral Hall* (later renamed the *Ocean Room*) erected in 1939. Unemployment was a problem in Gorleston as elsewhere, and the men were put to good use. Works for the unemployed in 1926 included the construction of the model yacht pond and paddling pool. Relief Works in 1930 included the development of Gorleston Cliffs estate including the provision of a sewer, at a total cost of £21,000.

The cinema became the most popular recreational activity between the wars. Judith Ferrier of Hemsby recorded in her diary a visit to a Gorleston cinema, which was run by a family friend:

> Saturday 22 March. A good lot of snow. Mother & I went into Yarmouth by the 11 train for my music lesson. PM I went to Gorleston on my own to see Miss Shaw at the *Coloseam* [sic] and all the way there snowed hard (I went by tram). Miss Shaw was very nice and gave me cosy tea in her little room while I watched the picture through her little window, they were very good. They were 'The Kiddies in the Ruins', a story about the French children in the war which was very pretty. There was also a very good story called 'Polly of the Circus' which was very exciting as it had a very good horse ride in it. I was very [sad?] not to be able to see the end. I caught the 6.10 [train] from Gorleston. At Yarmouth I was met by mother and the rest and we all came home.[25]

99   *A holiday treat: a ride in a charabanc, that is, an open motor bus.*

100 *Aerial view of central Gorleston, 1948.*

The High Street had every facility for shoppers from Gorleston itself and from nearby villages. Maurice Smith remembered what it was like in the 1920s:

> Shopping was pleasanter in my Gorleston-on-Sea days as everywhere gave personal attention – there was no self-service. I can picture the grocer's shop of Bussey's in the High Street with canisters ranged on shelves behind the counter and in front of it a line of biscuit tins set at an angle with glass tops to reveal their contents. If you sometimes concentrated your gaze on a particular tin, a friendly assistant would suggest you might like to sample one, an offer that was never refused. Goods were sold loose and there were magnificent scales in polished brass standing on the counter and one that could be pulled down from a fitment in the ceiling. Commodities were weighed out and put into bags of a traditional colour: currants in maroon, sultanas in yellow, raisins and sugar in blue.[26]

Gorleston continued to develop its facilities. A new Hospital was built on Lowestoft Road in 1937. This closed when the James Paget Hospital opened, but the building is still used in community health care. In 1939, a new Roman Catholic church on London Road opened. Its architect was the sculptor, Eric Gill; this is his only church. He designed the incised brick portrayal of Saint Peter on the outside of the north porch: the actual carving was done by Anthony Foster. The church cost £6,000 to build, and could not be consecrated until the building debts were finally paid in 1964.[27]

The Second World War saw many heroics on the part of lifeboat men. Six vessels in a southbound convoy were stranded on the Middle Happisburgh Sands on the night of 5 August 1941. Twenty-three men were taken off the *Aberhill* by the *Louise Stephens*, while the two Cromer lifeboats attended the other ships. In October of the same year, the lifeboats were once more in action together. The *English Sailor* went ashore on Hammond Knoll, 25 miles east of Cromer. The two lifeboats took it in turns to attend

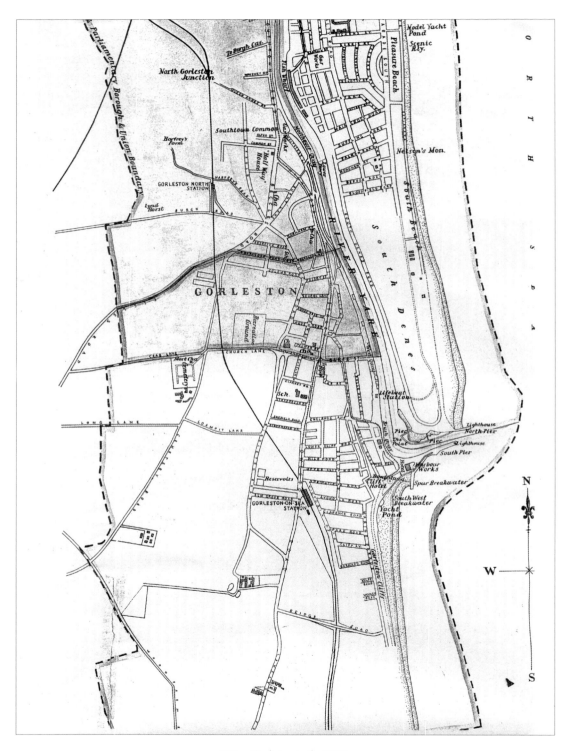

101 *Gorleston in the 1920s.*

102 *The Shrublands estate in Gorleston.*

the wreck, and the Cromer lifeboat under Coxswain Blogg eventually brought off 44 survivors, who were landed at Yarmouth. The *Louise Stephens* had gone to the wreck a second time but found it deserted.[28]

Maureen Miller recalled life as a child in wartime Gorleston:

> I remember queuing at the water cart for the day's ration of a jugful each time a water main was hit; being given tiny black bananas from the lady at the pub along the road, all the time watching and listening, reassured by those immortal words, 'it's all right, it's one of ours'.... But while the days afforded much interest, it is the nights I remember most vividly. They began in the cupboard under the stairs. I shall never forget the night the East Anglian School for the Blind received a direct hit. Our neighbours were actually in the shelter at the school! They crawled through the rubble and the dust to seek sanctuary at our house – white-haired ghosts of a bomb-torn haven. They were accompanied by a white spaniel whimpering with fright.[29]

Gorleston suffered from air raids, and there were casualties. In the great raid of 7-8 April 1942, two large bombs fell on the Southtown Road creating huge craters which effectively cut Gorleston off from Yarmouth: fortunately this possibility had been taken into account by the planners. On the following night ten houses in Nelson and Upper Cliff Roads were destroyed in a raid: six people were killed. Almost 250 incendiary bombs were dropped on Gorleston on the night of 18 March 1943, but no serious

103 *Gorleston Secondary Girls' School, the gymnasium.*

104 *'Snaps'.*

105 *Proposed bridge linking Gorleston and the South Denes, 1946.*

fires were started. Unusually, Yarmouth Borough Council gave due respect to the men, women and children killed in air raids. They provided gravestones for the civilian dead, with the borough logo on them: several of these can be seen in Gorleston cemetery.

The war produced at least two local heroes, Ralph Jones and Frederick Smith. Jones, born in Gorleston, emigrated to Australia and settled in Teuna. During the war he was one of the guards at a prisoner-of-war camp occupied by Italians and Japanese. In August 1944, over 1,000 prisoners attempted a breakout and tried to seize a Vickers machine gun. Jones and another man grabbed the gun before the prisoners could reach it and turned it on them. Eventually the pair were overrun by the prisoners, beaten and stabbed to death, but by that time they had rendered the gun useless. Two other Australians were also killed as were 231 of the prisoners, with another 378 escaping, almost all of whom were captured within a few days. There is a monument to Jones in Cowra, and a street in Gorleston has been named after him.[30]

Smith joined the Royal Navy in the 1920s. In 1942, he was serving on the destroyer *Grove* escorting a supply convoy to Malta. The ship was torpedoed and sank within minutes. Smith was one of 66 survivors of the attack, but hearing a cry from the bows he went back to try to save the man: the ship sank taking both men down with it. His wife was presented with the Albert Medal by King George VI at Buckingham Palace in June 1943.[31]

The character of Gorleston changed completely after the war as the Yarmouth authorities decided to relocate the former inhabitants of the Rows across the river: from this date, the history of the two parts of Yarmouth must be considered together. The town jealously preserves its own history and heritage, and still merits the slogan given to it in a tourist board leaflet:

> Gorleston is Anglia's best-kept secret.[32]

Southtown

This is the settlement that grew up on the west bank of the river, where the upper ferry crossed and where the Haven Bridge was put up in 1417. It was commonly known as Little Yarmouth. It was in the county of Suffolk, and in the Middle Ages had its own parish church – St Mary's. However, in 1511 the parishes of Gorleston and Southtown were united: this means that inhabitants of Southtown used Gorleston church and their baptisms, marriages and burials are recorded in the Gorleston parish registers. St Mary's was pulled down in 1548 and the stone used in building the pier at the mouth of the Haven.

There was at least one wealthy man in early 14th-century Southtown, Nicholas Siwhat. We know of him from a court case in 1315. John Darreys and Margaret Bully were caught in Aylsham with the enormous sum of 30 shillings of silver. They were charged with burgling Siwhat's house in Southtown and taking £40 in silver, four pieces of silver, 18 silver spoons, three silk belts, 12 brooches and nine good rugs. Few people in medieval Yarmouth could have possessed this standard of living and it can be little wonder that his house was a target for thieves.[33]

In the time of Queen Elizabeth, the people of Yarmouth were prohibited from drinking beer in Southtown – and complaint was made that butchers 'openly sold flesh there in Lent', which was against the law and could not happen in more tightly regulated Yarmouth.[34]

106   *Southtown in the 1740s, from the Bucks' panorama of Great Yarmouth.*

107   *Southtown station and Haven Bridge, 1966.*

In 1656, William Paston proposed that Southtown be incorporated into Yarmouth, but the town resisted the idea. In 1666, William's son, Robert Paston, reached an agreement with the town, and in 1668 Paston he issued proposals to build a new town:

> The proprietors in the ground are willing to erect a convenient market and chapel in the old place at their own proper costs and charges. The place to be built so far as fronts the town of Great Yarmouth to the quay, is near a mile in length, and near a quarter in depth. The place is convenient for merchants of all sorts, coopers, fishermen, ship-carpenters, firkin makers, ship-chandlers, sail makers, curers of red herrings, curers of white herrings, coal and wood mongers, pully makers, cable makers, smiths or any other trades, which do particularly belong to navigation; as also for drapers, mercers, grocers and other retailers.

Paston published his proposals in Dutch as well as English, hoping to attract investment from Holland, but there were no takers. The many disputes between Southtown and Great Yarmouth about harbour dues and related matters were resolved finally in 1681 when Southtown became part of the Borough of Great Yarmouth.

The long road from Southtown to Gorleston has had its dangers throughout history. In the 13th century, all trees and bushes within 200 yards of the road were cleared to prevent evildoers lying in wait for passing travellers. In 1748, John Towne was hanged for robbing Mrs Halden on the Southtown Road. According to legend, the road

108 *High Mill Southtown. This is a tower mill: the main part is fixed and only the cap and attached sails moves round to face the wind.*

was haunted by Old Scarfe, a giant black dog. The road became a turnpike in 1775, and the first houses were built along it in the same year. As the area continued to develop, there was once more demand for a church in Southtown: a new St Mary's was opened in 1831, at a cost of £3,000, on a site given by the earl of Lichfield.

Shipbuilding was an important part of the Southtown economy. The first shipbuilding yard in Southtown was built by Isaac Preston in 1782: over 40 years he built 153 vessels. His son followed him, building 102 ships between 1823 and 1841 including the *Maria Somes*, according to Palmer the largest vessel ever launched in Yarmouth. Ships were also built in Southtown from the early years of the 19th century at a dock constructed by James Lovewell. He died in 1824 and the enterprise was taken over by the Fellows family who built ships here well into the second half of the 20th century. Many of the ships were built for the ship owner Frederick Everard (a German who changed his name from Eberardt in 1914), whose fleet of motor coasters and steamships was based at Greenhithe in Kent: two of Everard's sons worked for Fellows.

109   *Southtown Road in the early 20th century.*

In 1806, a Naval Arsenal was built in Southtown at a cost of £15,000: the architect was James Wyatt. The officers lived in houses with gardens fronting the Southtown Road. The Arsenal closed in 1826, and the admiralty disposed of the site in 1891. Two lodges and the seven-bay Arsenal building remain, but two large buildings running between this and the river were destroyed by bombing in 1941.

Southtown boasted the tallest windmill not just in Britain but in all Europe. Known as High Mill, it was built in 1812 by Thomas Woolsey. It was 122 feet high and of 11 storeys. It had a lantern at the top which acted as a lighthouse. The mill drove four pairs of grinding-stones. The building was owned by the Press family from the 1870s. Damaged in a hurricane in 1894, it was sold on the death of B.H. Press in 1904. It was no longer advertised as a mill but as a property suitable for builders and speculators, with the house and mill described as 'building materials'. The property sold for just £100, and the mill was demolished in 1905: nos. 35 and 36 High Mill Terrace, Gatacre Road, now occupy the site.[35]

The town is noted for its number of 'crinkle-crankle' walls. These are brick walls built in gentle curves rather than in straight lines. They are used to protect fruit trees, but are also less likely to blow over than straight walls and so are used in sandy or marshy areas. A few survive in Gorleston and Yarmouth but the greatest concentration is off the Southtown Road: in 1974, there were 23 crinkle-crankle walls between 28 and 76 Southtown Road.[36]

Southtown railway station opened in 1859. Land between the station and the river was developed as a fish-wharf so that fish could be transported to London by rail. Two large icehouses were built in 1859-62. However the success of the scheme was short-lived: ice was last landed in 1899. One icehouse was pulled down in 1968 but the other still stands, close to Haven Bridge. Southtown railway station was badly damaged in an air raid on 9 July 1941.

110 *Taking up the tramlines in the Southtown Road.*

Although Gorleston and Yarmouth were the places for entertainment, there was the occasional festivity in Southtown as well. In 1903, Buffalo Bill's Circus came to Southtown with 500 horses. The arena could seat 14,000 people.

The contribution of Southtown people to the First World War can be seen in the memorial in the Edward Worlledge Central School listing all the pupils and teachers who had served in the War. It has 456 names, including those of 16 women whose work as nurses is rightly recognised. Of the people named, 51 died in the war. The memorial was uncovered in 2006 after having been hidden for 15 years: the school building is now occupied by Great Yarmouth College.[37]

Cobholm

Cobholm was originally an island, separated from Southtown by a channel called Lady's Haven, which ran where the roads called Mill Road and Lady Haven Road now are. The channel was navigable in early times: in 1668 it was 50 feet wide on average, and the two bridges which crossed it, connecting the island to Southtown, had opening sections to allow ships to pass.

The first known record of Cobholm is in the Hundred Rolls of 1273-4, when it is described as marsh. The Corporation had taken it over by the 15th century and rented it out as land for grazing: in 1481, for example, the Corporation leased it to Robert Ashton at four shillings a year. The first mention of salt making is in a lease by the Corporation to John Brown in 1539: he is described as a *saltier*, or maker of salt. Among the conditions of the lease are that Brown was to take action to prevent the island being flooded at spring tides, and to allow people to store masts and ships' tackle there. Brown was forbidden to dig out any earth for brick making. The salt was used in preserving fish, so it became a vital component of Yarmouth's main business:

111 *Everard's ship launch at Fellow's yard, Southtown, performed by Mrs Fred Everard.*

Corbridge's map of 1724 shows seven saltpans in Cobholm. The salt was even exported to Newfoundland for the fishery industry there in the later 18th century. However, by the mid-19th century all the saltpans had gone, replaced by three boat-building yards.

House building on the island began in the 1860s. In 1861, the island's owner, William Worship, started to sell parts of the land in small plots for building purposes. Among the buyers were John Joseph Isaac and George Tyrell, whose names survive in the street names of Cobholm. The houses drained into the Lady Haven, which had become an open sewer by the 1870s. In May 1874 there were 714 people living in Southtown and in the following year the population was estimated at 800. It was an unhealthy place to live, however: in May 1874, it was reported that six people had died of fever since January. In November 1880, conditions were even worse. The Medical Officer, Dr Bately, found several inches of water permanently under the houses with more at high tide – and with small fish swimming in it! Houses were sixty feet or more from the nearest water tap. Drains and a pumping station were installed in 1881.

A flood in January 1905 brought to light the dreadful poverty of many in the area. In one cottage, a dead child was found on a table surrounded by water in the front room: another child lay sick upstairs. There was no fire in the house and no means to make one. In another cottage, squalid with wet and filth, there were ten children and no food or fire: the husband was in hospital.[38]

112   *Saul's Wharf, Cobholm.*

The spiritual needs of the people of Cobholm were slowly beginning to be met. A small church, St Luke's, was built in 1898, followed by a Methodist chapel in 1923: by this time the population of Cobholm was 6,000.[39]

During the Second World War, Cobholm suffered several air raids. Twelve people in Elsie Road and Coronation Road were killed by bombs falling at five in the morning on 18 April 1941. Three weeks later, a saw-mill and two public houses in the area were badly damaged. Six people were killed at Mill Road in a raid on 14 July 1941: St Luke's church was also damaged.

Life Stories

BRIDGET BENDISH (IRETON)

Bridget was born in 1649/50, the daughter of General Henry Ireton and granddaughter of Oliver Cromwell. After Ireton's death in 1651, his widow, Bridget married another of Cromwell's generals, Charles Fleetwood, and Bridget was brought up by him after her mother's death. In 1669, when she was 19, she married Thomas Bendish, a lawyer: they lived in Southtown. The couple had three children. Thomas died in 1707 but Bridget continued to live in the Southtown house. Samuel Say, a dissenting minister, has left an account of her, published after her death:

Accustomed to give her personal attention to business, she might be seen from early morning till the decline of day superintending her workmen and labourers at her saltpans, not disdaining herself to take part in the drudgery. When the labours of the day were over, she would eat and drink heartily; then throw herself on a couch and fall into a profound sleep, from which she would arise with renewed vigour, dress herself in silk which had probably appeared at the court of her grandfather, the Lord Protector, and then drive in her chaise or ride on her pad to Yarmouth, and then join the Assemblies at the Town Hall, where all gave her place and precedence; or she would visit the houses of some of her numerous friends, at which she was always a welcome guest. When perplexed by any question, she was accustomed to pursue the method which she said her grandfather used with success under similar circumstances. To obtain a solution she would shut herself up in her closet, till by fasting and prayer her mind became peculiarly impressible; and then whatever text of scripture occurred to her she would consider it an infallible guide as to the course she ought to pursue; and when once her resolution was taken no persuasion could turn her from it, however erroneous it appeared to be. In this manner and by her imperious temper she was led into numberless extravagances; but she was always generous and charitable, and ready to serve all whose necessities and miseries required relief, however undeserving they might otherwise be.[40]

Bridget died in Southtown in 1728 and is buried in St Nicholas' church.

GEORGE WILLIAM MANBY

Manby was born at Denver in the far west of Norfolk in 1765. He moved to Yarmouth in 1803 to take up the position of barrack-master. His first invention was a mortar that would fire at a sinking ship, and carry a line along which those on board could be brought ashore. He was inspired to do this when he saw the *Snipe* sink just 60 yards off Yarmouth in a storm in February 1807, with the loss of 67 lives including French prisoners of war and a number of women and children. The ship was so close that people on the shore could hear the desperate cries of those on board, but in practical terms, as Manby himself wrote, the ship was 'as distant in effect as if she had struck a rock in the middle of the Atlantic Sea'.

Manby's invention first saw action on 12 February 1808, when the brig *Elizabeth* was stranded within 150 yards of Yarmouth beach. Manby was able to fire a line to her, by which means the crew of seven were brought safely to shore. By 1816, his invention had been placed at 59 stations around the coast of Britain, and by 1823 it had saved well over 200 lives: the House of Commons awarded him £2,000.

Manby also experimented with improvements to lifeboats, with equipment to rescue people who fell through ice, and with devices to reduce the damage caused by fire on a ship. Like many people involved with the sea, Manby was a non-swimmer. Once, when he was trying out an 'unimmersible' boat in the river, he was thrown into the water when the boat capsized. A Gorleston resident, John Sayer Bell, plunged into the water and saved him, not without reward. As Manby recalled in his own memoirs: 'his gallantry won him the heart of an amiable lady who was present, and who ultimately bestowed her hand on so good and deserving a man.' Manby himself married twice but had no children. For many years he lived at High Road in Southtown and he died there in 1854: by the time of his death, his mortar had saved more than 1,000 lives. He is buried at Hilgay.[41]

JOHN SELL COTMAN AND JOHN JOSEPH COTMAN

John Sell Cotman was born in Norwich in 1782, and became one of the greatest artists of the early 19th century and one of the leading members of the movement known as the 'Norwich School'. He came to live in Yarmouth in April 1812 at the wish of his patron, Dawson Turner: he taught Turner's daughters the art of painting in the family home at Bank House on the Quay. The Cotmans lived at Southtown in a house 'over the Bridge, pleasant, respectable and not too small': it is now marked with a plaque. Five of his children were born in the house. One of them was John Joseph Cotman, born in 1814. He recalled: 'Yarmouth was the place of my birth, or rather Southtown, on a road about a mile from Yarmouth. My parents had settled there and had already two children, a boy and a girl. The earliest scenes of which I have any recollection are those of garden and meadows, then extensive but now found to be small indeed.' The Cotman family returned to Norwich in 1823. John Sell Cotman died in London in 1842. John Joseph Cotman continued to live in Norwich, painting landscapes in watercolour and oil. He suffered from deep depression and became an alcoholic, dying penniless in Norwich in 1878.[42]

PETER SHORE

The *Two Bears* is a prominent building by the Southtown side of the Haven Bridge. Thousands pass it every day, but very few of them are aware that it was the birthplace of a cabinet minister. In the 1920s, the inn was run by Robert Shore, a former captain in the merchant navy. It was here that his son, Peter, was born on 20 May 1924.

Shore became MP for Stepney in 1964, the year in which Harold Wilson became Labour Prime Minister. Wilson was a great admirer of Shore and brought him into his cabinet only three years later. He became associated with a single issue, opposition to Britain's entry into the Common Market: a strong speech by him on the subject in March 1970 cost him Wilson's friendship. In 1975, he returned to the front bench as secretary of state for trade. In the same year, a referendum was held on entry into the Common Market: Shore was naturally a leader of the 'No' campaign, which, however, was heavily defeated. He was appointed secretary of state for the environment by James Callaghan in 1976. Shore stood twice for the leadership of the Labour party, on Callaghan's resignation in 1980, and on Michael Foot's resignation in 1983: however, he received only a very few votes on each occasion.

Shore is supposed to have been the author of the phrase 'the longest suicide note in history' as a description of the 1983 Labour Party manifesto, which contained radical – and vote-losing – proposals.[43]

Shore's life was blighted by a private tragedy. His son, Piers, a heroin addict, died after an overdose in 1977: he was just 20 years old. Shore was made a life peer in 1997 and became a leading critic of Tony Blair and his concept of 'New Labour'. He died in 2001.

Chapter Six

The Island of Flegg – The Northern Villages

The northern boundary of present-day Greater Yarmouth runs along the Hundred Stream, the ancient boundary between Flegg hundred and Happing hundred. Although the stream no longer reaches the coast, this has been a place where the sea has broken in many times over the centuries.

Place-names tell us a good deal about the early history of the northern villages. The word 'caister' comes from the Latin word *castra*, meaning fort or camp, and refers to the Roman camp discussed later. Others have Old English names. The 'burgh' of Burgh St Margaret refers to a fortified settlement, but it seems unlikely that this was ever more than a defended manor house. The 'ham' in Runham and Martham is a very common place-name element, meaning simply 'home'. 'Mart' derives from the marten, an animal now found only in remote moorland areas but once common throughout the British Isles. 'Run' could be from a personal name, or perhaps from a word implying a bridge consisting of a single tree trunk. The name Thurne comes from the word thorn or thorn-bush.[1]

Other villages whose names convey an important message are Somerton and Winterton. As they suggest, one settlement was originally occupied in summer, the other in winter. Names like this usually imply transhumance, the moving of cattle at different seasons. In this case, however, Winterton was probably occupied at the season its name suggests not for livestock, but for fishing. W.G. Hoskins tells us why: 'Winter quarters … [were] for the purpose of catching the larger codling which move inshore as the colder weather sets in. This sort of food, in a primitive economy, was too valuable to ignore … Huts provided the winter quarters in the first place, probably more like a camp than a regular settlement.' This must have taken place in Saxon times: by the time of Domesday Book (1086) Winterton was a typical farming settlement.[2]

Many names in this area are not Old English, but Scandinavian, suggesting that they were founded by Vikings in the ninth and tenth centuries. This does not mean that the English inhabitants were driven out amid scenes of rape and pillage. As the water levels were falling, just as at Yarmouth itself, as we have seen, so it was gradually becoming possible to settle in these marshes: people from Scandinavia were the first to seize this opportunity and establish family settlements. Flegg itself takes its name from a Danish word meaning marshy ground, overgrown with reeds and similar plants.

The villages include many with the ending –BY, a characteristic of Viking settlement. The first elements of the names are usually the personal name of the original settler. This applies to Herringby, which does not refer to the fish so important in the economy of Greater Yarmouth, but to a person with the name Hering. A few of the village names *could* have other derivations: the first element of Stokesby might be from 'stoc', an outlying farmstead, the first part of Filby could be a word for a bridge in the marshes, and the first element of Ashby may indeed refer to the tree of that name.

The earliest settlement in the area of which anything survives is Caister Roman Fort, founded in the third century as one of the chain of forts defending the Saxon shore. The whole fort covered 30 acres, with an inner heavily defended area of ten acres. The fort fell into decay with the Roman withdrawal from Britain at the end of the fourth century. Like many other Roman forts, the defences were later used by the Saxons and Danes for their own security: about 150 burials have been found outside the walls, dating between A.D. 650 and 850, and continuing into the middle 13th century. Interestingly, about a dozen of the burials

113 *Caister Castle, home of John Fastolf and of the Paston family.*

were found to be covered with ships' timbers, the poor man's version of the grand ship burials found at Snape and Sutton Hoo in Suffolk.

Many settlements in Flegg obtained salt from the sea or from tidal inlets. According to Domesday Book, there were no fewer than 39 saltpans at Caister and a large number at Rollesby. Horsham St Faith abbey near Norwich obtained its salt from an estate at Mautby in the Middle Ages. The First World War pillbox north of the Acle Straight near Ashtree Farm is standing on a mound which has been excavated. Under it was found pottery of the 11th century and the slag from wood fires: the site was identified by the excavator as a possible saltpan of the kind mentioned in Domesday Book.

The main medieval monuments are of course the parish churches. To tour these is to make a journey through the building history of East Anglia. All are built almost entirely of the local stone, flint. Round towers can be found at West Somerton, Repps, Rollesby, Clippesby, and at Mautby, which, unusually, is square inside. Norman work can be seen at the north doorway at Clippesby, and at the south doorway at Ormesby St Margaret. Early English is represented at Rollesby and in the thatched nave at West Somerton, Decorated at Filby, and in the south doorway at Thrigby. Perpendicular is seen in Winterton church tower, 130 feet high, rebuilt by prosperous merchants such as Adam de Tunstead who left six marks (£4) in 1387, and also in the nave at Hemsby, with a mid-14th century porch with carved bosses showing biblical scenes including the Nativity and the Resurrection. Hemsby also boasts a medieval wayside cross, now a scheduled ancient monument: the carvings on it are of the four evangelists, and are similar in style to those on the 15th-century font in the church.

High-status medieval houses can be illustrated by Caister Castle. The main building work was done between 1432 and 1435: the 'Master of the new work' or architect was William Gravour and over 1.5 million bricks were used, many made from local clay, with the kilns fuelled by peat. The detailed work took 30 years to complete: according to William Worcester, Fastolf's secretary, the last parts were only roofed and tiled in 1468, by which time Fastolf was dead and Sir John Paston in occupation. In the following year, 1469, the castle saw military action, being besieged by the Duke of Norfolk in a dispute about its ownership. Margaret Paston wrote to her son: 'Daubeney and Berney be dead, and divers others greatly hurt, and they fail gunpowder and arrows, and the place sore broken with guns of the tother part.' The defenders were starved out and the Duke took possession, but the Pastons regained control on his death in 1475.

Fastolf's bedroom at Caister included a featherbed with mattress, sheets, blankets and Arras hangings. There were further hangings on the wall, chairs and a hanging candlestick. (Candles were expensive. Poorer people economised by using a rush-light where a strip of rush was dipped into melted waste fats from the kitchen: these gave a very poor light.) The kitchen included many brass pots for cooking, two spits, two brass pike pans, mortar and pestle – and '1 vinegar bottle'. The buttery held dishes, plates, bottles and pots for beer, several kinds of knives, linen and 14 laten candlesticks. In the larder were three great standing tubs, two salting tubs and a barrel: meat and fish were stored for use in winter and, in the case of fish, in Lent.[3]

Flegg was in the forefront of the greatest achievement of early medieval technology – the windmill. Edward Kealey writes: 'At that time the invention of the windmill must have seemed utterly marvellous – literally something new on the horizon. What may be startling today is that it was English, rather than Continental, technicians who first tamed the whistling free air and cleverly exploited its immense commercial potential.'[4]

Windmills are supposed to have been brought to Europe by the crusaders, but what they saw in the Middle East were really wind tunnels as the wind always blew from the same direction and the vanes spin in a horizontal plane. The European post mill was very different: the blades turn in a vertical plane, needing complex gearing to harness the energy, and the device can be turned completely around to harness the wind from whichever direction it is blowing. A sloping tail pole at the back of the cabin is pushed to turn the central structure upon its central post. The post on which the structure is built must be very large and immensely strong to withstand the pressures and vibration of the spinning sails and grinding stones. It needs to be supported by buttresses, and by beams or cross trees laid beneath the ground.

Kealey has identified 56 windmills in England before the year 1200, all in the eastern half of the country, and including two in Flegg. These were part of a group associated with the priory at Hickling, which was founded in 1185. In about 1200, Beatrice of Somerton gave the priory her windmill with its site in Rollesby. The exact of location of the mill is given in the charter: 'standing at Tokesgap near the road which extends from the bridge of Bastwick up to the bridge of Burgh [St Margaret].' The donation was made for the salvation of her soul and those of her relations. At around the same time, Walter of Herringby gave his mill in the village of Herringby to the priory. At the

114   *Cottages in Rollesby.*

time he could only give half of the land on which it stood as a man named John Fitz Hodbert was renting the other half, but soon this also passed to Hickling Priory.[5]

Large parts of Flegg were owned by monastic houses, and their accounts record details of medieval rural life. Norwich Cathedral owned land in Hemsby, Ormesby, Scratby and Martham. They had dairy herds, presumably grazing on the edges of the marsh, as well as horses, bullocks and oxen. The Cathedral also had a flock of sheep on the Broads from the early 13th century: it grazed for most of the year at Fowlholme, on the marshes east of Acle, except for ten weeks after harvest when it was taken to Martham to feed on the stubble – and to enrich the Martham fields with its manure. The medieval pattern of farming was one of tiny strips of land: at Martham in 1292, there were over 2,000 parcels of land, two-thirds of which were less than half an acre in size. The population was growing rapidly which created a great pressure on land: by the early 14th century those who had land held only two to five acres and most people were 'near landless small-holders'. The Black Death, declining fertility and migration to towns led to a great decline in the rural population by the late 15th century. By 1497, there were only 77 holders of land in Martham, compared with 376 two centuries earlier. Eleven men held 43 per cent of all the land, and only six holdings were less than one acre in size compared with 153 in 1292.

The commons and open fields of the area were gradually enclosed over the centuries to become privately owned fields. The accounts of Caister Castle in 1433-4 refer to the making of new ditches and the planting of hawthorn and other shrubs. This enclosure could be done informally, as when the lord of the manor of Clippesby reached an agreement with some of his tenants to fence off part of Clippesby Common for his own use in 1573. In other villages it could lead to problems: in 1589, six Ormesby men took to the Court of Exchequer their complaint that the lord of the manor, Sir Edward Clere, had locked the gate leading to Barrow Lowes common and had taken 30 acres of it into his own use. Other enclosure took place by Act of Parliament, such as Stokesby, enclosed under an Act of 1720, the earliest of its kind in Norfolk. Not all enclosure was this early: there was still a good deal of open field in Ormesby as late as 1838.[6]

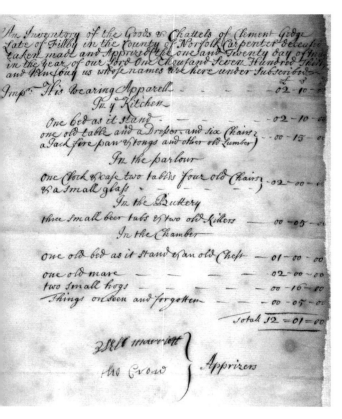

115 *Probate inventory of Clement Gedge, carpenter, late of Filby, 1739.*

Most writers follow W.G. Hoskins in seeing a great rebuilding in the English countryside in the late 16th century. This is true of Flegg and some fine examples of 16th- and 17th-century houses still survive. The best are probably Clarke's Farm House in Staithe Road, Martham, and the house of the Clere family, Stokesby Hall. The latter has a three-storey brick tower porch. Other examples include Billockby Hall, Stokesby Manor Farm and Ormesby Old Hall. Lower status dwellings of the same date can be seen at Rollesby, where the aptly named Old World Cottages have the date 1583 in the eastern gable, together with the words 'God bless us, T G and M G'. Nearby is the early 17th century Church Farmhouse. Originally farms were roofed with local thatch, but from the late 17th century this was often replaced by a roof of *pantiles*, curved tiles introduced from across the North Sea.

The builders often re-used timbers from wrecked ships, as Defoe noticed: 'I was surprised to see, in all the way from Winterton, that the farmers and country people had scarce a barn or a shed, or a stable, nay, not the pales of their yards and gardens, not a hogstye, not a necessary-house, but what was built of old planks, beams, wales and timbers etc.; the wrecks of ships and ruin of mariners' and merchants' fortunes, and some places were whole yards filled and piled up very high with the same stuff laid up, as I supposed to sell for the like building purposes, as there should be occasion.'

Right of picking up material washed onto beaches was technically reserved to the lord of the manor, but people were naturally always quick to help themselves where they could. A more recent example occurred in the winter of 1946, when the MV *Bosphorous* bound for Hull stuck on Scroby sands. The crew jettisoned the cargo – thousands of Jaffa oranges, which washed up on the beach at Hemsby to the great delight of the locals, many of whom had not seen oranges since before the outbreak of war in 1939!

The wild coast of Flegg has always been a haunt of smugglers, prepared to risk the dangers to bring in cargoes of spirits, tea and tobacco. A favourite route was to bypass the customs officials in Yarmouth and unload on the shore at Winterton or Hemsby, take the goods over the sand hills onto wherries which would sail down the rivers Thurne and Bure to North Walsham where carts would take the contraband into Norwich. Smart officials found hidden cargoes on several occasions. In November 1777, a customs officer found 400 pounds of tea and three barrels of gin buried in

Filby open field, and in the following month 3,300 pounds of tea and 113 barrels of gin were captured in Billockby after a skirmish with the smugglers. In 1816, 77 casks of spirits were found hidden in a marsh boat on the Thurne. Nine years later, almost 300 casks of spirit floating in the sea were picked up by customs men and taken to the Custom House at Yarmouth, to be sold off. Sometimes cargoes were hidden in sand dunes until they could be recovered: in Hemsby there is a tradition that one such cargo was hidden in the dunes by smugglers and never recovered: perhaps it is still there![7]

Danger and death were a part of growing up on such a coast. Winterton-born singer Sam Larner recalled – in good Norfolk – an incident there in 1884:

> I can recollect when I was about six years old when four sailors were washed ashore drownded on this beach. And they were tooken up into the old church barn, they, and that was the mortuary then. They took 'em up in a corner, four laid beside each other, laid in the barn. And we were birds-nesting and when we were up on the balks after the sparrow's nest, we could see 'em laying there covered up ya know, but we could see 'em layin' up in the corner, ya see. Four of 'em layin' there dead. Yes. Thass true. That was in May, May gale … . Gale o' wind come down, and they were mackerel-faring out there after mackerel, and they were lost in all hands. I heard my mother say they were shrieking in the riggings, they couldn't get no help no where, couldn't get 'em. And the old man, when he got to Yarmouth and he heard this news, he say; 'They're all gone, all gone'.[8]

The poor were the responsibility of each parish until a House of Industry for the area was built at Rollesby in 1775. The inscription above the doorway survives, summing up the many purposes of the building: 'For the Instruction of Youth, the Encouragement of Industry, the Relief of Want, the Support of Old Age, and the Comfort of Infirmity and Pain.' The Workhouse, like others in the countryside, had a farm on which the inmates could work: this is still called Union Farm.

The 'Daily Bill of Fare' for the paupers in the House of Industry survives:

	Breakfast	Dinner	Supper
Monday	½ pound of bread; 2 pints of milk broth	6 ounces beef and dumpling, 8 ounces vegetables, with gravy and salt	½ pound bread; 1 ounce cheese
Tuesday	½ pound of bread; 2 pints of beef broth	1¼ pounds suet pudding per man, 16 ounces per woman	½ pound bread; 1 ounce cheese
Wednesday	½ pound of bread; 2 pints of milk broth	Pea soup and bread	½ pound bread; 1 ounce cheese
Thursday	½ pound of bread; 2 pints of milk broth	6 ounces beef and dumpling, 8 ounces vegetables, with gravy and salt	½ pound bread; 1 ounce cheese
Friday	½ pound of bread; 2 pints of beef broth	8 ounces dumpling, with potatoes and gravy	½ pound bread; 1 ounce cheese
Saturday	½ pound of bread; 2 pints of milk broth	½ pound bread, 1 ounce cheese	½ pound bread; 1 ounce cheese
Sunday	½ pound of bread; 2 pints of milk broth	20 ounces suet pudding for a man, 16 ounces for a woman	½ pound bread; 1 ounce cheese

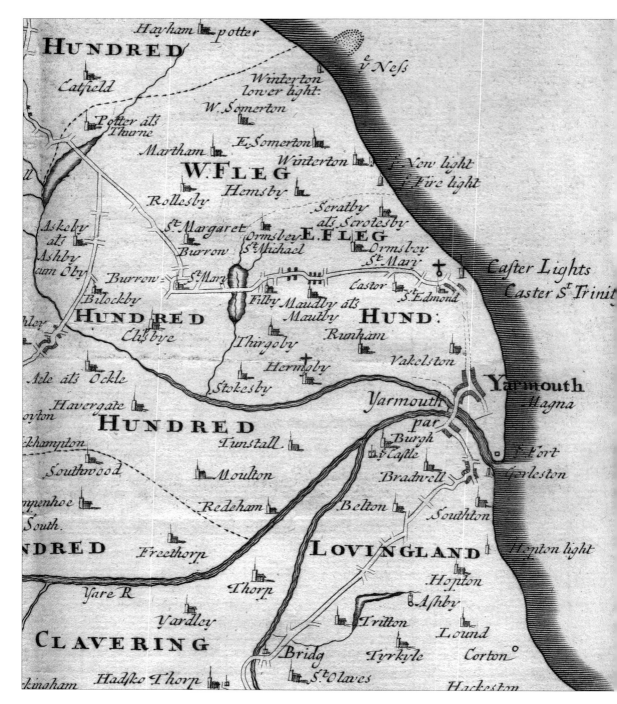

116 *Morden's map showing the Greater Yarmouth area.*

117 *Local children beside Stokesby windmill: there has been a mill on this site since about 1720.*

Two pints of table beer per day were given to men above 60, and one pint to all under 60 years. There were 175 people in the house, at an average cost to the ratepayer of 1s. 11d. per person per week – but the Governor's salary was an extra expense at £150 a year![9]

By the 18th century, the power of the wind was being harnessed for draining marshland: these are the mills that still survive in Flegg. The earliest known is Oby, which has a date stone labelled 1753. Five mills stand along the river Bure in Runham, all brick-built, as are the two survivors at Thurne. That on the east bank at the latter village, Morse's Mill, was built in 1820 and heined (Norfolk for heightened, as we saw in Chapter Two) in 1849: if a mill has a conical lower part and a cylindrical upper part, this is usually because it has been heightened in this way. Morse's Mill has all its machinery and fittings and is under the care of the Norfolk Windmills Trust.

By the mid-19th century, people were using the Broads for leisure activities. One attraction was the proximity of the sea, as Walter White noted during a cruise on the Broads:

> The Captain crept softly towards me, and said in a low tone, 'D'ye hear that roar?'
> I listened, and was presently aware of a solemn throbbing sound, that seemed as if it were the echo of continuous thunder.
> 'That's the sea,' whispered the Captain.
> Yes, it was the voice of the great sea, borne to our ears across seven miles of level pasture by the easterly wind. There was no room for trivial thoughts after listening to that voice, and looking up at the stars.[10]

Even on these quiet lakes, there could be dangers. In 1895, six young men were drowned when their sailing boat capsized on Rollesby Broad.

Each village had its Anglican parish church, 17 in all. The bigger towns had large congregations, as the 1851 Religious Census records: 400 at Martham, 150 each at Caister and Winterton. Some churches were serving villages with tiny populations, and attracting about half the populace: 20 at Thrigby out of a population of 49, 29 out of 65 at Billockby.

118   *Winterton lighthouse, from 'A Polite Guide to Martham'.*

There were Methodists in Martham in 1801, to the disquiet of the Anglican rector who reported to his Bishop: 'they have one teacher whose name is Chamberlain & who by business is a weaver & comes from Norwich. Their doctrines and principles are productive of much disorder among the lower orders.' The Wesleyan Methodist chapel at Burgh St Margaret still exists: it was built in 1841.[11]

The RNLI took over the lifeboat at Caister in 1857, and established a second station there in 1867. The most famous rescue from Caister is described by Alfred Hedges:

> It was from this spot that the pulling and sailing lifeboat *Beauchamp* was launched on 13 November 1901 in mountainous seas to go to the aid of the Lowestoft smack *Buttercup*. The launch was accomplished only with the greatest difficulty and then – largely as the result of an accident with the mizzen sheet – the *Beauchamp* capsized. In those atrocious conditions nine of the crew were drowned, two of them being aged but 18 and 21 respectively. At the subsequent enquiry, the view was expressed that as conditions were so extreme, the rescue attempt should not have been pursued with. To this, a former assistant coxswain, James Haylett, then aged 78 who had rescued his son-in-law and grandson from the surf but had lost two sons in the disaster, replied scathingly, 'Caister lifeboatmen never turn back'.[12]

The boats saved almost 2,000 lives before being closed in 1969 on the grounds that the *Khami* at Gorleston could cover the area more efficiently. Local people did not like this break in tradition and raised enough money to fund a private lifeboat, the *Shirley Jean Adye*, which was formally launched on 5 August 1973. The RNLI also had a lifeboat at Winterton from the 1860s, and a second one from 1880. Lifeboats from the two stations saved 406 lives before they were closed in 1924 and 1925.[13]

119 *Caister Camp, in the background are old trams re-used as chalets.*

In 1906, the world's first holiday camp, Caister Socialist Holiday Camp, was founded by John Fletcher Dodd. The camp was set up because Dodd wanted to give working-class people from the London slums a chance of a seaside holiday. It provided accommodation in tents, with a clubroom and organised games. At first the camp was basic, to say the least – people slept on bales of straw and shared a cold-water standpipe! No alcohol was permitted and political debates were held each Friday night. Originally the camp only catered for men but families were allowed after 1911: however, there was no mixed swimming – men and women had separate bathing times. The camp developed over the years – the first chalets were built in 1928, and a dance hall was added in the 1930s.[14]

The First World War had its effect on the area. Not everyone behaved well: in 1917, the Vicar of Ormesby was charged with hoarding. He was found to have 33 pounds of butter, which had been sent him from Cornwall, when the allowance for six adults was just 1.5 pounds a week.[15]

Many families lost young men in the war. William and Rebecca Sadler family of West Somerton suffered a double loss, as recorded on the War Memorial and on a tombstone in the churchyard. Thomas Sadler, aged 19, was killed in France in October 1915, and his 29-year-old brother a year and one week later: both men were in the 9th Battalion, Norfolk Regiment. The Martham memorial includes the name of one female, Blanche Garman: this is very rare for a First World War memorial. According to her death notice in the *Eastern Daily Press*, Blanche, 'the beloved and youngest daughter of Mr and Mrs W Garman' died on 30 June aged 21 at Gatehouse in Martham. Her burial is recorded in the parish register, but she does not show up on the Commonwealth War Graves Commission website.

Left: **120**   *Aerial view of Caister looking towards Breydon Water, June 1961.*

Opposite: **121**   *Beach Road, Winterton.*

The diaries of Judith Ferrier of Hemsby have already been mentioned. They contain fascinating details of growing up in Flegg in the years after the war, and showing how the railway had brought close links with Yarmouth:

Friday, 10 January 1919, pm. Mother and I went to Yarmouth to see 'My Four Years in Germany' which is now to be seen in the whole as before it was in parts. We went to the *Gem* which [was] a ripping little place, I think much nicer than the *Empire*, much cosier.

Tuesday 4 Feb 1919. This morning we heard and also saw in the paper that Arnold's shop was burned down last night! We went in to Yarmouth by the 8.30 [train] to shop & then go to my music lesson. We went down regent St and saw that Arnold's big corner shop & their arcade as well as Samon and Gluxlain tobacconist, & then Weg then another tobacconist, then the umbrella shop & the scotch Wool Shop & then an office all burnt-out! It was still alight when we seen it. Up King Street the whole of Arnold's shop as far as the Row which divides it from Jarrold's. I tried to take a photo of Arnold's corner.

Monday 10 Feb 1919. Today it was lovely & sunny & with everything white from the frost it looked lovely.... We set out across the fields to Little Ormesby, the Broads are all frozen and bear [the weight of people walking on the ice] for the first time for over 3 years.

Wednesday 19 Feb. Went to Yarmouth by the 11 train. We walked down to the beach. PM: we went to Yarmouth had a look round and then we went to the *Gem* and saw 'The Study in Scarlet' by C Doyle, simply rotten. We came home and had a jolly tea and played the gramophone etc.[16]

There was a dramatic event off the coast in January 1919, when the *Nimrod* (Sir Ernest Shackleton's old Antarctic exploration ship) was caught on the Barber Sands and battered to pieces by the storm. One lifeboat was washed away and the second was unusable because of the ship's list. The crew crawled into it hoping that a wave would wash it off the ship: it did but the lifeboat capsized. Three men managed to grab the upturned boat: one was washed away but the others maintained their grip until it came ashore. Exhausted, they might well have died on the beach but were found by a man walking his dog in the early morning. The two recovered but a total of ten men died in the disaster.

The most prominent building in Flegg between the wars, and still a dominant feature of the landscape, is Caister water tower. Water is pumped up into a large tank in the tower, and from there supplies the houses of Yarmouth by gravity. The water tower was the largest in the country when it was built in 1932: it is 162 feet high and its top 225 feet above sea level: it has a capacity in the inner and outer tanks of over three-quarters of a million gallons.[17]

The railway was an important factor in the economic life of the area. Filby became famous for its raspberries, many hundreds of pounds of the fruit being taken to London by train in the 1930s. As holiday camps developed along the coast, small stations were opened at Caister, California and Scratby: a 'Holiday Camp Express' operated from London on summer Saturdays from 1934.

The Second World War brought several dramatic episodes to Flegg. Two German pilots named Wappler and Schnabel had an extraordinary adventure. On

122   *West Somerton.*

123   *Caister Water Tower, from the bypass.*

24 November 1941, they escaped from a POW camp at Shap Wells and caught a train to Carlisle. Then, with the innocent help of a young apprentice, they managed to steal a small trainer aeroplane. They flew out over the North Sea, but had to turn back because of contrary winds and shortage of fuel. They landed in a field in Caister, not far from the *First and Last* public house. Mistaken for English airmen, they were given tea and sent to the RAF station at Horsham St Faith. Here they were also welcomed as Englishmen at first, and were about to be sent on their way when a signal arrived from the north and they were arrested.

Johnny Wiseman, the son of a Martham farmer, was killed in action over the English Channel on St Valentine's Day 1943, while escorting a crippled Royal Navy Motor Torpedo Boat off Cap Gris-Nez: he is commemorated in a plaque outside Grange Farm, where he lived as a child. The Martham War memorial also commemorates one civilian casualty, Beryl Applegate of 14, Council Houses, who was badly hurt in an air raid at her home on 4 September 1940, dying of her injuries two days later. She was just 12 years old. The burial register notes that she was 'the first fatal casualty in Martham. The house was struck by a German bomb and the family of 5 were covered with the debris, 4 badly hurt and this one fatally'.

The railway continued to be a key part of the local economy for a decade after the war. The 'Holiday Camp Express' stared once more in 1948. However, the great age of the holiday camp was coming to an end: the express ceased to run in 1958, and the entire railway line between North Walsham and Yarmouth was closed down in 1959.

The growth of environmental awareness can be illustrated by the history of Martham Broad, originally made by digging out clay for building purposes. The *Polite Guide*, written in the mid-19th century, says: 'There is a most beautiful and romantic Lake, called in the provincial phrase 'The Broad', interspersed with islands, shaded with trees and shrubs, which altogether give them the appearance of Fairy Land while various species of the aquatic tribe of wild fowl are seen enjoying themselves in security on the surface of the water, as we may presume are fish of various descriptions beneath such as the pike, perch, tench, roach, dace. Of the last of these there is a great profusion, which makes a day's sport to the angler here a most envied enjoyment.'[18]

The Broad was privately owned. In the mid-19th century, it belonged to Joseph Hume of Burnley Hall, and Hall and Broad remained in the same ownership until 1957, when they were put up for sale by Captain Kenneth Watt. He had taken a great interest in the broad, as the sale particular makes clear:

> The Broad is the regular breeding place of very rare birds, including the Bittern, the Bearded Tit, the Garganey, Water Rails etc. Of unique interest to ornithologists, it gives a home to large numbers of duck of various species. The Swallow-tail Butterfly is found here.
>
> The whole of Martham Broad has for many years been treated by the Vendor as a Wild Fowl sanctuary and will become a NATURE RESERVE when the negotiations now in progress have been formalised between the Vendor and the Nature Conservancy, which will embody an Agreed management Policy, and payment by the Conservancy of an annual sum representing compensation in respect of the Fishing and Sporting rights reserved to the Nature Conservancy and the restriction or curtailment of the Landowners full use and enjoyment of the property.[19]

Martham Broad became a nature reserve in 1971. Winterton Dunes, 105 hectares of coastal sand, had been granted this status in 1956. Winterton Beach achieved fame in 1976 when it was used in the film *Julia* to portray Cape Cod on the eastern seaboard of America as it was in the 1930s: Jane Fonda and Jason Robards were in Norfolk to shoot scenes in the area. The film went on to win three Oscars.

The northern villages have always been economically linked to Yarmouth: in the Middle Ages, traders from Ormesby had special privileges on Yarmouth market. By the 1970s, it was becoming clear that Flegg was not a viable unit of government, and in 1974 the whole area became part of Greater Yarmouth. The story since 1974 is told in Chapter Eight.

Life Stories

SIR JOHN FASTOLF

Fastolf was born in 1378-1380 and achieved national fame in the war against France: he was present at the great battle of Agincourt in 1415, and at the sieges of Caen and Rouen. He was made a knight-banneret in 1424 and a knight of the garter two years later.

Fastolf married Millicent, the daughter of Lord Tiptoft and widow of Sir Stephen Scrope. His Yarmouth house was on the North Foreland, on the land now between George Street and the river: he also had houses in Norwich and London. In 1443 he obtained a licence to build Caister Castle, and he took up residence there in 1449.

A catalogue survives of the books kept by Fastolf at Caister – all hand-written manuscripts, of course. They include religious books for the chapel in the castle and for private study, tales of knights and historical chronicles, and other works showing a wider range of interests such as a work of Aristotle and the *Meditations* of Saint Bernard.

Fastolf died on 5 November 1459, leaving Caister and his other lands to Sir John Paston for the foundation of a college of priests. He was buried at St Benet's Abby, in a specially-built chapel, which has totally disappeared. His dream of a college at Caister also came to nothing: after ten years of legal dispute some of the property was instead awarded to Magdalen College in Oxford. Much of this land was in Gorleston and was built over after the Second World War: this is the origin of the name 'Magdalen Estate' in the town, many of the streets being named after Oxford colleges.

MARGARET PASTON

Margaret was born in Mautby, the daughter and heiress of John de Mautby, a prominent local landowner. In about 1440, she married John Paston and thus became part of the family whose letters tell us so much about 15th-century life. They were of course a very wealthy family, with houses at Norwich and Drayton as well as Caister Castle. The couple had six sons and two daughters, one of whom, Margery, upset her parents by becoming betrothed to the family bailiff, Richard Calle. Calle was never accepted as part of the Paston family and Margaret deliberately ignored the pair in her will, although she did leave money to their eldest child.

Margaret's correspondence tells us about provisioning and other aspects of women's work. In one letter she tells her husband that she has bought a horse-load of herrings for 4s. 6d., but that she can get no eels. The letter was written in March and she was buying up food for Lent, when no meat could be eaten. Day-to-day supplies could be purchased in Yarmouth or Norwich, but Margaret often writes to her husband in London asking for more exotic produce such as spices, dates and sugar loaves, and also for cloth of a quality not obtainable locally.

The letters show that religion was a serious matter to a woman like Margaret: she went to Walsingham on pilgrimage at least twice. She was concerned with making a decent funeral monument for her husband, who died in 1466 and was buried at Bromholme Abbey, and also very interested in her own tomb, which she decided was to be in the parish church of her home village. The anniversary of her death was to be celebrated there for a period of 12 years, with four candles, each weighing four pounds, to be burnt around her tomb each year. Her tomb itself was to be marked with a memorial made of marble within a year of her death.

Margaret died on 4 November 1484 and was indeed buried in Mautby church: however, nothing survives of her tomb.

124   *Sarah Martin, prison visitor.*

SARAH MARTIN

Sarah Martin was born in 1791 in Caister, where she was bought up by her grandmother after the death of her parents. She worked as a dressmaker in Yarmouth, walking the three miles there at the beginning and end of each day. She taught in Sunday School and visited the Workhouse to read scripture to the sick and elderly, but is forever associated with her work in Yarmouth prison. In 1819, she went there to visit a mother convicted of beating her child and read to her from the New Testament. This led on to scripture readings to other prisoners and she then began to teach reading and writing within the prison.

In 1823, realising the problems of idleness within the gaol, Sarah began to teach female prisoners to sew and to make items of clothing, which were sold, providing the women with a little money to support them on their release. Men and boys in the prison were also taught how to make caps and shirts. She was also responsible for divine service in the gaol on Sundays, which had been completely neglected before her arrival. A prison inspector making a visit one Sunday in 1835 reported:

> Attended divine service in the morning in the prison. The male prisoners only were assembled; a female, resident in the town [Sarah Martin, of course], officiated; her voice was exceedingly melodious, her delivery emphatic, and her enunciation

exceedingly distinct. The service was the liturgy of the church of England; two psalms were sung by the whole of the prisoners, and extremely well, much better than I have frequently heard in our best appointed churches. A written discourse, of her own composition, was read by her. During the performance of the service, the prisoners paid the profoundest attention and the most marked respect, and, as far as it is possible to judge, appeared to take a devout interest. Evening service was read by her afterwards to the female prisoners.

Sarah's grandmother died in 1826 and she then moved into Yarmouth. She had been left an annual income of £10 or £12, and could now devote her whole time to the prison, spending up to seven hours a day there. She also held an evening class for factory girls in St Nicholas' church, attended by as many as 50 girls. Her health began to fail in the 1840s and she died on 15 October 1843. She was buried beside her grandmother in Caister, where her grave can still be seen. A window was erected in her memory in St Nicholas' church. The Bishop of Norwich subscribed to the cost, remarking, 'I would canonise Sarah Martin if I could'. The window was destroyed in the Second World War but Sarah Martin will always be remembered in Great Yarmouth.[20]

ROBERT HALES

The tomb of Robert Hales can be seen still in West Somerton churchyard. His claim to fame was his size: 7 feet 8 inches tall and weighing 33 stone, he was known as the Norfolk Giant.

Hales was born in West Somerton on 2 May 1813. His parents were also large people: his father, a local farmer, was 6 feet 6 inches tall and his mother well over six feet. The couple had nine other children, all extremely tall. Hales served in the navy as soon as he was old enough and travelled as far as Calcutta, but the cramped conditions of seafaring life were totally unsuitable for such a giant frame. For a while he travelled as a freak show, with his sister Mary who was herself over seven feet tall. While on a tour, Mary died of pneumonia in Guernsey.

In 1848 he tried his luck in America, travelling on the steamship *Canada*. One evening, he was entertaining the passengers by dancing a sailor's hornpipe when a small child fell from his father's arms and into the water. Hales dived in, grabbed the child and held him aloft until a boat could be lowered to rescue him. In America, he worked for P.T. Barnum, who was producing a freak show of dwarfs and giants: the well-known dwarf General Tom Thumb was another of the show's attractions. Hales was a huge draw – in Philadelphia over 28,000 people flocked to see him during his 13-day stay. He was presented to Queen Victoria at Epsom races in 1840, and again at her court in 1851; six of the royal children were present and the smaller ones found this enormous man very scary, especially Princess Louise who was only four years old at the time. Queen Victoria presented him with a watch and chain as a memento of the occasion.

Hales' later years are not well documented. He appears to have become a pub landlord, probably in London, but later to have returned to Norfolk and lived in a caravan in Beighton. In the summer of 1862, he could be seen at the Britannia Pier in Yarmouth. He died in Yarmouth on 22 November 1863, at the age of 50: his body was brought back to his home village for burial.

DAVE STRINGER AND DALE GORDON

Dave Stringer was born at Southtown on 15 October 1944. As a child, he played football for Edward Worlledge and Alderman Leach schools. He signed as a Norwich City B player in February, turning professional in 1963 and making his first team debut on 10 April 1965. He was an England Youth International, and made 501 appearances for Norwich City, scoring 23 goals. He became manager in December 1987. Dale Gordon was born at Caister on 9 January 1967. A winger by trade, he became an apprentice in May 1983, turning professional in January 1984 and making his first team debut in August of that year.

Stringer and Gordon were the key figures in the 1988-9 season, which was then Norwich City's most successful in their proud history. As late as April, the team were in with a real chance of a League and FA Cup double. They finally lost to Everton in the semi-final of the FA Cup (an event overshadowed by the Hillsborough disaster on the same day), and, despite obtaining only six points from their last six games, finished fourth

125   *Dale Gordon, footballer.*

in the league. This would normally have given them a place in Europe, but at that time English clubs were banned from European competition.

The two Greater Yarmouth men made this season for Norwich City. Stringer was manager, Gordon player of the season. He was an ever-present in his number seven shirt, playing all 38 league games, all six FA Cup games and all three League Cup games, scoring a total of eight goals.

This was the high-point of the careers of the two men. City transferred Gordon to Glasgow Rangers in November 1991, for £1,200,000, equalling the then record fee received by the club for a player. He played for several other clubs before returning to his roots for a spell at Yarmouth Town, where he became manager. Stringer resigned as Norwich City manager in May 1992, but continued to work for the club until his retirement. Their achievement has since been beaten by Mike Walker's team which finished third in the Premier League in 1994, but the 1988-9 team and the contribution of two men of Greater Yarmouth will never be forgotten by supporters of Norwich City.

Chapter Seven

Lothingland – the Southern Villages

The southern villages now incorporated into the Great Yarmouth local authority are Burgh Castle, Belton, Bradwell, Hopton and Fritton. In addition, St Olave's, historically part of Herringfleet, was detached from this parish and added to Fritton. They formed part of the hundred of Lothingland, once an island of about 83 square kilometres between the Waveney and the North Sea. It is almost cut in half by the valley in which Fritton Decoy lies, and which was formerly an outlet to the sea: it is the part of Lothingland that lies north of this valley that in 1974 was transferred to the county of Norfolk and the district of Great Yarmouth.

The names of the southern villages are as interesting as the northern ones in suggesting their origins: the ancient names of Gapton and Browston should also be considered even though they never became separate parishes. The most striking difference is the absence of Scandinavian names – the village names in Lothingland are Old English. The '–ton' element in several of the names means simply 'homestead'. 'Hop' suggests an enclosed area, perhaps in marsh or fen, and 'Frit' also means enclosed or fenced in. The meaning of the 'Bel-' element in Belton is not known but may also come from a word meaning 'space', that is, a gap in a forest or a piece of dry land in a marsh. Gabba and Brocc are personal names, presumably of the founders of the settlements (the latter, from which Browston originates, means 'badger' so may well be the founder's nickname). The final two names are different: Bradwell means 'broad water' (the word 'well' in Old English can mean any area of water, not just a well as we now think of it) and probably relates to the ancestor of nearby Breydon Water; Burgh Castle refers of course to the Roman fort, but the 'burgh' element could indicate that this was the centre of a large early Saxon estate out of which the other settlements were later carved. Romantically inclined antiquarians have linked two of the names with pagan gods and goddesses, associating Fritton with Freya and Belton with a word for a (funeral) fire as in Beltane: there is no evidence to support such speculations.

The oldest visible signs of human occupation are the Bronze-Age burial barrows at Bell Hill and Mill Hill on Belton Heath. Rather later, but far more spectacular is the Roman fort at Burgh Castle, which once looked across seven miles of shallow sea to Caister. The fort covers six acres, with walls 15 feet high and up to ten feet wide on three sides. It is made of local flint, with bands of brick on the inner and outer faces. We owe its survival to the generosity of Sir John Boileau, who was President of the Norfolk and Norwich Archaeological Society when the Castle was put up for auction in 1846. Boileau paid £1,500 of his own money for the site and later presented it to the nation.

126 *Burgh Castle: Roman fort, Saxon monastery, Norman castle.*

The main archaeological work was carried out by H. Harrod between 1850 and 1855, when the question as to whether the fort ever had a fourth wall remained unresolved:

> Some argue that the presence of the river, which would be sufficient protection against direct assault today, was all the more sufficient fifteen hundred years ago when the river was wider and deeper and the forebuildings, quay or whatever they were, of which some traces have been found, were complete. Others say that Harrod did find traces of a west wall when he excavated, and that before and since then the materials, being accessible there, have been carted away for repair of adjacent buildings, which is likely enough.[1]

In fact, traces of west wall foundations were found in 1961. The *Chorography of Suffolk* says of Burgh Castle:

> Once called Cnobesburgh that is as Bede interpreteth it Cnoberi Urbs, Cnober's Towne, which as Bede sayeth was a castell most pleasant by reason of the neerenes of the sea & of the woodes in the which was once a monastery built by Furseus, a Scot. Now only remayne ruined walls & bushes of bryers. Here many tymes are Romish coins found by them that digge in that place'.[2]

There is archaeological support for the Saxon monastery at Burgh – evidence has been found of oval huts and a tiny church. There is also evidence of Norman occupation after 1066 – an early Norman motte was constructed over a Saxon cemetery in the south-west corner of the abandoned fort. It was probably built by Ralph the Engineer, mentioned in Domesday Book as owning land here. The mound was completely removed in 1839.

Domesday Book gives us our first written account of these villages, but it is not easy to interpret. Bradwell is not mentioned, coming within the entry for Browston. The villages are held by freemen with good Saxon names, such as Wulfnoth, Sprotwulf and Godwin. All the settlements have sheep, all except Belton have a few pigs and cattle, and all except Burgh

Castle have some woodland. The other details give the villages their distinctive character: only Burgh Castle has a church, and it alone has salt-houses, no doubt on the edge of Breydon Water. Hopton and Fritton have beehives. Most people are described as freemen, villagers or smallholders. Four people are recorded in 1086 as being slaves, three at Fritton and one at Belton: they were presumably closely tied to the land that they worked.

The main medieval unit of landholding was the manor, and the manorial owner was often a monastic institution. The manor of Hopton was granted to the priory of the Holy Trinity Norwich (Norwich Cathedral) in the late 11th century. The manor of Gapton Hall was owned by Leigh Priory. Burgh was owned by Bromholme Priory, which had right of wreck, view of frankpledge and assize of bread and beer.

Each village had its own parish church, built of flint and several with the round tower characteristic of East Anglia. Many people think that they are round because of the difficulties of building a square tower in flint, but it is more likely that they are simply a preference reflecting an age when the North Sea was a highway and not a barrier: there are similar round towers in North Germany and Denmark. They may also have had a defensive purpose like the round towers of Ireland: villagers might retreat into the tower when pagan invaders landed. There are round towers at Belton (rebuilt in 1849), Bradwell, Burgh Castle and Fritton. They are difficult to date: that at Burgh Castle may indeed be Saxon, physical confirmation of the Domesday Book reference to a church here.

The nave at Fritton has been rebuilt, but the chancel is Norman and, unusually, is tunnel-vaulted. Pevsner calls it 'both interesting and impressive in its lowness and darkness'. Burgh Castle church incorporates Roman bricks and tiles taken from the walls of Burgh Castle, and contains a 600-year-old font. Other medieval features include wall paintings at Belton – a large St James and St Christopher of the 14th century, overlaid by later painting of the Quick and the Dead, now almost invisible. Bradwell has two medieval bells and a 500-year-old font.[3]

The only medieval monastic house in the area was St Olave's, founded by Roger FitzOsbert as a house for Augustinian canons in about 1216. It was deliberately situated on the main road at the crossing point of a major river, the Waveney. St Olave, more properly called St Olaf, was a Scandinavian saint, so there was probably already a chapel here dedicated to him, as Roger would be unlikely to have chosen this dedication otherwise. The priory was in fact jointly dedicated to Olaf and to the Virgin Mary. From 1225 the priory held an annual fair on St Olaf's Day, 29 July. The house was never large, consisting of a prior and six or seven canons. They were all priests and served the nearby parish churches at Hales and Herringfleet. Income was derived from land in Fritton, Belton and Bradwell.

Like all small monasteries the house was dissolved in 1536: its contents were valued at a mere £27. The prior was given an annual pension of ten marks, the remaining canons released to fend for themselves. A year later King Henry VIII sold the site of the priory and its possessions to Henry Jerningham for £92 8s. 6d. The priory buildings were pulled down in 1780, but the undercroft to the refectory (the canons' dining room) survives, and is worth a visit. It was excavated and restored by its tenant, Dr Smith-Wynne, in 1904. The central column was found to be resting on a large Roman millstone, over four feet in diameter. The stone is made out of lava and was imported from Saxony by the Romans: it was probably brought here by the canons from Burgh Castle to be re-used, another early example of re-cycling![4]

127 *The crypt, Saint
Olave's priory.*

Other signs of prosperity are markets and fairs. A charter for Bradwell market and
fair was granted in 1252. Leigh Priory obtained a grant in 1270 for a market and fair
at Belton.

After the Reformation, church building lost impetus, but there are a few interesting
fittings. At Bradwell, the tomb of William Vesey, who died in 1644, shows Vesey between
two wives, a child behind each, with four girls and their brother below. Fritton church has
a Jacobean three-decker pulpit. Most people were putting their money into houses rather
than churches. Browston House in Belton is a fine 17th-century manor house, with three
grand plaster ceilings. Old Hall, also in Belton, boasts a Georgian façade of red brick and
Old Hall Farmhouse in Burgh Castle is a 17th-century building, with a centrally placed
Dutch gable and Georgian doorway. Hobland Hall, Hopton, was a late 18th-century
house with a fine staircase, and park: the house was destroyed by fire in 1961. Hopton
Hall dates from about 1825 – the porch has two pairs of Doric columns.

Two features of the landscape especially associated with this part of England are
mills and decoys. We have seen the importance of mills in the economy of the northern
villages: there were mills in Lothingland too. Bradwell corn windmill, shown on a 16th-
century map, was still standing in 1903, while Black Mill and Caldecot Mill in Belton
and Fritton Marsh Mill are now-derelict drainage mills. Priory Mill in Fritton (before
1974 in Herringfleet), also now derelict, was built as late as 1910, illustrating that this
form of technology was still being exploited even in the early years of the 20th century.

Decoys are lakes adapted for catching wildfowl: the birds are lured or chased down
narrow 'pipes' of water, ending in detachable nets where they can easily be dispatched.
The earliest in England were in Broadland. That at Hemsby dated from about 1620, with
that at Fritton being formed about fifty years later, and followed by others at Mautby,
and, in 1807, at Winterton. Almost 3,000 birds a year were being caught at Fritton in
the years at the end of the 19th century. Fritton was also the only one of the decoys in
Greater Yarmouth to continue into the 20th century, still being worked in the 1950s.[5]

The social and economic lives of the villagers can be gleaned through parish records
and related sources. The 1801 census provides our first head-count: Belton was the

128 *Browston Hall.*

largest of the villages, with a population of 350. Each of the other settlements had a population of around 200. Such small villages depended on travelling salesmen to supply anything beyond the most basic requirements. A servant at Browston Hall wrote to her sister in the early 19th century:

> We had a visit from Old Ben last week when he went around the village. He had all sorts of goods in his cart and in packs on his two horses. I bought some cloth to make a dress, a hat and a pair of gloves for Sundays. Cook bought pots and plates but nothing for herself. I am in her good books now as I told her she should buy herself a hat, as Ben will not be back in the village for two months.[6]

The isolation of the area meant that it had its own customs, which have long died out. John Nall happened to be visiting Bradwell church in the 1860s, when a wedding was taking place:

> As the wedding party came out at the South Porch, the girls of the village lined the pathway, strewing the gravel walk with fern leaves. They had mustered all the hand bells of the neighbourhood to greet the happy couple with a wedding peal. In the lane the young men had prepared a rougher salute of guns and pistols, and the clergyman who had joined us after the service, assured us that as the evening drew on a continual discharge of firearms would be kept up, a custom peculiar to the villages of this coast.

Health is not well recorded: parish records suggest that the villages were not immune to outbreaks of plague. In Belton, just three people were buried in 1663 and four in 1664. The figure jumps to 13 in 1665, of whom seven are specifically recorded as being plague victims. The number of burials then falls back to two in 1666 and just one in 1667. In Bradwell, however, the surge is in the following year, 1666, when 20 burials occur compared with the usual three to five each year. None of the 1666 burials is assigned to the plague, but this may simply be because the clerk here did not choose to distinguish plague burials from other entries.

Most people were very poor, of course, and, if ill or elderly, would become dependent upon their local parish officials for relief. One example is Robert Pycraft of Hopton. In 1731 he became sick. His worldly goods were assessed by the parish, presumably to see

129 *Servants at Belton Rectory in the later 19th century.*

if he was in genuine need of parish relief. They were meagre indeed, consisting of: two bed mats, bed and bedstead and hangings, one pair of sheets and one pair of blankets; one table and two chairs and a jointed stool; a chest; a spinning wheel and reel; a frying pan and a pot; and a warming pan. A doctor was called, who charged the large sum of £4. The parish paid his bill, and from then on paid Pycraft's rent for his cottage plus an allowance of two shillings a week: they raised the money by collections in church.

Pycraft died in 1744. We then learn for the first time that the money paid – and the possessions listed in 1731 – were not just his, but those of a married couple. Small payments are made to his unnamed widow until she followed him to the grave in 1745. The expenses of her burial are given in detail:

Paid for her Coffen	7/-
paid more for the buriing of her	3/3
and looking after her and laiing of her forth	5/-[7]

Life for the poor altered in the 18th century, when the southern villages all became part of the Mutford and Lothingland Incorporation, established in 1763. The poor were no longer looked after in their own villages but sent to the Workhouse, or House of Industry, which was opened at Oulton in 1765, with space for 300 inmates. The workhouse was extended in 1836 and an infirmary was added in 1881. In the 1930s it became Lothingland Hospital, which provided mental health care.

The coaching route between Yarmouth and London ran through Lothingland. *The Sun* at Bradwell was the last inn along the route at which horses were changed, and thus saw many travellers stopping there for refreshment. The most famous of these was King Charles II, on his way to Yarmouth in 1671, and Bradwell's only known royal visitor – so far!

For those wealthy enough to have leisure time, the area was becoming an attraction by the early 19th century. The Yarmouth merchant William Youell recorded in his diary for 10 July 1810 that he went for a day's outing, past Gorleston church, along the Browston road to the Four Crossings and then down to the St Olave's road and back by Bradwell Mill. David Davy travelled from Gorleston in June 1832: 'We went thro' an unpleasant country to Burgh Castle, situated in a most retired spot near the marshes, & apparently having little communication with the neighbourhood…. [At Belton] not far from the church, but too near some swampy marshes, a tolerably good house has lately been erected, or repaired & improved, in which resides a Mrs Fowler. Near it in some marsh ditches I observed *stratiotes aloides* [water soldier, now almost extinct] growing in some abundance.'[8]

Few amenities for tourists had yet developed, however. John Nall described a visit to Fritton in 1866. He praised the beauty of the lake, with its birch and oak trees sweeping the margins of the water, but pointed out that there were only two boats available for hire and that it was 'absolutely necessary to prevent disappointment, to write beforehand to secure them', adding 'the trouble, however, will be amply repaid'.[9]

The isolation was broken to some extent by the arrival of the railway. The line between Yarmouth and Beccles opened in 1872, with a station at Belton, and also one at St Olave's where there was a swing bridge over the Waveney. The line along the coast between Yarmouth and Lowestoft, with a station at Hopton, opened in 1903.

By the mid-19th century, some villages boasted amenities that communities of this size would be unable to emulate 150 years later. Public houses named in the 1869 trade directory were the *White Hart* in Hopton, the *Burgh Castle Inn*, the *Sun* in Bradwell and the *King's Head* in Belton: there were also several other beer retailers in the villages. There were two shopkeepers in Fritton, serving a population of 209, and also two wheelwrights. Belton was larger, with a population of 516, and had a large number of market gardeners supplying the market in Yarmouth: the railway would enable them to transport their produce with greater speed. Services included a butcher, a baker and a blacksmith. There were two shoe makers at Bradwell (population 387). Burgh Castle (458) ran to industry with cement and brick makers as well as carpenters, a boot maker and a general shopkeeper, and also a miller working the windmill. Hopton (297) had no shopkeepers, beer brewers or tradesmen.

As Yarmouth expanded, there was an increasing need for bricks, and this led to the founding of the Burgh Castle Brick and Cement Company by William Claxton in 1859. At its height, the firm employed 150 people. Clay was dug near the river, producing both red and white bricks, which could be transported by wherry. From 1875, cement was also made: chalk was brought from Whitlingham by boat, mixed with mud dredged from Breydon Water and baked in kilns, the resulting clinker being ground into cement powder.[10]

Life for the children of the southern villages changed forever as the first schools began to be opened. A parish school was established in Burgh Castle in 1836. Local people gave their support: John Bowgin of Southtown gave three acres of land to the trustees, the proceeds to be used for the school, in 1849. In 1857, Mrs Nesbitt gave £100 to the Rector for the benefit of the school and the money was invested in another two acres of land. However, the school could only take 40 children and was not on a suitable site for

130 *A late 19th-century farm kitchen, Browston.*

expansion. A new school was opened in 1863, with the help of a grant of £181 from the Government: it was named after Bowgin. There was another small school in the village, run by the rector and known as the 'Little School'. It closed in the 1880s, and money which had accumulated from its endowment was transferred to Bowgin's School.[11]

A parish school was established at Hopton in 1861, and a national school at Bradwell in 1867. Another was set up in Fritton to serve the children of both Fritton and Herringfleet. Fritton school was enlarged in 1895, Hopton school in 1902.

The Inspector's Reports for Hopton school survive for the last 40 years of the 19th century and give us a clear picture of the struggle to provide education in a small village – and how dependent this was on the quality of the teaching staff. The following extracts are typical of the comments made:

> 1864: the school promises well.
> 1867: the first standard has passed very badly in Reading, Writing and Arithmetic. The ill effects of such bad grounding will, unless great efforts are made, be seriously visible in future years.
> 1870: the elementary instruction is improving in the first and second Standards, but it is still very unsatisfactory in the upper classes. The children are in good order.
> 1871: Reading and Spelling are improving. Handwriting and Arithmetic are still unsatisfactory. There is more life in the school than I have noticed on former occasions. Intelligence has yet to be developed.
> 1872: the school has improved very much under Miss Powell. Arithmetic is still inaccurate. The order, Physical exercises and Needlework are very good. Maps must be provided.
> 1876: the School is in fairly good order, but the Instruction is still very defective – only five passes in Arithmetic have been made in the whole School. The frequent changes in the Teaching Staff during the years have been most injurious to the School and the newly appointed Mistress will have to devote great care and energy to rendering the School efficient.
> 1879: the School is in good order and the instruction is in a creditable state.

131 *Children and teachers at Belton school, 1880s.*

132 *School House, Belton.*

1880: the girls are tidy and neat, the School is clean and the behaviour is good – generally it is a pleasure to be in the School. The Infants, except in calculation, did well; the Standards would have merited similar praise but for the weakness in the arithmetic of the two higher standards, and in a certain want of intelligence throughout, except in the first standard.

1882: the order continues to merit high praise and the neat and tidy appearance of School and Scholars are very creditable indeed. It is a pleasure to be in a School like this.[12]

The Victorian period was one in which religion still mattered, and the distinction between 'church' and 'chapel' was an important part of village life. The most dramatic incident in an Anglican church in the area was when St Margaret's Hopton was destroyed by fire in 1865. The cause was the church stove, which became overheated after the morning service on Sunday, 8 January: 'John Hodge, the worthy sexton, seated at his dinner close by noticed a smell of fire, saw the sparks, gave the alarm but there was no power of checking the flames which roared through the tower like a chimney and licked up seats, books, everything in fact the Church contained.' The church tower, like many along the coast, was a landmark for sailors. Two wooden lighthouses were set up to replace the church; they ceased to operate in 1871.[13]

The site for the new Anglican church in the village was given by Daniel Gurney. The building, costing £3,472, was designed by S.S. Teulon and built of flint and stone, with blank arches of red and yellow brick in the nave. The stained glass in the chancel is by the firm of Morris and Burne-Jones, and dates from about 1881 – the 1891 directory attributes the east window to Edward Burne-Jones himself.

The only Nonconformist chapel recorded in the 1869 trade directory is the Independent Chapel half a mile from the village of Hopton. However, this under-estimates the Nonconformist strength of the region. The Primitive Methodists were a powerful force in villages in Norfolk and Suffolk, often meeting for prayers in fields before there was enough money to build a chapel. They built a chapel in Belton in 1859, and another was established at Bradwell in 1891 by followers of the local preacher James Amis. Other branches of Methodism also obtained a foothold: a Providence New Connexion chapel opened at Burgh Castle in 1864, for example. Other religious groups were of course catered for in the large conurbation of Yarmouth to the north.

Parish registers tell us about changes in patterns of mortality over the 19th and 20th centuries. In Bradwell, twelve of the 57 people buried between 1813 and 1822 were less than two years old, and a further nine were under ten, including three members of the Hart family aged between four and seven buried within five days of each other in 1813. However, some people did live to a good age in 19th-century Bradwell: 14 of the 57 burials were of people over 60, including Mary Biggs, described as 'either 103 or 108 years old', and Susannah Drake aged 96. Hopton had a similar pattern, with 21 of the first 60 burials after 1813 being of children under ten, and 14 of people aged over 70. By the later 20th century the pattern had changed dramatically, with a great decline in infant mortality and an enormous increase in the number of people reaching the age of 70: out of a sample of 60 burials at Hopton, just two were of children under 10 while no fewer than 37 were of people over 70.[14]

Burial registers sometimes give the cause of death, and these can give us an insight into daily life. Those of Burgh Castle are a good example. Drownings were relatively

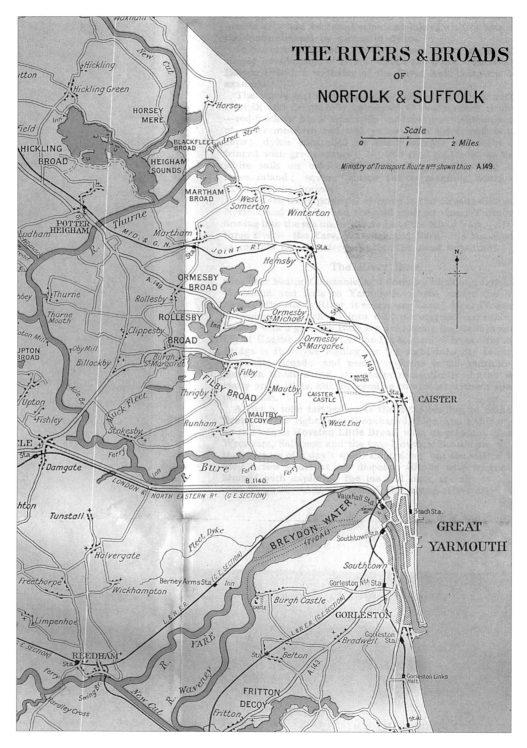

133   *Plan of the Greater Yarmouth area, showing rivers, broads and railways, 1947.*

common – John Milligan of the Berney Arms cement works drowned in 1866, Albert Poole in 1895. Richard Davey, aged just 21 months, drowned in Stepshort Dyke in 1874. George Vincent, aged 23, drowned himself in 1921. Accidents reflect changing forms of communication: Anne Killett was killed after being run over by a cart in 1760. James Preston died after falling from a waggon, which then ran over his body, in 1790: his son suffered the same fate seven years later. Edward Brown was killed on the railway in 1877 and Rose Burrage in 1889. In 1905, George Nelson died after being kicked by a horse which had been alarmed by a passing motor car.

The end of the 19th century saw major changes in local government. East Suffolk County Council was created in 1888, followed by the Rural District Council of Lothingland and Parish Councils for each village, both in 1894. At Bradwell the landowners were anxious that 'the wrong people' might get onto the parish council: they made sure that they were the leaders on it, whereas at Burgh Castle the landowners were happy to stand back and let others to the work. In Belton, the election was run on political lines, with the Liberals winning all 11 seats against the Conservatives. These elections were conducted not by secret ballot but by show of hands at a public meeting, so that there was plenty of opportunity for intimidation.

Village life began to change at the end of the 19th century. Populations had gone up between 1861 and 1891, Hopton by a mere seven, but the other villages by 30-40 per cent on average. Hopton now had a few tradesmen – blacksmith, carpenter and shoemaker – and a thrashing machine proprietor had appeared at Belton, William Beare working at Browston. There were still working windmills at Bradwell (Robert Disney, miller) and at Burgh Castle (Harry Everitt). A few indications of leisure interests had begun to appear – a Church Club and Institute at Burgh Castle run by the local schoolmaster, Frederick Chambers, and an Institute and Reading Room at Belton: this was erected by public inscription in 1885, at a cost of £300. In 1899, Captain Prickett, the owner of Browston Hall, put up a corrugated iron hut in the village to serve as a Methodist chapel: it was also used as a secular meeting room.

Tourism was beginning to become a factor in the local economy. Fritton was described as follows in 1900:

> Fritton Lake, about three miles in length, is closed to the public from September to April, as it is still in use as a decoy for wild-fowl. Duck, mallard, widgeon, teal, herons, breed in the neighbourhood. In the summer months boating and angling are favourite pastimes; and surely the woods, where the giant beeches, exchanging courtesies with branching oaks, were made for happy lovers. You may wander for hours up those grassy glades, or sit down on a tree stump, and take out your favourite author – your only visible neighbour a furry squirrel high above you, or a woodpecker at his favourite tap tap. Fritton for anglers! Fritton for weary toilers! Fritton for sweethearts![15]

By the time of the First World War, populations had risen again, but not spectacularly: the total number living in the five villages was 2,710 in 1911, compared with 1,867 in 1861. Hopton had a population of 304 and a railway station, but just one shopkeeper is recorded – Thomas Whittley at the Post Office. Fritton had one shopkeeper for a population of 227. The only shopkeeper in Bradwell was Alice Amis: she was the daughter of the James Amis already mentioned and ran the Post Office here for 35 years.

134 *Fritton Lake and Gardens.*

The largest village was Belton, with a population of 850 and several amenities – a railway station, a doctor (attending on Thursdays only) and 20th century trades – a van and cart builder and a cycle dealer. Bradwell and Belton had many market gardeners by this date, and some were developing specialist enthusiasms. Edward Adcock at Poplar Farm, Bradwell was described as a'tomato grower', and William Russell was advertising his farm as 'Belton Pleasure Gardens; planted with fruit trees and flowers'. Burgh Castle had a grocer and two general shopkeepers. It also boasted the beginnings of a leisure industry: Edmund Beeching was running a boarding house at the Manor House and Emma Willis offering apartments at The Lodge. Private residents at Fritton include Arthur Large at Myrtleberry and Major-General Russell Upcher at The Warren: wealthy people were beginning to retire to the area.

The First World War affected all the villages, with conscription coming in for the first time, and with its dreadful toll of life. Fifteen Bradwell men were killed in the war: their names are recorded on a brass tablet in the church. Three of them lie in the churchyard, including another member of the Amis family, F.C. Amis of Star Farm. Thirteen Hopton men are commemorated on the village war memorial. They include Albert and (Edgar) John Adcock, two sons of William and Ellen Adcock of Seaman Cottages, Hopton. John was a deck hand on H.M. Trawler *Tugela* and was killed in on 29 February 1916: the extra day of a leap year brought him no luck.

The population of the five villages actually fell slightly between 1911 and 1921, to only 2,635. The main loser was Hopton where the population fell from 506 to 383. Bradwell saw a rise of 56 to 654, the other villages were more or less static. Ernest Whittley had expanded the Post Office at Hopton to 'grocer, confectioner, stationer, tobacconist, petrol store and garage, Post Office'. Robert Whittley was dealing in photographic material. The doctor at Belton now visited twice a week and the town boasted a coal merchant and two fish merchants. The blacksmith continued to function at Bradwell but the new era was shown in the presence of two motor garages and a haulage contractor. Fritton had just one shop but also now had a Village Club.

In fact, the character of Hopton had totally changed: it now hosted the Constitutional Holiday Camp, Potter's Seaside Holiday Camp, a refreshment rooms and a village club. Herbert Potter had won £500 in a Sunday Chronicle prize in 1913. He fought in the war but returned to set up a holiday camp at Hemsby in 1920, and another at Hopton: it moved to its present site in 1934. Moody's Camp opened in 1928. A smaller camp was the Beach Approach Holiday camp, with room for about 120 visitors and owned by the Burgess family between 1936 and 1946.

The area was the scene of two dramatic incidents in the Second World War. On 25 August 1944, an American bomber flying from Rackheath crash landed at Belton while returning from a bombing mission to Germany. Six crew members baled out as the plane flew over Bradwell and Burgh Castle, losing height all the while. They were taken into local houses. The plane finally came down at Goffins Lane, now Sandy Lane, in Belton. Many local residents saw the crash. Walter Sharman was working in a nearby allotment: being deaf he could not hear the noise of the approaching bomber. He recalled, 'the sky went dark and I looked up to see this great plane pass just about rooftop height over my head. Then it crashed in a great cloud of dust or smoke in the next field. I rushed over to see what I could do.' Two crewmen who had not baled out were taken to Yarmouth hospital: they were only slightly hurt.[16]

The other incident was at Hopton just five weeks later. There was an enormous explosion just west of the railway station at 2.40 on the afternoon of 3 October: the sound could be heard right across Greater Yarmouth as far away as Caister and Hemsby. It turned out to be one of Hitler's newest secret weapons, the V2 rocket, which travelled so fast that there was no warning before it fell. Fortunately there were no serious injuries, although 28 houses in the village were damaged.

The 50s and 60s saw the closure of amenities such as railways and schools. Bowgin's school closed in July 1969, the children transferring to Waveney Primary School at Belton. In May 1971 the building was sold at auction for £5,100 for conversion into houses. Bradwell, meanwhile, was expanding rapidly as a dormitory town for Yarmouth, with over 2000 residents in 1961. The church-controlled voluntary school did close in the 1960s, but was replaced by a new voluntary aided school in Homefield Road. The previous school building became the first village community centre. The railway line between Yarmouth and Beccles closed in September 1959, and the coastal line through Hopton closed in 1970.[17]

Hopton remained a holiday village: Hedges described it as 'a village dominated by holiday camps, chalets and static caravans'. The Constitutional Holiday camp was badly damaged by fire in March 1963: the dining hall and bar were destroyed, but the rest of the buildings including the kitchen and the dance hall were saved. By the 1970s the holiday camps in Hopton were losing some of their popularity. In 1972, three camps covering between 15 and 20 acres were sold for housing – Moody's, Hopton Holiday Camp and Mariners' Park. Two camps, the Majorca and Speedwell, announced that they were to amalgamate as Holimarine. There were still four other camps in Hopton, however, including Potters.[18]

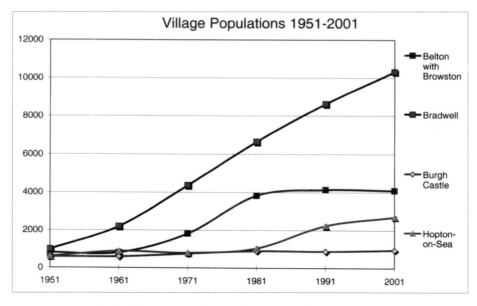

135   *Changes in population in the southern villages, 1951-2001.*

The 'southern villages' were by now linked inextricably with the economy of Yarmouth. The case for joining the conurbation had been considered seriously since the end of the war. A public meeting was held at Bradwell School in October 1946. Mr Matthes presented Yarmouth's case, pointing out that when the planned second river crossing was built, Bradwell would be closer to new factory development on the South Denes than parts of Yarmouth were. Mr Bunnewell supported him: 'My main interest is social welfare, and I honestly think that the breaking of these old-fashioned barriers between town and countryside would be an advantage to the country folk, as at the moment people in the country are paying for some of the amenities which the townsmen are enjoying.' The villages formally became part of Greater Yarmouth in 1974, and their history since this date is discussed in Chapter Eight.[19]

Life Stories

SAINT FURSEY

The conversion of the Saxon kingdom of East Anglia began with King Sigebert, who had become a Christian while in exile in Gaul. The king welcomed Felix when he was sent by Archbishop Honorius to convert the East Anglians – Felix was a Frenchman. He was made bishop of 'Dommoc', traditionally thought to be Dunwich, but now thought likely to be at or just outside Felixstowe. There was another strand of monasticism, however, which also affected East Anglia. This spread from Celtic monastic communities in Ireland. Sigebert welcomed the Irish monks Fursey and his brother Foillan into his kingdom in about A.D. 636: they had entered monastic life at Louth in about 627. He gave them a site to build a monastery at a place called Cnobheresburg, almost certainly Burgh Castle. Bede tells the story:

Once when he was ill, God granted Fursey to enjoy a vision, in which he was directed to continue his diligent preaching of the word, and to maintain his accustomed vigils and prayers with indefatigable zeal; for although death is certain, its coming is unpredictable, as our Lord says: *Be watchful, for you know neither the day nor the hour.* Stimulated by this vision, Fursey set himself with all speed to build a monastery on a site given him by King Sigebert, and to establish a regular observance in it.[20]

According to Bede, the visions were so strong that when Fursey told others about them, even though he was wearing a thin garment in the middle of an East Anglian winter, he 'sweated as though it was the middle of summer'. Bede was writing in a monastery in far away Northumbria about a century later, but he tells us how he knew: an old monk living with him had as a young man known someone who had actually talked with Fursey. This is a fascinating example of how information can be passed down from generation to generation in the days before written records were common.

In 648, Penda, the pagan king of Mercia, attacked East Anglia. Sigebert had given up to the throne and retired to a monastery: he emerged to help in the battle but his principles would not allow him to arm himself with anything more lethal than a stick. He was killed in the battle, together with his successor as king, Ecgric and the kingdom was lost. Fursey and Foillan retreated to northern France. Fursey died there in the following year, and is buried at Peronne.

JOHN AND EDITH 'ANNETTE' MILLS

John and Edith Mills were children of a schoolteacher, Lewis Mills: Edith was born in 1894, John in 1908. Mills senior became headmaster of the village school at Belton, so that both children spent an important part of their growing years there. John Mills became one of Britain's best-loved character actors, starring in films such as *In Which We Serve* and *The Colditz Story*, and winning an Oscar for his role in *Ryan's Daughter*. He died in 2005. His sister Edith adopted the name of Annette Mills and became an international dancer until breaking her leg on stage in Cape Town. She then became a cabaret artist and comedy entertainer. She wrote several songs popular in the Second World War, including 'Adolf' and 'When we're home, sweet home again'. After the war she saw success with a puppet called Muffin the Mule, which led to television appearances and children's books and annuals. She was a strong supporter of animal rights and vice-president of the Anti-vivisection Society. She died on 10 January 1955.

Mills said in an interview: 'I remember Belton very well – my father was head master of the little village school … . I remember a zeppelin coming down in flames off Great Yarmouth and people streaming out in their nightshirts…. We used to go to Gorleston from Belton with one of my little aunties, take our baskets, spend a day at the sea and then walk back, so we would walk ten miles in a day and thought nothing of it.' At the age of 90, Mills recalled that he first performed in public at a concert at the Belton Institute organised by his father: he danced a hornpipe dressed in a sailor's suit. It was this first taste of show business that made him want to become an actor. At the age of ten he played Puck in the school's production of *A Midsummer Night's Dream*: his mother made the costume. In later life, he retained an interest in the area, writing the foreword to Dorothy Smith's *History of Beton*.[21]

Chapter Eight

Greater Yarmouth since 1974

G reat Yarmouth Borough District Council was created in April 1974, and comprises the former Great Yarmouth County Borough and 22 parishes formerly in Flegg or Lothingland, stretching from Winterton in the north to Hopton in the south. The parishes formerly in Lothingland were of course in the county of Suffolk, and were thus transferred to Norfolk for the first time – a change still regretted by some inhabitants of the area.

The new council had 48 members: the first elections were held in June 1973, with the Conservatives winning control. A.W. Ecclestone was chosen to act as first chairman, until the council was properly set up in April 1974 and Jack Bishop was elected first mayor of the new Yarmouth Borough. He had been born in Yarmouth, moved to Hemsby at the age of 19 to start the Seacroft Holiday Camp, and was a member of Blofield and Flegg Rural District Council for 25 years.[1]

The holiday trade remained the main source of income for the whole region. There have been many new developments to attract customers. In 1976, it was reported that 50,000 people had visited Fritton Lake the previous year. The owner, Lord Somerleyton, planned to improve the facilities adding a cafeteria and planting thousands of shrubs, including rhododendrons. He also planned to create a new valley through a whaleback hill, giving views of the lake from the Old Hall.[2]

In 1979, the Marina open-air theatre and cinema were replaced with the Marina Leisure Complex. This opened in 1981 and boasted amusement arcades and an indoor swimming pool complete with wave-making machinery. Modern developments tend to have short shelf-lives, however: by 2006 it was planned to replace it by a new facility. The Sealife Centre was opened in 1991, and has proved a very popular attraction. Other developments in the 1990s included Crazy Golf, a Ripley's 'Believe It or Not' attraction in the Windmill cinema building, and an Indiana Jones experience called 'Treasure World and the Temple of Doom'. Gorleston also saw changes. In 1981, Dick Condon of the Theatre Royal in Norwich took over the Pavilion and ran a 'Seaside Special' there. Carl Adams, an entertainer from Burgh Castle, ran the Pavilion for a decade from the later 1980s, and was succeeded by Kevin Lynch in 1995. A £350,000 refurbishment was announced in 1999, involving new seats, lights and sound. Lynch said, 'it will take the theatre into the new Millennium and hopefully for another 100 years'.

The British holiday industry is flourishing, and may well experience a boom as foreign holidays become less popular due to fears of terrorism and environmental concerns. Greater Yarmouth is ready: already the Pleasure Beach is one of the five most popular

136   *Fun at the Fair – the Waterslide.*

paying attractions in the whole of Britain. The holiday camps have responded too by offering a range of specialisms: Wild Duck boasts that it is set in 97 acres of woodland, while Potters offers health and fitness clubs, and hosts world championship indoor bowls. The facilities for inhabitants are also being improved with a refurbishment of St George's Park including a water feature to commemorate the town's 800th 'birthday' (the granting of its first charter) in 2008. Yarmouth Stadium opened a new £2.5 million grandstand in 2006.

After the death of the fishing industry, the town soon found another source of income, as we have seen. North Sea Oil was piped ashore from 1975. By the end of 1979, there were nine fields in production including the massive Brent and Alpha fields: Brent, one of the earliest crude oils produced in the North Sea, is still used as the standard reference for pricing oil. By 1980, Britain was producing 100 million tonnes of oil a year, on a par with countries such as Nigeria, Kuwait and Iraq. In the 1980s the area was increasingly exploited as rising prices made it more economically viable to do so, but production peaked in 1999 and is currently falling. Major oil producers have turned to newer discoveries in the Gulf of Mexico, Brazil and West Africa. Thanks to the North Sea fields, Britain was a net exporter of gas until 2004 and will continue to be a net exporter of oil until about 2010. However, many millions of barrels of oil remain under the North Sea, perhaps awaiting new technology to make their exploitation worthwhile.

The discovery of oil and gas sparked a whole new industry. Major energy operators and contractors flooded in, resulting in the development of a pool of innovative entrepreneurs and a skills base renowned throughout the world. More recently, as gas

137   *South Quay during the oil and gas boom of the 1970s.*

reserves mature, the industry has had to change. AMEC, which operates out of Great Yarmouth, joined forces with Dutch partners Jacobs Engineering and Stork to win a seven-year, £475 million contract to provide support services to facilities in the North Sea.[3]

One important role for the new council was provision of housing. Yarmouth Borough Council began building houses on a large scale in 1919, and in March 1974 owned 6,178 dwellings. The new borough had nearly 8,000 council dwellings, with a further 300 being built in Yarmouth and Gorleston. The programme for 1974/5 allowed for 119 new houses in Yarmouth, 40 in Burgh Castle and 40 in the former Flegg parishes. In addition, money was ear-marked for alterations to houses in Filby, Fleggburgh, Rollesby and Ormesby, as well as a district heating scheme in Middlegate in Yarmouth.

In June 1974, it was recommended that the Council purchase 13 acres of land in Bradwell. The Local Plan for the area had not yet been formalised, but it was felt that, even if permission was not forthcoming, the land would be useful for other purposes. In February 1975, the Council decided to acquire 11 acres of land south of Bell Lane in Belton, and sell five acres on to the Norfolk County Council for use as a new Middle School, and half an acre to the local Community Council for use as a Community Centre. However, the County Council refused to co-operate, saying that the new school would not be needed for five years: it was rumoured that in fact they had found a cheaper site for the school. At the same time, seven out of 11 chalets at Waveney Farm were declared unsuitable for human habitation: eventually it was recommended that all 11 chalets be demolished but the Council decided against purchasing the land for

138　*Tree-planting ceremony, East Anglian Way/Shrublands Way, Gorleston, 1994.*

housing. The possibility of a Council caravan site at Waveney Farm was also rejected as there were no suitable schools close by.[4]

In November 1988, the Council approved the development of eight or ten flats within a two-storey building at Koolunga, to secure the completion of renovation work on the main house, and on condition that there was to be no more building on the site and that the grounds were landscaped.[5]

The concept of re-using historic buildings for housing has also reached the town, most notably with the adaptation of St Nicholas' Hospital for apartments. An example on a more intimate scale is Boulton's furniture store on North Quay, a 17th-century merchant's house. After much debate in the early 1960s, the building was 'saved by a whisker'. The council bought the property in 2003, and spent £140,000 on a facelift. In 2006, the property next door was bought as well, and a full refit begun to turn the premises into 19 flats, at a cost of £1.5 million. The property is just one of 98 projects in Yarmouth under the Township Heritage initiative directive aimed at the restoration of old buildings – the plans will add 120 residential units to the town's housing stock.[6]

On 9 April 2006, 'an ambitious beacon development for Yarmouth … heralding a new era for the regeneration of the town' was announced. The development at Runham is to consist of 28 four-bedroom houses, 19 three-bedroom houses and 58 two-bedroom flats, with underground parking and views over the River Bure and Breydon Water. This is the first of a series of riverside schemes to reinvent Great Yarmouth. The buildings form an 'S' shape, with heights of between three and seven storeys. The Broads Authority has opposed the scheme on the grounds that it would ruin the views from the river and from Breydon Water. However, the Borough Council supported the development, which is to be built by Heritage Developments and completed in late 2008. Councillor Penny Linden commented: 'It's a saucy design, it's cheeky and I like it.'[7]

The need for a new hospital for the east coast had been recognised by 1945. In 1961, the Northgate Hospital was suggested as the site. In 1969, a site at Wood Lane in Gorleston was chosen, but the Ministry of Agriculture objected, suggesting that the Hospital be built in Bradwell, Belton or Burgh Castle. The final site was agreed in 1974. The first phase had 250 beds and cost £13 million. The James Paget Hospital opened in 1981, the name chosen by a local consultant physician, Doctor David Wayne: some people would have preferred that of a member of the royal family. The Hospital has a 20-bay east front and a structure built round a series of courtyards. The architects, McDonald, Hamilton and Montefiore, had already used the design for hospitals at King's Lynn and Bury St Edmunds. A second phase of building to double the number of beds began immediately, at an estimated cost of £5.5 million. The number of patients in 1999/2000 was 29,320, with 14,875 day cases.[8]

The old General Hospital in Yarmouth and the Nurses' Home in Alexandra Road closed in 1981. The Home was sold and eventually demolished. The site of the Hospital was sold at the end of 1983. When the building was being demolished, a time capsule was found that had been put under the foundation stone in 1887. It was opened live on BBC TV's *Look East*: it contained a hospital annual report of 1886, an *Eastern Daily Press* for 18 May 1887, and some coins.[9]

In 2006, the Hospital was awarded foundation status, giving it autonomy from the regional health authority. The Hospital immediately announced that it would be spending £40 million on improvements. First priority was to gut all the six-bed wards. These were only 24 years old but already out of date: they are to be replaced with four-bed wards with modern facilities, including en-suite bathrooms. David Hill, Chief Executive, said: 'From now on it will be up to us to decide what benefits patients and instead of talking about it, we'll be able to get on and do it. We'll be able to make the right decisions based on what the people of Yarmouth and Waveney need, and put these decisions into practice far more quickly.'[10]

Transport was another responsibility of the council. The old Borough Council had run 64 buses on 13 regular services in Yarmouth, Caister and Gorleston. Now it had to provide buses for the rural areas to the north and south of this densely populated region as well.

Responsibility for the roads within the southern villages area passed to the new authority from Suffolk County Council. In 1976, the go-ahead for the Hopton bypass was announced: the cost would be £408,000. The work took 12 months and completed the dual carriageway between Yarmouth and Lowestoft. Many locals welcomed the road, which had originally been planned as long ago as 1937. Others were not keen as they were concerned at the loss of passing trade to shops in the village. The opponents thought the new road was a waste of money and that all that was needed was a set of traffic lights where Station Road joins the A12.[11]

An experimental pedestrianisation of Yarmouth Market Place took place for six months from July 1988. It went down well, with 79 per cent of those interviewed favouring the scheme. Permanent covered stalls have been erected at the southern end of the market, and it is currently intended to expand the covered area. Regent Road,

139   *A pedestrianised Regent Road.*

the main link between the Market Place and the sea, has also been made largely traffic-free, and in season is crowded with holidaymakers seeking refreshment or souvenirs.[12]

The ferry across the Yare was in terminal decline. In April 1974, the Trades Council complained of the harmful effects to employees of restricting the weekend running of the ferry to Saturday mornings only. The operators said that there was not enough demand for the ferry on Saturday afternoons and Sundays. Some councillors thought that the ferry should be run as a public service, but the Council decided against subsidising it at weekends. However, subsidies soon became an accepted fact: £3,000 in 1987/8 and £5,000 in 1988/9, by which time the County Council was also subsidising the ferry to the tune of £10,000 a year. Its closure was inevitable.[13]

A second road crossing over the Yare *was* eventually constructed, but much further north than originally planned: Breydon High Bridge opened in 1985. It was a major piece of engineering: the lifting section is 34 yards long, 12 yards longer than any other bridge in Britain at the time. However, the scheme for a southerly crossing, now called the *third* river crossing, is still considered a key element in the expansion of Yarmouth as a port. In 1988, a feasibility study was conducted. Obviously it would have to allow ships through: it was estimated that a double-leaf swing bridge with four lanes would cost £20 to £25 million. If the width of the navigation in the channel was reduced, it could be built for £10 to £15 million. However, if the Harbour expanded as hoped, to allow the ships through the bridge would have to be closed to motor traffic for up to 19 minutes every hour in winter and for 25 minutes in every hour in the summer! A tunnel would be more practical, but also more expensive, at £30 to £35 million for a single carriageway in a tube-type tunnel.[14]

The international ferry service between Great Yarmouth and Schevingen in Holland also came to an end in the 1990s: ironically this was because the service was so successful that the operator had to relocate to a UK port with deeper water and less restricted access.

We have seen how newcomers have benefited the Greater Yarmouth area over the centuries. The town continues to celebrate diversity, with incoming communities adding to the cultural mix. A sizeable Greek Cypriot community has built up in the town since the Second World War. Among the first to move to Yarmouth from London were the Socratous family who established the Rainbow Corner and Café au Lait restaurants in 1947, and Loucas Chryssafi who set up the Savoy restaurant in the 1950s. In 1967, the Church of England entrusted the community with St Peter's church, which had been acting as the Anglican parish church while St Nicholas' was reconstructed. The community has dedicated the church to Saint Spyridon, a very popular Cypriot saint: he was a fourth-century peasant who became a bishop. Other Cypriots joined the Yarmouth community from Cyprus itself after the island was invaded and partitioned by Turkey in 1974. By 1992, there was a school based at the church where Tassos Karlis was teaching almost seventy pupils the language and heritage of their land. The community has added colour to the life of Yarmouth with their annual celebration of epiphany in January: a cross is thrown into the sea and young people dive into the icy water to retrieve it.[15]

In 2006, members of black and ethnic minorities made up 2.8 per cent of the adult population of Greater Yarmouth, but 4.1 per cent of those under 16, an increase likely to continue in future years. As Eastern European countries have joined the European Community from 2004 onwards, many migrant workers have settled in the area, finding jobs in agriculture and in the holiday industry. Most of these people are aged between 20 and 30 and stay a relatively short time. Many people from Portugal have also moved to the area, as evidenced by the number of Portuguese-speaking children in local schools. In 2005, the go-ahead was given for the town's first mosque, an adaptation of holiday flats on Northgate Street for use as a place of worship.

The southern villages have mushroomed as part of the conurbation of Greater Yarmouth. Belton was the largest of the southern villages until 1951, when Bradwell caught it up: both had just over 900 inhabitants. In 2001, however, Belton had 4,500 residents but the population of Bradwell had grown to 14,500. None of the northern villages saw such a dramatic increase in population, although Caister rose from 3,029 in 1951 to 8,756 in 2001. The populations of the largest northern villages – Hemsby, Martham and Ormesby – each more than doubled in the half century, to somewhere between 3,000 and 4,000. However, smaller communities actually declined over the fifty years – Rollesby falling from 435 to 395, Stokesby from 366 to 293 and Somerton from 317 to 257 people.

The villages have naturally been keen to retain their own identity within the framework of the new Greater Yarmouth. One form of expression of this feeling was in the erection of village signs. Hopton village sign, unusually, is double-sided, both sides showing a view of the church. It was designed and painted by Richard Gadsby. It was erected on 24 June 1980, when a time capsule was buried intended to be opened up a century later: 'This capsule consisted of a tube which contained a tape recording of village life and the ceremony of the sign, a newspaper of the day, a specially written

140 *Village pride: Bradwell community hall and village sign.*

poem, records from village organisations, school work, coins and shop lists and prices. The tube was sealed, placed at the base of the sign and covered in concrete.'[16]

A series of festivals was held at Bradwell in the 1960s and 1970s. The first centred around an exhibition in the Village Hall in 1964. Ten years later, 1974 saw a flower festival in the church, a fête and children's sports, followed in 1976 by a festival on a Victorian theme. The fourth festival was held in 1978 to raise money to provide a stage for the Community Centre. Exhibitions were held and there was a parade and a comedy cricket match. When Norfolk County Council decided to close the village library in 2003, the local community responded by setting up their own.[17]

Martham is another community that takes pride in its individuality. In the 1980s a resident remarked:'There's a lot going on. People come into Martham from all round for this – ballet classes, dog-training, buying mushrooms at the farm, the comprehensive school, Women's Institute, bingo, badminton, youth clubs, sailing on the Broads. In many ways it's more like a small town than a village.'[18]

Towards the end of the century, Yarmouth was becoming increasingly aware of the importance of boosting its historic heritage. Two good examples are the Norfolk Pillar and Time and Tide Museum. The story of the restoration of the Norfolk Pillar in the early 21st century is fascinating. In 2000, responsibility for it was transferred from Norfolk County Council to the Norfolk Historic Buildings Trust. Tests showed that the majority of the stone was sound, but that the mortar joints had been scoured out to a depth of 300 millimetres or more by the wind. Repairs included re-pointing the mortar and replacing stone in the plinth and pedestal where damage had been caused

141   *The Green, Martham, 1989.*

142   *Tolhouse and Public Library: the Tolhouse is now a museum.*

143 *Cherry Tree Holiday Park, Burgh Castle.*

by rusting stone clamps. The most important change to the setting of the Pillar has been the restoration of the original railings: 19th-century photographs were enlarged and used to recreate the original form and ornamentation of the cast iron railings and gates. New interpretation boards around the site provide visitors with an understanding of the monument and the work involved in its restoration. An interactive website gives people the opportunity to take a virtual tour of the Norfolk Pillar, a distinctive feature of the Great Yarmouth landscape for 200 years.[19]

Time and Tide is an excellent example of how a museum can be both informative and fun. It is set in a former fish-curing works, and the unique smell of smoked herring adds to the maritime atmosphere. Here it is possible to take the wheel of a coastal drifter, hear tales of wreck and rescues, and walk through a recreated Row to see how a Victorian fishing family lived. The museum includes many sorts of local craft, but it is important that working vessels are also preserved, such as the *Lydia Eva*, the world's last surviving steam-powered drifter. In 2006, the Borough Council bought the *Horace and Hannah*, the last seaworthy shrimper, which will be put to practical use in training Sea Cadets.

A less-considered aspect of heritage is dialect. The Norfolk dialect was denigrated by most schoolteachers throughout the 20th century, but is now beginning to be appreciated. One of its most distinctive characteristics is the dropping of the 's' at the end of the first person singular verb, 'he go' rather than 'he goes' for example. Norfolk words in common use include 'loke' for a lane, 'quanting' for punting a boat, and 'staithe' for a quay along a river – and of course 'squit' for a light-hearted conversation or an unbelievable tale.

144   *Old and New: the restored shrimper* Horace and
Hannah *sails past the drilling rig taking samples for the
EastPort development, September 2006.*

The future of Yarmouth is reflected in two developments, the wind farm and the
Outer Harbour. Edward Kealey has pointed out: 'in 1973, the world energy crisis
suddenly made solar, hydroelectric, geothermal, and wind power popular again. People
rediscovered that such power is safe, locally derived, inexhaustible, and non-polluting.
Like the broad, sweeping sails of the old mills, the available resource alternatives have
thus been buffeted full cycle.'[20]

Two major projects have been developed in Greater Yarmouth. In 1992, a wind farm
was planned for West Somerton, with ten turbines each 30 metres tall. The Broads
Authority opposed the scheme because of its effect on the landscape, but the Borough
Council voted in favour and it was running by the end of the year. Each turbine weighs
24 tonnes and cost £200,000 to install. The amount of electricity produced was said
to be sufficient to supply 1,700 homes, but in 1994 it was reported that less electricity
was being produced than expected because of insufficient wind! The large Somerton
Wind Turbine followed in July 2000. This turbine is 67 metres tall, and its blades are
33 metres long: it provides electricity for over 4,000 local people.

Scroby Sands wind farm is 2.5 kilometres off the coast of Caister. Construction
began in October 2003, at a total cost of £75 million. The farm produces enough
electricity to power 41,000 homes. There are 30 turbines on towers rising 68 metres
above sea level: the blades of the turbines are 39 metres long. Dutch links helped once
more: steel piles for the wind turbines were installed by Mammoet Van Oord's jack-up
installation barge.[21]

In 2006, there were concerns that the wind farms were not fulfilling their potential.
This was put down to teething troubles, and the new technology was already a tourist
attraction: over 35,000 visitors went to the Visitors' Centre at Scroby in the year
2005.

EastPort is a £40 million regeneration project supported by Norfolk County
Council, Great Yarmouth Borough Council and the Great Yarmouth Port Authority.
It has financial support from the European Union, and from the East of England
Development Agency. The public funding element is in the order of £12 million, with
the balance being provided by private investment.[22]

The new outer harbour can cater for ships too large to enter Yarmouth's present
harbour, both general cargo and specialist offshore vessels. It offers the shortest route
between England and the Netherlands, and it is planned to run a ferry service operating
three times a day between Yarmouth and Ijmuiden: the distance is just 103 nautical
miles, and could be accomplished in less than five hours using modern ferries capable

145 *Scroby Windfarm, taken from the air by Mike Page.*

of over thirty knots. The new harbour is also intended to provide all-year employment in Yarmouth and play a major part in the redevelopment to the town. EastPort will open in 2008, exactly 800 years after the charter of King John had established the borough.

The natural route from the Midlands of England to Yarmouth and across to Europe involves crossing the marshes west of Yarmouth on the Acle Straight. Proposals have been made to dual this road to improve the access to the town, at a cost of about £25 million. Many people feel that this is essential if the town is to grow in the 21st century, but others are strongly opposed on the grounds of the damage that would be done to the tranquillity and the wildlife of the area. The matter remains highly controversial, and has no obvious solution.

The challenge for Greater Yarmouth is to provide a balance between economic growth and the enhancement of its fragile environment. Every resident and every visitor has a part to play in ensuring that the future of Yarmouth is a story of continuing success.

Life Stories

JACK CARDIFF

Jack Cardiff was born in Yarmouth in 1914. His parents were both music hall performers who occasionally played in films. Cardiff became a child actor at the age of four, starring in *My Son, My Son* in 1918. His most dramatic part came in 1922 in

Billy Rose, in which he played a boy who dies trying to obtain a rose for his mother. The last film in which he acted was *Tiptoes* in 1927.

In the following year he worked on *The Informer*. Although he later recalled that his main task was to provide Vichy water for the director, he did get to handle a camera, and this led to his career as a cinematographer. He worked on some of the most important British films of the 1940s and 1950s, including *Black Narcissus*, *The Red Shoes*, *Scott of the Antarctic*, *The African Queen* and *The Vikings*. He won an Oscar for his work on *Black Narcissus*, and was expected to win one for his stunning camera-work in *The Red Shoes* in the following year, but was not even nominated: general opinion was that Americans did not want to see an Englishman receive the award in two successive years.

In 1958, Cardiff turned to directing films, of which the most well known was *Sons and Lovers*, made in 1960. In the 1970s he returned to cinematography: the most popular film he made in this period was *Death on The Nile* (1978). In later life, he was awarded a second Oscar, this time for his lifetime achievement in films. He joked that he would regard it as a long overdue award for *The Red Shoes*.

MYLEENE KLASS

Myleene was born in Gorleston in 1978, the son of a ship's captain. She began playing piano and violin at the age of four. She went to school at Notre Dame Roman Catholic School in Norwich and at Cliff Park High School in Gorleston. In 2001 she was one of the five winners of the ITV programme Popstars who together formed the group Hear'Say. Their first single, 'Pure and Simple', was the fastest selling single in UK chart history, and remained in the charts for six months. The band recorded several more hits over the next couple of years before fading: it finally disbanded in the autumn of 2002. Myleene's talent was such that she was then offered both a pop music contract and a classical music contract. She chose the latter, and her album 'Moving On', on which she plays the piano, was released in October 2003. It stayed in the charts for 32 weeks, peaking at number three. She has since become a presenter for both Classic FM radio and GMTV. She also does a great deal of charity work, involving herself in 'The Year of the Volunteer' in 2005, and taking part in a show in London Fashion Week in aid of the 'Save the Children' charity.

In 2007, she appeared in a TV reality show, had a number one classical album (*Myleene's Music for Romance*) and starred in BBC TV's *The One Show*. Not bad for a 'Gorleston Gal' – and her career has only just started.

From Saint Fursey to Myleene Klass, men and women connected with Greater Yarmouth have made many contributions to the life of Britain over 14 centuries. The town's contribution has been a great one too, as a fishing port, a centre of trade and a premier holiday resort. The future is an exciting one, with the opening of the new EastPort offering many opportunities for development. As long as these opportunities work with the environmental background described in chapter one, rather than trying to fight against it, the future for Greater Yarmouth as a place to work and a place to enjoy leisure time will be bright indeed.

Further Reading

Archives

Yarmouth Borough archives are held at the Norfolk Record Office, The Archive Centre, Martineau Lane, Norwich NR1 2DQ. This Office also holds many records of firms and private individuals in the Yarmouth area.

   Archives relating to the northern villages are held in the same place. The southern villages were in Suffolk until 1974, so that much historic material is held at the Suffolk Record Office. However, parish records and parish council records for these villages are also in the Norfolk Record Office.

Printed Books

Bennett, H.S., *The Pastons and their England* (1968 edition)
Callan, Brian, *Belton from its past to its present* (undated)
Davies, Dr Paul, *A History of Medicine in Great Yarmouth* (2003)
Ecclestone, A.W. and J.L., *The Rise of Great Yarmouth* (1959)
Ecclestone, A.W., *Gorleston* (undated, but published in 1980)
Goodman, Nigel (ed), *Dawson Turner* (2007)
Hedges, A.A.C., Boon, Michael, and Meeres, Frank, *Yarmouth is an Antient Town* (2001), a revised and expanded of the original book by Hedges.
Meeres, Frank, *Norfolk in the First World War* (2004)
Meeres, Frank, *Norfolk in the Second World War* (2006)
(Both the above have a great deal on Great Yarmouth in wartime)
Palmer, C.J., *The Perlustration of Great Yarmouth* (1874)
Temple, C.R., *East Coast Shipwrecks* (1974)
Williamson, Tom, *The Norfolk Broads: a landscape history* (1997)
Yarmouth Archaeology – essential for keeping up-to-date with the latest local research

Notes

CHAPTER 1

1. Ogley, Bob and others, *The Norfolk and Suffolk Weather Book* (1993) p 12; *Norfolk Chronicle* (hereafter NC) May 1865
2. Robinson, Bruce and Gregory, Tony, *Norfolk Origins – Celtic Fire and Roman Rule* (1987), p.81.
3. Armstrong, Patrick, *The Changing Landscape: the history and ecology of man's impact on the face of East Anglia* (1975), p.126.
4. Ecclestone, A.W., *Henry Manship's Great Yarmouth* (1971), p.34; Rackham, Oliver, *The History of the Countryside* (1986), p.359; 'The Norfolk Sea Floods' in *Transactions of the Norfolk and Naturalists' Society*, volume xiv, part iv, 1938.
5. Pollard, Michael, *North Sea Surge* (1978), p.16.
6. Ecclestone, A.W., *Yarmouth Haven* (1981); and *The Rise of Great Yarmouth* (1959), *passim*.
7. Mottram, R.H., *The Broads* (1952), p.237; Pollard, Michael, *North Sea Surge* (1978), p.16.
8. Contemporary pamphlet quoted in Ecclestone, A.W., *Henry Manship's Great Yarmouth* (1971), p.34.
9. Ecclestone, A.W., *Gorleston* undated (1980), p.63.
10. Lamb, H.H., *Climate, History and the Modern World* (1995 edition), pp.193-4; Bentham, Harvey, *Once Upon a Tide* (1955), pp.107-8 (he puts the movement south of the herring in the 15th century); Scott, Susan and Duncan, Christopher, *Biology of Plagues: Evidence from Historical Populations* (2001), *passim*. They argue that the plague was not in fact bubonic, too technical a question to be considered here.
11. 'The Norfolk Sea Floods' in *Transactions of the Norfolk and Naturalists' Society* volume xiv, part iv, 1938.
12. Ogley and others, *op. cit.*, pp.15, 18
13. Pollard, Michael, *North Sea Surge* (1978), p.16; Lamb, *op. cit.*, p.260.
14. 'The Norfolk Sea Floods' in *Transactions of the Norfolk and Naturalists Society*, volume xiv, part iv, 1938.
15. *Eastern Daily Press* (hereafter EDP), 2/9/49.
16. Summers, Dorothy, *The East Coast Floods* (1978), p.80.
17. Summers, *ibid.*, p.59.
18. EDP, 18-20/10/1987.
19. EDP, 22/2-1/3/1993.
20. *Yarmouth Mercury* (hereafter YM), 29/6/2006.
21. Quoted in articles on fishing collected at Yarmouth Library.
22. Rackham, Oliver, *The History of the Countryside* (1986), p.360.
23. YM 8/9/2006.
24. *Great Yarmouth and Gorleston Advertiser*, 17/12/92; YM 4/6/99.
25. Allard, Peter and others, *Nature in East Norfolk* (2000)
26. Tooley, Beryl, *John Knowlittle* (1985), *passim*.
27. *The Guardian*, 5/04/2005.

CHAPTER 2

1. YM 11/3/1949; Fox, Harold, *The Evolution of the Fishing Village: Landscape and Society along the South Devon Coast* (2001), pp.137, 178.
2. Rutledge, Paul, *The Court Rolls of Great Yarmouth*, a paper read to the Norfolk Research Committee, 1963.

3. *Pers comm.*, Dr J.R. Alban.
4. Rutledge, Paul, *The Court Rolls of Great Yarmouth*, a paper read to the Norfolk Research Committee, 1963.
5. Rutledge, Paul, *Great Yarmouth Assembly Minutes*, Norfolk Record Society, 39 (1970), p.9.
6. Stephens, W.E., 'Great Yarmouth under Queen Mary' in *Norfolk Archaeology* 39 (1946), pp.143-54.
7. Nall, J.G., *Great Yarmouth and Lowestoft* (1866), p.43.
8. Mottram, R.H., *The Broads* (1952), pp.78-9.
9. Spencer, Colin, *British Food: an extraordinary thousand years of history* (2004 edition), pp.16, 54.
10. Rutledge, Paul, 'The origins and early development in Greater Yarmouth: further evidence', *Yarmouth Archaeology* (hereafter YA), 1999.
11. Poole, A.L., *Domesday Book to Magna Carta* (1955 edition), pp.94-6, 420-1.
12. Lewis, Charles, 'Whaling from Great Yarmouth 1627-1797' in YA5 (1983), not paginated.
13. Rutledge, Paul, *The Court Rolls of Great Yarmouth*, a paper read to the Norfolk Research Committee, 1963.
14. Ecclestone, A.W., *Henry Manship's Great Yarmouth* (1971), p.66.
15. Rutledge, Paul, *The Court Rolls of Great Yarmouth*, a paper read to the Norfolk Research Committee, 1963.
16. Swinden, *Yarmouth*, p.149 (spelling modernised); http://www.gorleston-history.co.uk/history-medieval.html.
17. Ecclestone, A.W., and J.L., *The Rise of Great Yarmouth* (1959), pp.175-6.
18. Tattersfield, *The Forgotten Trade* (1991), p.202.
19. Ketton, Cremer, R.W., *Felbrigg, the story of a house* (1982 edition), pp.84, 155; Dymond, David, *The Norfolk Landscape* (1985), p.234.
20. *Oxford Dictionary of National Biography* (hereafter DNB) entries; Waller, Maureen, *Ungrateful Daughters* (2002), p.142.
21. Dymond, *The Norfolk Landscape* (1985), p 235; Palmer, C.J., *The Perlustration of Great Yarmouth*, vol.1, pp.299-300.
22. Ecclestone, A.W., *Henry Manship's Great Yarmouth* (1971), p.58.
23. Rutledge, Paul, *Great Yarmouth Assembly Minutes*, Norfolk Record Society, 39 (1970), p.16.
24. Ecclestone, A.W., *Henry Manship's Great Yarmouth* (1971), pp.56-7.
25. Palmer, C.J., *Perlustration of Yarmouth*, vol.II (1874), pp.209-21; Preston, J., *Picture of Yarmouth* (1819).
26. Nall, J.G., *Great Yarmouth and Lowestoft* (1866), p.40.
27. Dymond, David, *op. cit.* (1985), p.171.
28. The text is quoted in Hedges, A.A.C., *Yarmouth is an Antient Town* (revised edition 2001), p.32. Authorship is discussed in Fiske, Ron, 'Who wrote the Norfolk Gridiron?', YA 2005, pp.19-21.
29. Swanson, R.W., *Urban Rectories and Urban Fortunes in Late Medieval England: the evidence from King's Lynn* in Slater, T.R. and Roper, Gervase, *The Church in the Medieval Town* (1998), pp.100-32; Duffy, Eamon, *The Stripping of the Altars* (1992), p.166.
30. Webb, Diana, *Pilgrimage in Medieval England* (2000), pp.117, 209, 235.
31. Cozens-Hardy, B., in *A Miscellany*, Norfolk Record Society, 22 (1951).
32. Jewson, C.B., *Transcript of three registers of passengers from Great Yarmouth to Holland and New England 1637-1639*, Norfolk Record Society, 25 (1954), *passim*.
33. Anonymous [Boon, Michael], *Celebrating 450 years in the life of Great Yarmouth High School* (2001).
34. Stephens, W.E., 'Great Yarmouth under Queen Mary' in *Norfolk Archaeology* 39 (1946), pp.152-3; Rutledge, Paul, *Great Yarmouth Assembly Minutes*, Norfolk Record Society, 39 (1970), p.21.
35. Rutledge, Paul, *Great Yarmouth Assembly Minutes*, Norfolk Record Society, 39 (1970), pp.45, 51; Blomefield, *History* vol 11, p.397.
36. Rutledge, Paul, *The Court Rolls of Great Yarmouth*, a paper read to the Norfolk Research Committee, 1963.
37. Ketton-Cremer, R.W., *Norfolk in the Civil War* (1985), p.59.
38. Norfolk Record Office (hereafter NRO), PD 28/4.
39. Ecclestone, A.W., *Henry Manship's Great Yarmouth* (1971), p.69.
40. Hanawalt, Barbara, *Crime in East Anglia in the Fourteenth Century* (Norfolk Record Society, 45, 1976), *passim*.
41. NRO, MC 97/1.
42. Richmond, W.R., *The Story of Great Yarmouth* (undated), p.42.
43. Cozens-Hardy, B., *A Miscellany*, Norfolk Record Society, 22 (1951), pp.1-40.

CHAPTER 3

1. Preston, J., *The Picture of Yarmouth* (1819), *passim.*
2. *A Georgian Holiday Guide*, quoted in Nobbs, George, *Bygone Yarmouth* (1971), p.9.
3. Cozens-Hardy, B., ed., *The Diary Of Sylas Neville* (1950), p.177.
4. NRO, MC 26/1.
5. Palmer, C.J., *The Perlustration of Great Yarmouth*, vol.1, pp.299-300.
6. NRO, BR, 185/3.
7. NRO, BR, 185/3.
8. NRO, MS 453.
9. Mann, Mary, 'His First Day at the Sea' in *Tales of Victorian Norfolk* (1992 edition), pp.107-11.
10. Gordon, D.I., *A Regional History of the Railways of Great Britain: The Eastern Counties* (1977 edition), *passim.*
11. Nall, J.G., *Great Yarmouth and Lowestoft* (1866), p.5.
12. *Yarmouth Free Press*, 23/8/1856, quoted in Box, Peter, *All At Sea* (1992), p.9.
13. Burley, T.L.G., *Playhouses and Players of East Anglia* (1928), pp.118-20.
14. *Lowestoft Journal*, 10/8/1889, quoted in Box, *op. cit.*, p.9.
15. Rouse, Michael, *Coastal Resorts of East Anglia* (1982), p.1.
16. Scott, Clement, *Poppyland*, quoted in Rouse, Michael, *Coastal Resorts of East Anglia* (1982), p.37.
17. Rouse, Michael, *Coastal Resorts of East Anglia* (1982), p.31.
18. quoted in Nall, *op. cit.* p.247.
19. Southwell, Thomas, 'Notes on an eighteenth century museum at Great Yarmouth', in *The Museums Journal*, vol.viii (1908) pp.110-23.
20. Nall, J.G., *Great Yarmouth and Lowestoft* (1866) p 112; Burley, T.L.G., *Playhouses and Players of East Anglia* (1928) pp.104-18.
21. *A Frenchman's Year in Suffolk*, Suffolk Record Society, vol.30, 1988, pp.214-5.
22. De Caux, J.W., *The Herring and the Herring Fishery.*
23. NRO, BR 137/1.
24. NRO, BR 137/1; Y/D 87/21; Lewis, Charles, 'Whaling from Great Yarmouth 1627-1797', YA 5 (1983), not paginated.
25. NRO, MC 97/1.
26. *A Frenchman's Year in Suffolk*, p.215; Woodforde is quoted in Seymour, John, *Companion Guide to East Anglia* (1970), p.112.
27. quoted in Seymour, John, *op. cit.*, p.112.
28. Palmer, C.J., *The Perlustration of Great Yarmouth*, vol.2, p.261.
29. Palmer, C.J., *op. cit.*, vol 2, p.339.
30. Quoted in Mottram, R.H., *The Broads* (1952), p.219.
31. Preston, Harold, *East Anglian Banks and Bankers* (1994), *passim.*
32. Gourvish, Terry, *Norfolk Beers from English Barley* (1987), p.48.
33. Cozens-Hardy, B., ed., *The Diary Of Sylas Neville* (1950), p.256.
34. *Chelmsford Chronicle*, 20/8/1880, quoted in Rouse, Michael, *Coastal Resorts of East Anglia* (1982), p.36.
35. NRO, Norfolk Windmill Trust archive.
36. *Norfolk News*, 1849, Davies, Paul, B., *History of Medicine in Great Yarmouth* (2003), p.552.
37. NRO, Y/TC 87/56; Nall, J.G., *Great Yarmouth and Lowestoft* (1866), p.176.
38. Y/HE 94/8.
39. NRO, COL 8/121.
40. Nall, J.G., *Great Yarmouth and Lowestoft* (1866), pp.113-5.
41. Leary, William and Vickers, John, *A Methodist Guide to Lincolnshire and East Anglia* (1984), p.31.
42. Hanson, Brian, 'The Dissenters Burial Ground', YA, 1998, pp.30-3.
43. NRO, Y/ED/S/2.
44. Palmer, C.J., *The Perlustration of Great Yarmouth*, vol.3, p.237; quoted in Mottram, R.H., *The Broads* (1952), p.176.
45. Gray, Patricia and Richards, Paul, *The True Life and Crimes of a Body-Snatcher* (1999), pp.11-16.
46. Palmer, C.J., *The Perlustration of Great Yarmouth*, vol.1, p.224. Palmer quotes the full statement, well over a page of delightful dialect.
47. NRO, MC 27/2.
48. Bull, Jack, 'The Runham Vauxhall School Board' in Ecclestone, A.W., ed., *A Yarmouth Miscellany* (1974), pp.173-5.

49. Dutt, William, *Highways and Byways in East Anglia* (1904), pp.78-88.
50. Pocock, Tom, *Horatio Nelson* (1987), p.242.
51. NRO, HMN 4/196.
52. Chitty, Susan, *The Woman Who Wrote Black Beauty* (1971), p.92.
53. Davies, *op. cit.*, pp.126-7.

CHAPTER 4
1. NRO, SO 141/1.
2. McBride, John, 'Buying the Wintergardens', YA 2000, pp.28-31.
3. EDP 22/2/1908; Ecclestone, A.W., *Great Yarmouth 1886-1936* (1977), pp.108-9.
4. EDP, 29/6/1908.
5. Temple, C.R., *East Coast Shipwrecks* (1974).
6. Berry, Richard Gordon, 'Great Yarmouth Textiles in World War 2', YA, 2001.
7. YM, 16/5/1952.
8. EDP, 29/6/1907.
9. EDP, 2/4/1974.
10. Wyatt, R.J., *Death from the Skies* (1990), pp.7-18; YM 5/5/2006.
11. NRO, Y/ED 478; YM 29/4/1916.
12. NRO, MS 4694/1/1.
13. YM 5/10/1918.
14. NRO, SO 141/3.
15. Barrett, E.L., 'Oh those happy days in Yarmouth fifty years ago' in *East Anglian Magazine*, September 1957, p.662.
16. Morton, H.V., *The Land of the Vikings* (undated, but 1928), p.72.
17. YM, 5/7/1919.
18. Tubby, David, 'Moving the Racecourse', YA 2005, pp.6-11.
19. NRO, FX 36/1.
20. Temple, C.R., *East Coast Shipwrecks* (1974).
21. YM 16/5/1952.
22. NRO, Y/TC 87/56.
23. Reproduced in Davies, Paul, *History of Medicine in Great Yarmouth* (2003), p.583.
24. NRO, Y/ED 331, 384, 406; Y/TC 88/5,6; Y/HE 49, 50.
25. Ashbourne, Terry, 'Great Yarmouth's First Garden Suburb', YA 2001; YM, 14/6/1919.
26. NRO, Y/TC 87/56.
27. NRO, FX 36/2.
28. NRO, Y/TC 87/56.
29. NRO, Y/TC 87/56.
30. Calvert, Dorothy, *Bull Battle-Dress Lanyard and Lipstick* (1978), pp.2, 3.
31. YM 16/5/1952.
32. Berry, Richard Gordon, 'Great Yarmouth Textiles in World War II', YA 2001.
33. Calvert, *op. cit.*, p.2.
34. YM 8/9/2006.
35. YM 9/1/1943.
36. http://www.bbc.co.uk/ww2peopleswar/stories/09/a3429209.shtml.
37. YM 16/5/1952; NRO, MC 2033; NRO, Y/ED 663a.
38. YM 14/7/67; Walding, Roy, *Words have Tongues* (2001); EDP 26/5/1961.
39. Jacobs, Norman, *Speedway in East Anglia* (2000), pp.43-54. The average cost of a ticket at the Palace match was two shillings.
40. Seymour, John, *Companion Guide to East Anglia* (1970), p.110.
41. Ecclestone, A.W., *Henry Manship's Great Yarmouth* (1971), p.68.
42. NRO, Y/ED, 663a.
43. YM 19/5/67: Temple, C.R., *Great Yarmouth and Gorleston* (1993), not paginated.
44. *The Official Guide and Handbook to the County of Norfolk* (seventh edition, 1973-4), p.59.
45. NRO, Y/ED, 643.
46. NRO, Y/ED 663a.
47. NRO, Y/TC 88/33, 4.
48. NRO, Y/ED 663a.

49. Anonymous [Boon, Michael], *Celebrating 450 years in the life of Great Yarmouth High School* (2001); NRO, Y/ED, 663a.
50. Pevsner, N. and Wilson, B., *The Buildings of England* (1997 edition), pp.494-8.
51. NRO, Y/ED, 663a.
52. Gordon, D.I., *A Regional History of the Railways of Great Britain: The Eastern Counties* (1977 edition), *passim.*
53. Gordon, D.I., *op. cit., passim.*
54. Smith, Russell, 'A Night to Remember' (The Great Flood of 1953), YA, 2000, pp.35-43.
55. Summers, Dorothy, *The East Coast Floods* (1978), p.60.
56. EDP 1/9/1932; 20/6/1933; 13/4/1936; 16/4/1936; *Yarmouth Independent* 4/9/1920; EEN 6/1/1968.
57. *Oxford Dictionary of National Biography*; Wyman, Bill, *Stone Alone* (1997 edition), pp.82, 86, 100.
58. *Oxford DNB.*

CHAPTER 5

1. Teasdel, R.H., *A History of Gorleston* (1933), pp.7, 8; Nall, J.G., *Great Yarmouth and Lowestoft* (1866), p.157.
2. Ecclestone, A.W. and J.L., *The Rise of Great Yarmouth* (1959), pp.164-70.
3. Teasdel, *op. cit.*, p.16; Cozens-Hardy, B., ed., *The Diary of Silas Neville* (1950), p.102.
4. Teasdel, *op. cit.*, p.28.
5. Teasdel, *op. cit.*, p.20.
6. Nishimura, M., *The Gorleston Psalter* (2001).
7. John Kirby's Suffolk, SRS xlvii (2004), p.24; Camden, *Britannia* (1586); Chorography of Suffolk, SRS, xix (1976), p.11.
8. Palmer, C.J., *The Perlustration of Great Yarmouth*, vol.3, p.350; Teasdel, R.H., *A History of Gorleston* (1933), p.40.
9. Teasdel, *op. cit.*, p.45.
10. Ashbourne, Terry, 'Hill House & the Garnham Estate', YA 1999; 'The Koolunga Riddle', YA 2000.
11. NRO, PD 671/15.
12. Ecclestone, A.W., *Gorleston* (undated, but 1980), pp.109-11.
13. Ecclestone, *Gorleston*, pp.47-50.
14. Gourvish, Terry, *Norfolk Beers from English Barley* (1987), p.39.
15. NRO, MC 26/1.
16. Smith, Russell, 'Gorleston Beach Company's Tragedies', *Yarmouth Archaeology*, 2001.
17. Cox, B., ed., *Lifeboat Gallantry* (1998), pp.216-37.
18. Ecclestone, *Gorleston, passim.*
19. Preston, Harold, *East Anglian Banks and Bankers* (1994), *passim.*
20. Ecclestone, A.W., *Gorleston*, pp.99-100; YM 16/5/1952.
21. Walding, Roy, *Words have Tongues* (2001).
22. Ecclestone, A.W., *Gorleston*, p.29.
23. Steward, Michael, *A Brief History of the Stewards in Gorleston* (2004).
24. http://www.gorlestonholidaycamp.co.uk/productssimple2.html
25. NRO, MC 587/9.
26. NRO, FX 36/1.
27. Ecclestone, *Gorleston*, p.18.
28. Cox, B., ed., *Lifeboat Gallantry* (1998), pp.289-91.
29. Miller, Maureen, 'A Child at War' in *Norfolk Fair*, July 1983, pp.60-2.
30. http://www.gorleston-heritage.co.uk/GORLESTON%20%20HEROES.html
31. http://www.gorleston-heritage.co.uk/GORLESTON%20%20HEROES.html
32. Walding, Roy, *Words have Tongues* (2001), citing a Yarmouth Tourist Board leaflet.
33. Hanawalt, Barbara, *Crime in East Anglia in the Fourteenth Century* (Norfolk Record Society, 45, 1976), *passim.*
34. Palmer, C.J., *The Perlustration of Great Yarmouth*, vol.3, p.258.
35. NRO, Norfolk Windmill Trust archive.
36. Rutledge, Paul, 'Crinkle-Crankle Walls' in Ecclestone, A.W., ed., *A Yarmouth Miscellany* (1974), pp.150-2.
37. YM 29/6/2006.

38. Ecclestone, A.W., *Great Yarmouth 1886-1936* (1977), p.98.
39. McEwen, A., 'The Story of Cobholm Island' in Ecclestone, A.W., ed., *A Yarmouth Miscellany* (1974), pp.122-8.
40. Quoted in Palmer, *op. cit.*, vol.3, pp.285-6.
41. *Oxford DNB*, Palmer, *op. cit.*, vol 3, pp.208ff, 364ff.
42. Kitson, Sydney, *The Life of John Sell Cotman* (1937), pp.163-5.
43. Morgan, Kenneth, *The People's Peace* (1991 edition), p.464.

CHAPTER 6

1. Sandred, Karl, *The Place Names of Norfolk Part Two The Hundreds of East and West Flegg*, Happing and Tunstead (1996), pp.1-83.
2. Fox, Harold, *The Evolution of the Fishing Village: Landscape and Society along the South Devon Coast* (2001), p.178.
3. Bennett, H.S., *The Pastons and their England* (1968 edition), pp.87-101.
4. Kealey, Edward J., *Harvesting the Air: Windmill Pioneers in Twelfth-Century England* (1987), p.7.
5. Kealey, *op. cit. passim*.
6. Williamson, Tom, *The Norfolk Broads* (1997); Dymond, David, *The Norfolk Landscape* (1985).
7. Hipper, Kenneth, *Smugglers All; centuries of Norfolk smuggling* (2001), *passim*.
8. *Now is the time for Fishing: songs and speech by Sam Larner*, Topic Records (1961, 1999).
9. NRO, MC 90/1.
10. White, Walter, *Eastern England from the Thames to the Humber* (1865), quoted in Mottram, R.H., *The Broads* (1952), p.110.
11. Quoted in Lee, Robert, *Unquiet Country – voices of the Norfolk poor* (2005), p.40.
12. Hedges, A.A.C., *What to see in Great Yarmouth and District* (1978), p.15.
13. Temple, C.R., *East Coast Shipwrecks* (1974).
14. YM 5/5/2006.
15. NRO, FX 36/2.
16. NRO, MC 587/9.
17. NRO, Y/TC 87/56.
18. NRO, MC 90/1.
19. NRO, MC 39/392.
20. Nall, J.G., *Great Yarmouth and Lowestoft* (1866), pp.123-32.

CHAPTER 7

1. Mottram, R.H., *The Broads* (1952), p.37.
2. *Chorography of Suffolk*, Suffolk Record Society, xix (1976). p.34.
3. Pevsner, N., *The Buildings of England – Suffolk* (1974 edition), p.225.
4. Dahl, Louis H., *The Roman Camp and the Irish Saint at Burgh Castle* (1913), pp.138-45.
5. Williamson, Tom, *The Norfolk Broads: a landscape history* (1997), *passim*.
6. Callan, Brian E., *Belton from its Past to the Present* (undated), p.95.
7. NRO, PD 563/1, 49.
8. *A Journal of Excursions Through the County of Suffolk, 1823-1844*, Suffolk Record Society, xxiv (1982), p.197.
9. Nall, J.G., *Great Yarmouth and Lowestoft* (1866), p.185.
10. Williamson, *op. cit.*, p.148.
11. Dahl, Louis H., *The Roman Camp and the Irish Saint at Burgh Castle* (1913), pp.231-4.
12. NRO, PD 563/64.
13. Guyton, Peter, *The Importance of Time* (*c*.1999), p.19.
14. NRO, PD 563/8; PD 581/17.
15. NRO, SO 141/1.
16. Callan, Brian E., *Belton from its past to the present* (undated), pp.171-87.
17. Gordon, D.I., *A Regional History of the Railways of Great Britain: The Eastern Counties* (1977 edition), *passim*; EDP 20/5/1971.
18. Hedges, A.A.C., *What to see in Great Yarmouth and District* (1978), p.7; EDP 13/3/1963; YM 30/9/1949; YM 13/10/1972.
19. NRO, PC 49/61/2/2.
20. The Venerable Bede, *A History of the English Church and People* (Penguin Classics edition), pp.167-71.

21. NRO, SAC 2003-3/1313; Callan, Brian E., *Belton from its Past to the Present* (undated), pp.108-10.

CHAPTER 8

1. *Yarmouth Mercury*, 29/3/1974; 5/4/1974.
2. *Norfolk Fair*, July 1976.
3. Norfolk County Council, *Norfolk and the Netherlands* (2005).
4. NRO, Y/TC 88/62.
5. NRO, Y/TC 88/76.
6. EEN 30/6/2006.
7. EDP 8/4/2006.
8. Davies, Paul B., *History of Medicine in Great Yarmouth* (2003), pp.447, 8.
9. Davies, *op. cit.*, p.447.
10. EDP 2/8/2006.
11. EDP 25/2/1976.
12. NRO, Y/TC 88/76.
13. NRO, Y/TC 88/62.
14. NRO, Y/TC 88/76.
15. YM 6/10/1967; EDP 3/1/1992.
16. *Norfolk Fair*, June 1983.
17. *ibid.*, November 1978.
18. Orton, Christine, *Martham in the Past* (1984), p.46.
19. Information from Michael Knights.
20. Kealey, Edward J., *Harvesting the Air: Windmill Pioneers in Twelfth-Century England* (1987), p.9.
21. Norfolk County Council, *Norfolk and the Netherlands* (2005).
22. Norfolk County Council, *Norfolk and the Netherlands* (2005).

Index

Killett, William, 136
Kindersley, Jemima, 91
Kirsp, Dioni, 46
Klass, Myleene, 204
Koolunga, 136, 196

Lacey, Johanna, 46
Lake, Frederick, 143
Lambert, Joyce, 7
Large, Arthur, 188
Larner, Sam, 163
Leach, Ethel, 130-1
Lees, Andrew, 21
Leggett, Christopher, 141-2
Leggett, James, 139
Lewis, Jessica, 115
lifeboats, 139, 145-6, 166
Line, Enid, 115
Lingwood, Joan, 46
Littlewood, Rosa, 117
Lokard, John, 34
lottery, 31
Loveday, Jack, 130
Lovewell, James, 151
Ludbright, 50
Lydia Eva [ship], 84, 201

Macauley, Jean, 115
Mackay, Elizabeth, 115
Macleod, Hannah, 115
Macmillan, Kenneth, 132
Magdalen College estate, 124
Manby, George, 156
Mann, Mary, 62
Mann, Vera, 115
Manship, Henry, 30, 36-7, 49
Mapes, James, 83-5
Market Place, 20, 33-4, 46, 66, 67, 73
Marten, Mr, 57, 137-8
Martham, 19, 158, 161-7, 171, 198-9
Martham Broad, 171-2
Martin, Sarah, 124, 173-4
Mautby, 159, 173
Maxwell, Louisa, 115
Meecke, Barbrey, 45
methodism, 65, 77-80, 137, 185
Miller, Maureen, 147
Milligan, John, 187

Mills, John and Edith ('Annette'), 191
Moore, Ivy, 115
Motte, William de, 44
Moulton, John and Henry, 46
Mumper [a dog], 32
murders, 82-5, 100-1

Neal family, 82
Nelson Monument see Norfolk Pillar
Nelson, George, 187
Nelson, Horatio, 88-90
Neville, Sylas, 56, 57, 73, 135
Nigrum, Felicia, 34
Nimrod [ship], 169
Norfolk dialect, 85, 163, 201
Norfolk Pillar, 56, 88-90, 199-201
North Gate, 23

Oby, 165
oil and gas, 193
Olivers, Thomas, 77
Ormesby, 5, 18, 77-8, 159, 161, 162, 168, 172, 198
Overill, Tony, 16
Oxney, William, 30

Paget, Sir James, 93
Paget, Samuel, 136
Palgrave, Mary, 92
Palmer, C.J., 87
Palmer, Charles, 59
Park, Ann, 46
Parr, Robert, 48-9
Paston family, 151, 160
Paston, Margaret, 172-3
Patterson, Arthur, 14, 17, 20-1
Payn, Thomas, 51
Pearce, Max, 118-9
Pearson, Joan, 115
Penrice, Thomas, 36
Perebrown, John, 53
plague, 33, 48-9
Poole, Albert, 187
Porthcawl [ship], 73, 109
Portsmue, John de, 34
Potter, Herbert, 189
Powell, Violet, 115
Preston, Isaac, 44, 151
Preston, James, 187